# ALONE IN THE NIGHT SKY

Aside from the strike fires there was only black night, no groundfire, and silence beyond the engine. Ron finished his strike, called for me to come on down, and I began my strike. I planned on four to five passes and started in with a forty degree dive for the first. The fires below were bright and made it easy to locate the target area. No one shot, no one said anything.

Now, if you ask a pilot to do a roll, chances are he will do it to the left. It's easier to move the stick that direction for right-handed people. So I made four left turns from my four passes. Then there was dive number five. The pipper glowed pink in the gunsight and through the glass I could see the roaring fires there below. I hit the release button and started to climb. And then it happened. A tiny voice, one that didn't belong to anyone I knew, but clear and distinct, said, "Turn right, not left." I did. I yanked the stick violently right and watched a stream of tracers streak by—just where I would have been—perhaps ten rounds of hot and hard metal a few feet away. Then I turned and flew back home.

# MY
# SECRET WAR
## RICHARD S. DRURY

**ST. MARTIN'S PRESS/NEW YORK**

DS
558.8
.D78
1986

**MY SECRET WAR**     15033087

Copyright © 1979, 1986 by Richard Drury

ISBN: 0-312-90503-3   Can. ISBN: 0-312-90527-0

Printed in the United States of America

First St. Martin's Press mass market edition/September 1986

10  9  8  7  6  5  4  3  2

I have been fortunate to know some of aviation's few, those to whom flight is a love affair, a passion—life. They are not all alive in the physical sense, nonetheless, they are real. They have dreamed "impossible" dreams and attained "impossible" goals. To those few this book is dedicated.

# Acknowledgments

The author wishes to thank all those who helped him in the preparation of this book. Too many to name, they all gave of their time in gathering photos, documenting facts and dates, typing, retyping, and proofing the galleys. Their constant support and optimistic spirit were essential to the successful completion of this project.

Many photographs and illustrations came from outside the author's collection. Thanks to Mike Machat for his illustrations and photo assistance, USAF/Russ Parrish photos, Douglas Aircraft Company/Don Williams and Harry Gann.

# PREFACE

**N**EARLY TWO DECADES have passed since I flew my last military combat mission. Even so, I can recall that time as clearly as yesterday. Those moments were dramatic, thrilling, and highly emotional, days and nights indelibly engraved in my mind forever. When I pulled the mixture to cutoff that last time, an era died for me.

As an aviator who loves his craft, I found those missions to be the unforgettable flying experiences of my career. Yet the Southeast Asian predicament was so perplexing, frustrating, and finally absurd I cannot forget those days for those reasons as well.

I started this book to express what it was like to fly in our different sort of aerial combat, to document a combat aviator's life, allowing the reader to be a part of the pristine love affair of a man and his medium, in this case, the sky. To accomplish that goal I wrote after nearly every flight, after any significant incident. My journal thus recorded my thoughts, the words— what affected me. I believe those ends have been accomplished.

But something else became evident as the thoughts and words came to paper and a design emerged. I began to see a "slice of life" portrait of a young man fulfilling his dreams, yet losing his faith and trust in the system that put him in the sky he wanted. The paradox grew as he faced ineffectual and obsequious leaders, policies which had no positive goals, an exercise which had finally lost its purpose. *My Secret War* is thus the true story of a pilot who fought ideas and principles over a battleground of illusion.

The book is also a memoir of combat missions flown in Laos, a country best described by Bernard Fall as a "political convenience." I flew from Nakhon Phanom, a joint U.S.–Thai base on the Laotian border in northeast Thailand from June of 1969 to May of 1970. While the Laotian war was shrouded in secrecy—indeed, no news media of any sort were allowed at Nakhon Phanom where our missions were launched—the greatest number of antiaircraft weapons of all calibers were solidly entrenched in Laos, and the magnitude of the operations there were only publicly advertised later in 1971, under the Nixon administration when United States armed forces crossed into Laos to pursue the enemy openly with news coverage. Losses were understandably high. They had been in previous years also, but went likewise unadvertised. Rather than pinpoint a major offensive or even a rescue as Laotian, the public was told "Southeast Asia," or simply "Vietnam." The United States denied Communist charges that America was waging a "special war" in Laos in 1969. But a State Department spokesman acknowledged later that year that we did have military personnel in Laos in conjunction with the supply of "certain military assistance and equipment" to the Royal Lao government. At the same time, Laotian Premier Souvanna Phouma announced the presence of more than fifty thousand North Vietnamese troops in Laos. And in 1970, a United States senator publicly announced that "the U.S. is up to its neck in

Laos." And so the politicians and news media, generals and official briefers, argued the issue, while we flew day and night combat missions over Laos in some of the most intense aerial warfare ever known.

Not only were we flying in Laos, we were doing it in airplanes designed over thirty years ago. The Douglas Skyraider prototype was designed in 1944, and the first aircraft flew in 1945. The Air Force started operating the A-1 in 1964, selecting it rightly as the best counterinsurgency attack aircraft available. The antiquity of the airplane did not mean that we were being forced to fly obsolete equipment. Most of us selected it ourselves. We were strictly volunteer in most cases, and many of us were there because we wanted to fly that airplane more than anything else. The A-1 was indeed an extraordinary machine, and I trust I have given some feeling of what it was like to fly it.

With the advantage of several years' hindsight, some passages of this book now appear simple, sometimes foolish, to me. I was tempted to make changes for the sake of wisdom and timeliness. Yet the text was written on the spot, many times after a flight when the adrenaline was still flowing and I couldn't sleep or relax. It was fresh, the way I went into war, and thus are preserved the thoughts I carried with me, what moved my spirit, how I related to my world. So I have resisted that impulse to change, to deny any of those moments as they were. That I could find beauty and inspiration in the sky, in an old airplane in the midst of war, is for me a beautiful irony.

I have made no attempt, then, at interpreting the war, neither lamenting nor applauding it. How I feel about it now is not part of this book. There has been no tampering with that early exuberance or the dreams, the feel of the machine or the wind's song. This is my story of Southeast Asia, eagerness and naïveté left intact.

RICHARD S. DRURY
Santa Barbara, California
1986

# ONE

**I**NSANITY! IT'S SHEER INSANITY to fly through that weather, I kept thinking. The storm front lay across the Mekong River, and the first hours of the night were filled with monstrous eruptions of lightning. It was August of 1969, just two months into my tour, and I was already battling thunderstorms as well as North Vietnamese. From our little building at Nakhon Phanom, Thailand, the storm had been miles away and silent. We were watching the colossus with the audio shut off.

Col. Al Martin and I launched into the night under bright stars with the storm still raging to the east. Our target was beyond the front, so we turned east and climbed sluggishly to eighty-five hundred and nine thousand feet, a five-hundred-foot separation between us. There was no way to top the storm in a fully loaded old Skyraider, so we started weaving through the open spaces between the building storm cells, Al Martin's aircraft invisible to me, only his white fuselage light my reference out ahead. Water started gushing in through the canopy rail as I lost Al's light. Outside was total blackness, broken by canescent splashes of lightning. With the white light gone I was virtually alone except for the radio. "You OK back there?" Al asked on the FM radio. "Yeah, so far so good. Let me know your headings," I replied. "Roger that. Will do."

1

Normally, keeping parallel headings kept us fairly close together, and with the assistance of our automatic direction finding radios we could rejoin in clear weather at the target. If that didn't work, the flash from detonating ordnance and enemy groundfire would let anyone know where the target was.

We drove on for another twenty minutes on instruments, chatting about headings, remarking about the weather. Many nights in a row it was a matter of outwitting the weather and basic fears and trying to get where we wanted to go in spite of things. We flew out the other side of the storm piece by piece until there was an overcast above and the moon glowing through like a projection lamp. For a while the weather was behind.

The night's forward air controller was flying a twin-engine C-123 transport at twelve thousand feet. With starlight-sensitive equipment, the FACs scanned the roads and selected geography for enemy traffic. We communicated on the VHF radio and were informed of a suspected target, another way of saying that a target might be down there, but then again, it might not. "Clear off to the south, and we'll throw out a flare and see what we've got," the C-123 pilot said.

Al and I turned south of the area and watched a flare ignite under its small parachute and drift down into the murk. The gloom gave way to its probing light, which was as bright as a welding torch at close range. I put my hand up to shield my eyes and scanned the ground, which took form like a prehistoric drawing. It was as if all the ocean water had been drained from an immense sea and we were seeing the bottom for the first time. I'd seen flares work before, but each

2

time the view was haunting. Laotian mountains jutted up into the dark, where we circled like primitive spacemen observing the dark side of the moon under the same sort of artificial light. There was a winding dirt road running between two karst mountains, disappearing into what must have been very dense underbrush. The flare burned out, and I went back on instruments until I could regain some of my night vision. "Keep holding south and we'll throw out a mark," the FAC said. Shortly we saw a red light on the ground, our target marker. I orbited above Al, keeping the marker on my left. "Your target is a suspected truck park which lies about two five zero degrees from the mark at about two hundred meters," the navigator in the transport relayed. "You can expect groundfire of all calibers through fifty-seven millimeter. Cleared in at your discretion."

The briefing was standard. One could always expect groundfire on the Ho Chi Minh Trail, and one could always expect mountains and rough engines and mechanical problems and a mighty list of other such standard delights. If any man flew with any other conception, he was deeply wrong. I armed my guns with the master arm switch, imagining the mechanism sliding back, the ammunition inserting, the bolts sliding back into place in the wings. I set the toggle switches to the ready position, then set the intervalometer to a five-hundred-pound bomb on station five. The A-1 had fifteen wing stations where ordnance was hung. The intervalometer was a rotary selector which the pilot set to a number representing a wing station. With varied loads of bombs, rockets, and napalm, it could be confusing as to what was where. Some of us carried diagrams so we'd know for certain. "Cleared in at your discretion," the man had said. The FAC could hold high and watch the action.

There was a slight pause. Then I heard: "OK, I'm in from the east." I banked on the left wingtip and waited. "I'm off, breaking south," Al called. Nothing happened. No bomb burst. No groundfire. Nothing. "Got a nape off, but it must have been a dud," Al said calmly. The red marker was getting dim, as if it were sinking in an ocean. "I'm in again from the east," Al announced. I sat on my wingtip again and saw the slow splash of napalm in an east-to-west direction, the splash tracing the airplane's direction. It was my turn four passes later, and still no groundfire. "Let's swap altitudes," Al directed. "I'm south of the target, heading east." I organized my mental picture and confirmed, "OK, I'm north, heading west. Starting down."

We performed this little maneuver with great aplomb, having done it so many nights before. The first time I wondered if I'd hit the other airplane. In an emotional moment during the strike it wouldn't be too difficult to misinterpret position in the dark. There had even been one collision in the past. I leveled and called, "I'm level at eight and a half and in from the north." Rolling into a forty- to forty-five-degree dive down into the dark, I flipped the master arm switch on and saw the dim pink dot of the gunsight materialize, projected on the round reflector glass. Through the sight I could also see the remaining fire from Al's napalm. As the air pressure increased on the controls and the scream of the dive intensified, I momentarily gave thought to the scene under the flare light. I was plunging down into that eerie sight, between the mountains, the altimeter unwinding rapidly. I always noticed a tingling sensation at such a moment, a distinct mix-

4

ture of fear and elation, a peculiar combination. I punched the red button on the stick and started my climb, jinking madly and looking about for any sign of groundfire, thankful there was none. Checking the rearview mirrors for any tracers that might sneak up behind, I saw the napalm ignite and fill the sky with a soft glow. "Pretty good hit," came the FAC's remark on the radio. "Try it about twenty meters to the south next time." Twenty meters! The man's obviously never tried it himself, I thought. How does one distinguish twenty meters of distance at night with an antique airplane and seat-of-the-pants delivery methods? It was all a wild guess, a WAG as we called it, a "wild-assed guess." If I could just overlap the last drop, I'd have the distance, I figured. It was the last pass, and with the release of my five-hundred-pounder I started my pullout while looking to the side. A single pink-red tracer shot up from below, and I turned aside as it swept past to explode perhaps a thousand feet above. It was as if someone were giving a last salute. "That's odd," I heard Al say. "Yeah, maybe he's a lousy gunner," I said, thankful that we had been spared this night. We turned to head back west, and there was my forgotten storm, waiting, hungry, lashing out with the lightning I had taken no notice of during the strike. I heard Al call on FM, so I moved my radio wafer selector to FM. "Heading west, and all switches off and safe." "Off and safe," I chanted back. I looked out at the wings, no longer encumbered by ten thousand pounds of ordnance and the immense aerodynamic drag the shapes produced. At least I wouldn't have to tote it all back through the storm. As I looked ahead I realized that the storm cells had grown and the same passages we had used in coming had closed and

5

become solid walls. "The lightning is less to the north-west," Al said. "Let's try it over there."

I tightened my shoulder harness and lap belt. Wisps of cloud flew past the canopy bubble like tendrils clutching for me. I reconfirmed my old thoughts that sometimes the weather scared me as much as the enemy gunners. I changed radio frequencies in accordance with Al's instructions, then tensely settled back to fight it out.

It is a strange feeling to face such a storm in any airplane, let alone a single-place, single-engine, prop type designed a quarter century ago. At first it is overwhelming. The storm covers the entire horizon, a line visible only because of light from the cells themselves. It is towering and immense and alive. You can't go under it in the mountains at night, and you haven't the airplane to go over it. Your alternatives are singular. You must go through it somewhere, somehow. If it were the good old U.S.A., you could perhaps set down and wait it out. Not so when the terrain below had no airfields and everything was enemy-owned anyway. After the trip had been made a few times in similar weather, I felt easier. It was a matter of accepting the fact that it had been done many times before, and that it wasn't new. It didn't lose any of its immensity, but I wanted to go home, and home was through the weather, and I was going to jump right in and navigate through it.

I did. The machine was jolted by the hand of a mad wind, cracking my head into the canopy and putting a deep gash into the helmet. My body tugged at the straps and my feet were blasted from the rudder pedals. The propeller surged, the pitch of the engine changed, and more rain came through the cockpit. I fought the storm as if my life depended on it. In a sense it did. The thought of going down and being captured was the greatest fear I had. I had projected a protective sort of mental shield around me every time I flew. It simply said to me, I will do everything to escape capture. I will fight every bit of groundfire and wind and rain and storm to get home safely. The storm was simply another test of my dedication to survival. The machine threw me against the side of the cockpit as it made a wild skid, then scrunched my body down into the seat as the force of rising wind raised the airplane several hundred feet instantly. I was struggling just to maintain the wings level. I had a thought that somewhere, that very instant, there was someone thousands of feet above us in a jet who was just crossing the storm in clear air and who would later describe the night as uneventful. I pictured him calling over to his wingman and saying, "Hey, look at that storm down there. Isn't that lightning spectacular?"

The first bolt of lightning spit out across the canopy and lit the airplane so brightly that I saw the imprint of combat boots across the wing where mechanics had spent hours working before the flight. Footprints traced in engine oil meandered across both wings, walking off into the night. The instruments vibrated and danced so that my vision of them was blurred. The only world of familiarity was the airplane, the cockpit, a red-lighted world measured in inches. The radios were there to my side, the frequency digits clear in their black print. The knurled knob connected to the rudder trim was placed to my lower left, waiting for my gloved hand to make slight adjustments. The oxygen flow blinker moving with my breathing, opening and closing, opening and closing, was a remote indication of my corporal existence. I was covered with a dark green flight suit with multiple zippers, a helmet and oxygen mask, survival vest with thirty-eight-caliber pistol, ammunition, and finally a pair of combat boots designed for the tropical war. They were out ahead of me, attempting to remain on the rudder pedals, covering the worn engraving of the Douglas company.

I was brawling with the elements when I suddenly broke out into a winding canyon between cells of the storm. My eyes went full open as though I had seen some miraculous vision. Each wall of the canyon was made of towering cloud which went up as far as the lightning could illuminate. Inside were the flickering waves of light. I was flying in an immense cavern, dodging the white stalactites and stalagmites. It was at once both curiously beautiful and awesome. The cavern was cold in the moon's light, and the pulsating electrical glow throbbed like a heartbeat. Banking around the trail was like working through a long maze, the sides of which were alive with electricity. "Like flying into Carlsbad Caverns," I said to Al on the radio. "Yeah, really weird," he said. "Just flew through there myself." We were a sort of cosmic eye, traversing that place like sightseers, exploring this mystery in the aerial version of the glass-bottomed boat.

Then there was a dead end and a plunge into a solid wall of icy-looking cloud. A line of electric blue-white fire spread across the nose of the aircraft, and I was momentarily engulfed in cloud and rain. I held heading as best I could while the airplane bounced along once again. The radio crackled with static, and a radar controller inquired as to what the weather was like. I banged into the canopy again and said in English broken and punctuated with turbulence, "I don't think ...I...can talk to you and...fly too." "OK, that gives me a good idea," he said. A good idea, I thought. You have absolutely no idea, my friend. Yours is a warm room and a cup of coffee. The rain falls on your roof, outside. The wind is recorded on your instrument. And with all your data, you have no idea what it is. And then, with startling abruptness, I flew from the storm directly into calm and clear air. It was as smooth as drifting underwater in a pool. All slow motion. Giant tongues of lightning licked out at me as if the master were angry at the little mortal who got away. The Mekong River was lit with moonlight and the airfield lights were out ahead. Aileron into the wind, rudder down the runway, I touched on the upwind wheel and rolled that way. The rain was finally reaching the base and hit my face as I opened the canopy at the end of the landing roll. It felt good, different than it had in the middle of the storm. I stopped the engine and climbed out onto the wing under the poncho of the crew chief. Al—now Colonel Martin—drove up in his jeep, and we went to the debriefing building where a huge bowl of popcorn and plenty of cold beer waited. As if I were being hunted, the wind moaned at the roof and banged at the door. But I wasn't up there anymore.

# TWO

NIGHT RACED ON, devouring the last finger of sunlight and extinguishing our single patch of blue sky. There was a vast sunset, orange and red through the distant clouds which hinted at thunderstorms. Just across the Mekong River in Laos, the limestone mountains changed from their unique shade of green to a purplish tinge. Nature was exercising its awesome power in quiet efficiency, and there was an all-pervading sensation of peace. Northern Thailand and Laos were a locale of great visual serenity, although this August evening of 1969 that settled quietly on that soft-seeming jungle concealed a brutal war. After dressing for the night mission, I opened the door, looked out, and suddenly, as if by surprise, it was night. There was a certain thrill to it. Even in my brief two months of combat operations I had been flying with most of the squadron pilots, and Jim Bender, a first lieutenant whom I had been flying with frequently, stood looking at the distant lightning flashes which were directly in the path we would be taking in another few hours. I often liked to watch the storms, so I took a chair outside my room and sat staring into the northern sector of the horizon. Thoughts of weather flying, being chased by clips of groundfire, and sidestepping lightning and turbulence in between were heavy little thoughts that kept us company when nothing else did.

Jim walked down the planking to where I sat, pulled up a chair of his own, and as we both scanned the northern storms he asked, "Do you ever wonder how you got here? I mean, did you ever think, way back when, that you'd be doing this for a living?"

Way back when, I had given little thought to much of anything except flying. A love for airplanes had possessed me since my kindergarten years. No one else in the family had been a pilot, and no one was really enchanted that I wanted to pursue aviation. I never had any great decisions to make or battles to fight, and generally led a youthful life free of complication. Except for putting together enough money for another hour of flying or talking my parents into driving me to the airport, flying was something entirely natural and easy. I was too young to drive, so there were some struggles to get to the airports, and since I was too young for power planes, I started with gliders. My parents were generally cooperative in the driving regard, often in the financial realm, and various odd jobs kept me in the air. I flowed into the Air Force as though it had been destined. I had even spent four years in the Air Force ROTC and got a commission as a Regular officer. My foremost thoughts were that I wanted to fly, to fly fighters, perhaps someday be a test pilot, maybe an astronaut. It was to be a career, the good old Air Force I had dreamed of, like a thousand old motion pictures—P-51 Mustangs, P-38 Lightnings, F-86 Sabre Jets, and finally Starfighters and supersonic fighters. It was something I wanted more than anything else; and it was duty and honor and country, and all that, too. It was the United States of America personified. And then one day for real I was standing in military ranks on the ramp of Williams

11

Air Force Base in Arizona with thundering jets in formation flight overhead. My heart was pounding, the marching band was playing the Air Force song, and wings were being pinned on my jacket. I was a pilot in the Air Force. It was all a neat little dream shared there with my classmates. We were invincible, leaving our helmets and checklists lying around so that people would know we were pilots. We strolled around the base with our new wings shining for everyone to see.

But then I began to emerge from my sheltered life and in my twenties faced the conflicts and skirmishes that constitute daily living. The way I had always felt about flying was not to be found in the manuals and books of regulations. I was frequently at odds with the system. My love was with a special type of flying, preferably where I could be alone with an airplane that had one engine. That was home in the sky to me. No one could reach over and touch anything, no one could say anything, no one could interfere with my flying. That was the lure of a single-seat airplane. When I saw the first pictures and read the articles and documents about the Air Force getting old Skyraiders for "military assistance" work, I knew what I wanted. Unfortunately, the Air Force had other ideas, and thus began one of the largest battles and heaviest decisions I had made in my life to that time. The decision was monumental. Here was a chance to fly the sort of aircraft I had dreamed of, yet I would be flying in a crude and tortuous war, an undeclared "conflict" where I could be killed or—worse, to my thinking—captured. As I began the hundreds of telephone calls and letters trying to get transferred to the small corps of Skyraiders pilots, I also realized that I was fighting for what I believed in for the first time. Flying was my "work," and the perspective it had given me had brought about almost a reverence for flight. With the great sense of freedom that came from flying I also began formulating a philosophy, a life-style, cementing my notions about freedom, communism, and the Indochina war itself. Even though I could see the factors of political subterfuge and Dow-Jones managers in the scene, I still managed to view the war as basically a freedom versus nonfreedom issue. And though the war was grossly mismanaged, eventually turning the conflict into a bloody waste, I thought of it quite differently at its inception.

I had achieved success by my perseverance. The orders were to Course 111101Z: A-1 Pilot, and it was a different world of aviation. There were no supersonic booms, no jet engines, nothing from the modern world. The old sound greeted me on arrival at Eglin Aux Field #9, Hurlburt Field, Florida. Four Skyraiders were entering the overhead pattern for landing, and the sound of four mighty reciprocating engines in formation was thunderously loud, pouring an avalanche of vibration into the sky. I stood like a statue, smiling as the vibration rattled windows and rippled through the air. And after landing, the four machines idled blap, blap, blap off the runway. I had time-traveled to my favorite part of aviation history.

Hurlburt Field has played a large and unadvertised part in aviation history. The Doolittle Raiders planned and practiced for the Tokyo raid there; the aircraft carrier length-markings were still etched across the "Doolittle Taxiway." And the Special Air Warfare pilots learned their trade there, as I was to do. I finally got my introduction to the A-1 Skyraider and found

13

it as expected, a time machine measuring fifty feet and one quarter inch, wingtip to wingtip. It was heavy for a single-engine ship, at twelve-thousand pounds empty, and it was big. The engine was a Wright R-3350-26WD and rated at nearly three thousand horsepower. It carried almost forty gallons of oil, most of which wound up on the aircraft surfaces and on the pilots. The A-1 also burned about a hundred gallons an hour of fuel. For all that, it barely went three miles a minute with an ordnance load. But speed was a relative thing and had lost its importance in the sort of war we would be in. With the A-1, I began to enjoy a full flying world: Breathing deeply, I could taste the oil, looking forward, I could see the yellow circle where the propeller tips were painted just as I had done with so many model airplanes. The aircraft was basically a World War Two attack fighter, once owned and operated by the Navy. When the Navy gave them up, pilots cried, books were written, and the Air Force finally decided to pick them up for their versatility and effectiveness in the conventional attack role. The airplane embodied a special airman's philosophy to me, which was one reason I had to fly it. Instead of myriad electronic systems and computers and instrumentation, the A-1 was a basic airplane. Its pilot had to rely on the old aviating skills for the most part. The airplane had a conventional landing gear configuration known as a taildragger. This feature, coupled with the immense engine, could make for some serious handling problems unless the pilot was sharp enough to keep well ahead of the machine. That held great appeal to me, as if the airplane simply said that if its pilot were good enough to understand it, he could find great joy in the taming. And it had one engine, and most models had but one seat. That about tied up the package, as far as I was concerned. Further, it didn't fly at high altitudes, didn't go super fast, and survived only by the capabilities of its pilot, a man who had to know more about flying airplanes than computer programming. I was totally hooked.

After we learned the basic handling qualities of the airplane, including aerobatics and formation flying, we learned to use it for its ultimate military purpose, as an ordnance delivery platform. There were rockets, dive bombings, strafing, and low-level placement. But the one thing that impressed me forever was the statement an instructor made on the first day. I was returning from the transition area where loops, rolls, and Immelmanns had been traced through a clear sky. "I want to show you how the gunsight works," the man said. The sight had simply been a small instrument above the panel, and I hadn't given it much study. With the arm switch turned on, I looked through the glass sight and there was a pinkish dot enclosed by parentheses, the pipper as it was called. While I stared the man bluntly said, "There's only one reason why you're wearing those captain's bars on your shoulders and those wings on your chest. You're looking at it." I believed in more reasons than that, but understood what he meant. That an airplane could be used as an instrument of war as well as a tool for joy was evident. It was both, and I accepted that. The airplane was alive in a special way. There were times when I could peer over the side to little towns deep in American textured land, pass miniature automobiles on superhighways, wave to children in schoolyards, absorb the deep green of young hills, and inspect the gashes of ancient canyons and immense mountains. I could reach out to the sky as if I were not in an airplane. There were moments when I could dive and feel the controls tighten with wind pressure, then pull upwards a few steps to heaven and feel the pleasure as we, the airplane and I, fell through the horizon inverted, where for precious seconds the world and the machine were silent and everything was united. Such freedom was profoundly good, yet I knew there were moments coming when the same airplane would deliver bombs and rockets and bullets dead on target because I believed in that freedom. That also made sense. It was the beginning of a change in my life. I was finally fighting for what I solidly believed in. *That's* why I was there. . . .

Jim and I glanced at our watches, put our chairs away, then made our way to the briefing, the personal equipment shop, and then trundled across the metal planking to the airplanes. The cockpit smelled of hydraulic fluid, oil, smoke, and leather, and I drank it in. After strapping in, I sat idly, giving Jim time to get ready in his own airplane. The weather was nasty up north, and I could even hear the rumblings from the thunder as I sat in the cockpit.

One of the perils, if it might be called that, was the knowledge that there was absolutely no assurance of coming back. There was no guarantee of getting through the weather on instruments, since our airplanes did not have the latest of anything. The North Vietnamese army operating in Laos was sincere in its efforts to kill, maim, or capture as many Americans as possible. We considered this fact a significant hazard. There was never a promise of outwitting the gunners, or even the wind that would sweep rain across the oily runway if one did get back. But those uncertainties were the things which made such a life so intriguing.

If a pilot wanted better odds, then he could perhaps improve his techniques and study harder. He could test his methods of escape against heavy groundfire any night of the week. Even so, he never got any assurances, only better odds. Jim and I laughed at our insanities. We said it would be safer to sell shoes, but we weren't ready to stop living yet, and by living we meant facing death and heavy challenge. It was contradictory at first thought, but it was an interesting premise. On the ground you could say anything, boast, lie, whatever. Once you were airborne, that sort of thing had to end. You fended for yourself, alone, in a single-seat, single-engine airplane, getting shot at. In so doing we felt more alive than ever before. We liked it greatly.

Presently I started the engine and Jim checked in on all three radios. Heading for the arming area, I adjusted my body into the seat, which was like trying to get comfortable while shackled to a cement slab. Night flying was more a mental activity than day flying and required more concentration. There wasn't a whole lot to look at outside the cockpit, and the world of flat black was only momentarily broken by lightning and groundfire. We both armed in relative silence, the arming crew below connecting the mechanisms, wind gusts shoving the stick around the cockpit, the rudder pedals straining under my feet as the control surfaces were being beaten by the advancing winds. Within five minutes we were airborne and striking out for a target an hour and a half ahead. There was still a battle to be fought along the way. I computed a rough estimate of the time we had to fly yet. It would be a long sit. Ten minutes after level-off, we seemed to be in limbo, a semimotionless existence, holding steady on course, looking out ahead into nothing, approaching the greatness of the thunderstorms in miniature celestial clipper ships. I played a Bach three-part invention, my eyes scanning the map under flashlight, the sky, and the instruments, while my thoughts raced through constructions of my own castles, rejected and accepted philosophies, swept away delusions and organized universals. And like the musical composition, the aircraft moved along perfectly.

Turbulence caught the ship with a giant swat, and I felt the combinations of skidding flight and the thrusts to either side of my selected altitude. I checked on Jim, who was behind and higher, then set about keeping my heading and altitude. It was another struggle with a heavyweight. An eerie glow built up along the wing leading edge. It was the omen of St. Elmo's fire, a discharge of static electricity which took the form of a silver-blue iridescence which could become wild sparks flowing around the aircraft. The black silhouette of the napalm canister on my right stub station and those along the outer wing stations were alarming shapes against the glow. I had once asked about it during my early night flights, wondering if lightning could set off the ordnance. The instructor had looked out to the wing, then back at me. "Gosh, I don't think so," he said. But I noticed that he kept looking at the wings as we progressed through the storm. I had carried the question to the ground but got the same answers. No one really knew. The final statement was: "It has never happened." I flew along, thinking about all the first times things had happened to people and others saying afterwards, "Well, I'll be darned."

The fiery glow spread and surrounded the entire machine. The propeller picked up the discharge and set about spinning it into solid electric silver. St. Elmo had seen the phenomenon back in the 1200s. It hung about a ship's mast when there were thunderstorms near. When men finally took to the air and ventured into storms, it became known to pilots as well as sailors. It was enveloping my airplane like a glove, pulsating with its intensity, tickling the ordnance under my wings, bringing a little extra sweat to my body. The airplane was an instrument of death, a sterling projectile in the storm, raw electricity spitting at it in rage, the surfaces painted dull black against reflection, not mirroring the bright flashes. It was total isolation, the action of a play designed for me alone, a solo actor without dialogue, special effects by God.

I called to Jim on the FM radio. His voice sounded distant and he said he was fighting it out just as I was. The time over target was close, and I attempted contact with the FAC who would be in the area. He confirmed that a marker was on the ground and was visible through a large hole over the target. I saw it just as I came into the ragged opening. Jim pulled into trail behind me, and we set up our orbit around the misty hole while the thunderstorm raged around us. Our arrival had been no secret to anyone, the sounds of two Skyraiders announcing us for some time. The FAC said the target was a truck convoy which had stopped on Route Seven near Ban Ban. I rolled on down through the mist, lined up the pipper on the mark, pressed the button, and started my pullup. Even before I had raised the nose very far there were clips of thirty-seven-millimeter groundfire piercing the sky. It came up from the murk like a stream of molten metal. I jinked away and climbed back into the clouds, which weren't too good a cover since I couldn't see the tracers but the gunners could

19

hear me. It made for a cloud condition we called cumulo metallum, or cloud full of metal.

We were over a segment of Ho's Trail, one of the better-defined ones. It was a North Vietnamese entry into northern Laos and a line of supply to troops many miles west and south. In effect, the southern part of Laos had been annexed by Hanoi. The North Vietnamese installed a labyrinth of routes into South Vietnam. We called it the Trail. In blatant violation of the Geneva accords, Hanoi had simply seized its neighbor's land and moved in an army. Now the road structure was carrying Hanoi's war materials. Our mission was to interdict the supply line by dive-bombing and strafing the targets as they were located.

The groundfire covered the sky, and I was hard pressed to roll in again without getting hit first. It was tiring work since there was lots of talk on the radio announcing more groundfire, clouds drifted through the target area, and I was trying to avoid taking any hits. It took total concentration to keep everything together and was always a strain unnoticed in the strike but realized afterwards when I relaxed on the way home. Groundfire had a queer way of looking pretty, the pink and red streaking from the ground, passing beside the aircraft, bursting above. And as long as it didn't hit the airplane it was sport to avoid the stuff. But it was also sudden death, and you couldn't see everywhere at once. It was highly possible to get it from behind when pulling off as a gunner opened up from your tail position. I hoped Jim would call out anything, so I kept my attention to his voice and on the business at hand. And while the groundfire could be intriguing from an academic standpoint, it could also be provoking. It was a means of communication, the worst one we could be using, albeit universally understood. It was a faulty statement of Chairman Mao that ran amuck. "Power lies in the muzzle of a gun." His disciples had taken it for truth; at least, lots of that "truth" came up through the night in the form of 23mm, 37mm, and so on. When villages were being overrun, international boundaries ignored, people slaughtered, and the reason was the supremacy of the gun barrel disguised as some sort of liberation, then it was time to communicate in return. I did. I set the intervalometer to station five and rolled in. To one side of my target I saw another gun position open up but judged its accuracy just enough off to allow me to keep going. The men were wrong down there. They were talking to me and I was talking back, crudely at best. You, sir, I thought, with your stupid gun and your imbecilic right-by-force idea, you will understand what I'm doing. Mao and Ho have told you so. Pay attention. You will understand it because your false belief has made you living death, clinging to an illusion. And all the while I knew that my bombs and guns were worthless in themselves, infinitesimal gropings in the dark. I didn't believe in them as the answer, but those below brought their own evil to bear upon themselves. I punched the release button twice, which moved the station selector twice, and two hunks of ordnance left the wings. I pulled off and climbed back into the night. It occurred to me that the men with the guns were quite simply punishing themselves. It was a highly religious, philosophical evening.

Jim swapped altitudes with me, and we passed each other once again invisible in the night. I held high with enough 20mm left to cover him and watched as he made pass after pass. Finished after nearly an hour, we climbed back through the overcast as the target closed over with cloud, and we could only see the results of our strike as a diminishing glow. "Come up channel eight and stand by," I called to Jim. "Head out to the south and you're cleared to eleven five." I talked with the FAC for another minute or so, then joined Jim on the radio as we slipped out of the area and pointed ourselves back towards Nakhon Phanom. The rain and surging winds returned, as did the glow of St. Elmo, although the wings were empty and free. Bluish silver swirled around the prop and hung about the airframe like frost. A giant circle of bluish discharge swung around the aircraft, then snapped away, as I started a descent to the base. I flew through several dissipating cloud formations, then descended into clear rain, the airfield lights glistening ahead like precious gems resting on black velvet. In a pilot's sense they were jewels of a different sort, the web of human life spun around them, a man's primordial thoughts rooted there, not a mile up in black airplanes thrashing about in thunderstorms and groundfire at night.

The final controller sounded urgent when he said the crosswind was strong. He even added that there was discussion about closing the field and diverting traffic to Udorn, another Royal Thai Air Force base in northern Thailand. I replied that they could close everything after we landed, preferably not before. I could understand the situation, though. Although headed down final with the nose adjusted well east, the airplane was drifting in a westerly direction. There was most assuredly a crosswind, and in the A-1, with the combination of its tailwheel configuration, the slick runway, and strong wind, a pilot had his hands full to the maximum. It was a rough proposition at best. All flying had to be perfect, and it occurred to me that a pilot lived in a world of perfection or not at all, which was easily demonstrated on a night like this. There was no traffic cop, no one to tell you how it had to be done, no one to help you to safety. It was all alone, no mistakes. I called Jim, who was in trail and turning final himself, and said, "No mistakes, old buddy." It has to be right the first time. He echoed simply, "OK, no mistakes."

I set up for landing with almost full left aileron and right rudder to keep the machine straight. My landing lights swung down and momentarily caught the wind sock pointed straight out across the runway. It appeared to confirm the direction we would be going if we bungled the landing. With near full control displacement I touched on the left main gear and rolled straight, the right wheel still in the air. The gusts were harsh, and I skidded in the rain when I got the right wheel down. Finally turning off the runway, I looked back and watched as Jim's lights found the runway; his airplane touched, rolled straight, then pulled up beside me. Jim was grinning.

I left the cockpit under the rumblings of another storm and tried to throw my poncho over my head, but the wind caught it and blew it across the ramp. I chased it, finally cornering the thing as it wrapped itself around the tailwheel of another airplane. The field was closed within minutes, and no other planes would make it in until the next day. The truck pulled up, with the windshield wipers doing little good against the downpour and wind. Jim was inside, still grinning, and he offered a little wave. It had been strange to have been so close for a few hours in the stormy night, yet not really see each other, to have fought it out with the elements and gunners, and return to a little blue truck there in northern Thailand.

"Well, neither of us made any mistakes on the runway," I said triumphantly.

"Well, there were a few moments there," Jim said, "when I thought I had."

We both laughed as the driver turned down the dirt road to maintenance debriefing. Jim ran through the rain, and I asked the driver to wait for us by the door so we wouldn't have to run so far in the monsoon showers. The Thai said, "No, sah, the tree." I looked up to the waving branches, but his statement didn't register. Perhaps it was another oriental custom, or some such thing. I said, "Yeah, great, trees. Just wait here." I was sitting at the desk when a giant howl of wind moaned under the roof, followed by a sharp crashing sound. We ran to the door and looked outside. The driver held up his hands, smiling. A thick branch was resting across the caved-in roof of the truck. Jim put his hand on my shoulder and said, "Well, my son, looks like you finally made that big mistake."

# THREE

**O**RDERS TO A-1 TRAINING IN HAND, I had played with the ultimate questions. What would combat really be like? How would I react to it? Would it be like the old war movies, lots of camaraderie and gallant words, or simply a sweaty, frightening, and miserable affair? I hadn't been in combat, so I could only speculate and wait. I did know for certain that I would be shot at almost every time I flew, that people would be plotting to kill me in the air or, even better for them, capture me and carry on whatever wild schemes they had a mind to, out of my element, on the ground. The thoughts left me with chilly dreams and more questions. Would I end up in the "Hanoi Hilton"? Tortured? Dead? We Americans, never having fought a battle on our own soil of the immensity of World War Two or the Southeast Asian War, had to suddenly come face to face with the real substance of war. Men are broken; some die. Some come home and some do not. Where would I fit in? Would I be scared? Would I be able to fly in combat and keep my wits?

Looking at my peers with their many different faces, personalities, and attitudes, I knew we all faced the same questions. Outward appearances didn't really mean a thing. Blasé demeanor apparent, we played through jungle survival school, accepting it as a game.

25

The rather uncomplicated journey to Southeast Asia was amusing. There was lots of beer and women and new surroundings, sounds and feelings and the rest that soldiers have seen since the first combat. But finally we boarded the last transport in May of 1969, headed north from Bangkok, and during the short flight attempted to construct whatever personal presentation we wanted when the door opened at the end of the line. I'm sure we all wanted to look and act like veterans but did not know the substance of the art. Indeed, we hardly knew what a veteran looked and acted like anyway. The fellow next to me said quietly, "This is probably the last time we'll fly that someone won't be shooting at us."

The C-130 transport made a fairly direct line from Bangkok to our new home, Nakhon Phanom, Thailand, with a rather quiet load of passengers. When the descent started we were all noses and eyes to the window trying to eke out a picture of what that new home looked like. There was very little to see. The base had been cut from a sparse jungle and consisted of a long runway, numerous buildings, the perimeter road and guards, then space. The Mekong River curved its fine line from the northern horizon past the town on the water's edge. The muddy Mekong continued south out of sight in the afternoon haze. In short order the Hercules transport scrunched onto the runway and the rear cargo door was lowered, giving us a view of the ramp as we taxied in. The A-1s were there for sure, parked side by side in the blistering heat.

In a line like all other military lines, we deplaned and walked on, looking for a familiar face. We were greeted by members of our new squadrons, our selections having been made prior to our arrival. There was a light rain in progress, and with my bulging B-4 bag it was a ponderous walk across some red mud under the weight of a heat beyond anything I'd known before. It was the humidity that made it so oppressive, as if we were carrying a hundred pounds extra load. There was a squadron truck into which we tossed our precious few goods, and off we drove across a base of red wood buildings, red mud, dust, and rain. We looked up once as a flight of Skyraiders came by for a landing, and I still had the same feelings about them as I had at first glance at Hurlburt Field and before. Our truck finally stopped long enough for us to lower our pants and receive copious injections of whatever substance it is that keeps one from hepatitis and so on. Then we drove on, threading our way between buildings until we arrived at a long series of structures which were the crew quarters. There was a large sign that announced Hobo Hilton. Ours was the First Special Operations Squadron, formerly the First Air Commandos, a name that had been changed to convey a less warlike image. Bag once more in hand, it was up a couple of wooden steps, then along a narrow wooden walkway to our rooms. I dumped my things in a tiny chamber which was to be one-half mine for the duration. It was a cubicle with two cots, two metal lockers, a chest of drawers, chair, desk, and noisy air conditioner. I wasn't really overjoyed by my initial impressions, and spending one year or so in that little room didn't sound all that great. As I stared inside the room, someone said, "OK, come on down to the hooch and meet the guys. Let's have a beer."

I walked past two Thai hoochmaids, who had been nicknamed Giggles and Popcorn. They took care of room cleaning, bed making, and even shoe shining, all for a modest monthly fee. At least a hint of the civilized was amongst the harsh realities of war, I thought, trying to be amused. Pity the Army lad in his wet trench. The girls were in the characteristic squat and were eating huge bugs with a side order of rice. Inspecting further, I discovered that they were, in fact, eating huge black rice bugs. As I learned shortly, the rice bug may be an ugly fellow, but is full of rice itself and is quite often part of the native diet. But not for me.

The hooch was a rectangular building, handmade mainly by the pilots, and was the general drinking and lounging place. There was a bar in the northern end, well manned by a Thai named Pete. The wall coverings ran the gamut from aviation to pornography, and the air was filled with cigarette smoke and the odor of liquor. Everyone was in a flight suit, many of which had salt-encrusted rings on the back, indicative of some hard work in a cockpit. It was about what I had expected and would satisfy any motion-picture director's demands for a movie set about pilots flying Skyraiders in a "secret war." We were introduced to the pilots, took our cans of beer, smiled, and said the appropriate things. But I noticed a curious distance between the old pilots and ourselves, a coolness behind the smiles. I soon realized what it was. The experienced combat pilots had been out there day after day, knew what it was to be shot at, knew what the art was about. They had nothing to prove. But we did. We couldn't even talk the language. A man in a two-plane formation in combat relies on the other man, his wingman, for protection, for cover, for many things. Having us, the unknown quantity, out there was tenuous. And so, laughing, tossing out dumb smiles, and trying to be accepted, I knew full well that what we would do in the air was the most important thing, and what words were spoken in the hooch were insignificant. One doesn't have to be very sensitive to know when no one really cares what you think or say about much of anything.

While the many thoughts of our new environment were spinning about in our minds, the traditional demands of the military began to emerge. "You obviously haven't met our squadron commander," one of the fellows said. "He's death on haircuts and sideburns." "I'll loan you my razor," another said. I finished my beer and headed for the dismal little room through a torrent of hot rain. In an hour I had sideburns of regulation length, or at least to the specifications of the commander I hadn't met. Then I prepared for a long night in damp sheets filled with the scent of mildew.

Morning was filled with many little chores that one must succumb to in the military: lots of paperwork and new forms and personal equipment. The day was a blistering tropical one in which I even sweated in the shower. Of immediate concern was the initial interview with the squadron commander, something I looked forward to with hesitation after the comments I'd already heard. Four of us marched into his office at the prescribed time, turned, and faced a creature who looked to me like the last surviving example of Neanderthal man. He had lieutenant colonel's leaves on his shoulders. His arms stretched across the desk like the limbs of a tree, and I entertained the thought that they might even reach the floor when he stood. He had no hair, or rather, any trace of growth had been removed with finality, as if it had committed an unpardonable sin. There was an American Flag in one

29

corner of the room, and little else. After he made some general comments about the superiority of the unit, the magnificence of its war record, and the usual patter about teamwork, he uttered some words which ascended from the bathyal zone of Paleolithic nonthink. "Well, I'm certainly glad none of you has long sideburns or long hair. That shows me a perverted mind. People with those things have mental problems. Now, we'll get you checked out as soon as possible because I'm sure you can hardly wait to get out there and kill somebody. That will be all." We saluted, turned, and left the room. I walked in somewhat of a daze, shaking my head, actually embarrassed. I had no idea how I would deal with that man. To him, long hair or sideburns were signs of perversion, yet apparently killing, per se, was just fun, to be enjoyed.

With a week to go before actual flying, I sat through the series of briefings and lectures concerning everything from the more bizarre forms of venereal disease common in the area to full descriptions of the Ho Chi Minh Trail. The former subject concluded with a brief statement that the malady was a matter of inverse economics: A higher price paid for a girl bought a more common disorder, and the lowest price usually resulted in the more exotic versions of the problem. In many cases, doctors had no idea what the strains were, much less how to cure them. The situation on the Trail was discussed in more detail and with greater interest. It wasn't at all humorous.

The Trail was a multithousand-mile interlacing transportation system including narrow dirt roads, rivers, perilous mountain trails, and the larger, more easily defined road structures which flowed down the eastern side of Laos. The Trail didn't simply work its way down through Vietnam. It left North Vietnam and entered Laos. Driving south and west, it drifted to the Plaine des Jarres as well as down into Cambodia through southern Laos. North Vietnam used this network like a busy ant colony and denied that it had any troops whatsoever outside Vietnam. To make this point clear, it refused to accept North Vietnamese prisoners of war since, in their manner of logic, if they had no people outside Vietnam, how could they receive their own POWs? The Lao prisons were full of North Vietnamese soldiers, but their own country wasn't admitting it. Thus they kept on with the statements about an in-country civil-war affair that the Americans interfered with. All the lies were obvious to those who were daily observers, but everything was well concealed from the American public. Part of my initial study concerned itself with facts and figures of the war, and I was surprised to see that not only did the Trail cross an international boundary or two, but it also handled some sixty tons a day of war materials from Hanoi. The main entry points into other countries were located at Mu Gia Pass and Ban Karai. Consequently, there were larger defenses erected at those locations. And as to defenses, the Trail network was the most heavily defended area of any war. There was more antiaircraft fire in the Vietnam-Laos area than had ever been seen in Europe or Japan. The anatomy of the Trail system had been mounted on large wall charts which could be pulled across an entire wall of the briefing room, providing easy inspection. The maps were covered with circles of different colors, the red ones pinpointing the locations of guns with recent firings. The board was covered with them. There were estimates that the antiaircraft guns numbered as many as two thousand. This didn't even count the smaller-caliber weapons. As the intelligence officer left me to study the various briefing guides, he remarked, "Just remember, it's only a little liberation movement to free all those people in the south. Just cover up Laos, Cambodia, parts of Thailand, Communist Chinese and Russian war materials, missiles and MiGs, and you will have just the picture the North Vietnamese want the world to have."

I opened the bound papers and read for hours. The rainy season, which spanned roughly May through October, slowed down the traffic and the groundfire. We were told to expect less resistance during those months, although the weather conditions kept the roads largely unusable, so the targets would be scarce. To keep the roads in constant repair, such as could be done, there were bulldozers and a constant stream of coolie labor to patch the holes and keep the roads clear. Most of the equipment, I noted, was American machinery, stolen or taken in battle. Reports by defectors were also interesting. One stated that it took him almost three months to come down the Trail, during which time every man suffered malaria and crushing exhaustion. Truck drivers were experienced in particular segments of the road system and drove only those areas. It was generally a headlights-off operation when there was moonlight, and shielded lights were used on the black nights. The men leaving Hanoi were propagandized into the notion that upon reaching South Vietnam there would be a welcome reception and a united fight, brothers together, against the "imperialist aggressors." Unfortunately for them, that wasn't the case. Also unfortunate was a complete lack of reverse-flow information. Only the approved data went south, and nothing unfavorable was to return. Whatever did manage to come back was denounced as lies. What took place was typical indoctrination, not true education. It resulted in classic xenophobia based on a severe lack of knowledge, as if a door had been kept closed and the occupants of the room, knowing only dark, accepted it as truth and fought to preserve the lie. It was tragic because any transfer of ideas was extraordinarily difficult. Very disheartening was the captured information that the American "antiwar" movement was to serve as added motivation to the North Vietnamese troops, that while they might think the Communist battle was lost, they must see that those Americans were helping from within to weaken the aggressors and help bring about final victory.

Studying further, I found obvious evidence of infiltration across international boundaries indicating a genuine interest in more than "southern brothers." The 17th-parallel DMZ was noted in the 1954 Geneva accords as a frontier barring direct infiltration by the North Vietnamese into South Vietnam. Hanoi reasoned that it could avoid the problem simply by going into Laos, another sovereign country, and around the DMZ. Of course, Laos's neutrality had been assured by the same agreement.

As I turned the pages, there were several photographs and tables. NVA tanks were driving across Laos into the Plaine des Jarres. Communist troops were swarming into Cambodia, and some teams had already started operations in Thailand. Any resistance was met with savage butchery, captured in disgusting detail in several photos. In one village where dissent was encountered, the chief and his family were dragged before the entire population. The bloody execution that

33

ensued would stay graphically in the minds of those people for some time, its effects upon children catastrophic. As a reminder that cooperation was expected, the remains of the family were put on public display. Public statements about active cooperation with the NVA and VC were rather obvious. Watching the tongues, eyes, and ears butchered from infants, people followed a numb course directed at physical survival. Laos was assaulted continually by Hanoi's army, its blackmail, its brutality. Unlike some members of America's "peace movement," Laotians did not suffer from the delusion that North Vietnam was a harmless, friendly minor power victimized by ruthless Americans. Any investigation of the war as a civil conflict would have to come to grips with the reality of the North Vietnamese army roaming Laos practically at will, and with its incursions into Cambodia in considerable force and its midnight sorties across the Mekong into Thailand. There was a statement by Laotian Prince Souvanna Phouma, who had requested American military intervention in the form of air strikes since 1964. At one point he declared he would be willing to accept continued use of the Trail by the NVA provided they withdrew from the rest of Laos. North Vietnam refused.

The Laotian conflict was first kept a secret in order to preserve the "neutralist" government of Souvanna Phouma. Then, since the United States had given no formal assertion of its interdiction efforts on the Ho Chi Minh Trail, it hoped to avoid offering any reason for Hanoi to commandeer *all* of Laos. If the remnants of the 1962 accords were repudiated by America, Hanoi would expand its Laotian war, creating increased fervor back in the United States. Three administrations of two political parties kept Laos a "secret war" in the hopes of maintaining a limited conflict.

There was another briefing titled "Rules of Engagement." Another interesting fact came to life. The rules, known as ROE, were apparently designed to minimize everything but the actual prosecution of actual combatants and associated equipment. In essence, the rules effectively prevented our waging a true war. There were no such things as targets of opportunity. Generally, by the time the entire situation had been discussed and studied, as was the policy, the target was either gone or there was disapproval to strike. Unless there was positive identification, calls to some higher headquarters, discussion and debate, there was no strike. This situation was bringing about a gross misuse of airpower. The majority of strikes in Laos were controlled and directed by a command many miles away, generally in Saigon, often in distant Washington, and decisions filtered down later. No one could move quickly except in the case of rescue. In some areas of Laos, the FACs had a Laotian with them in the aircraft to ensure positive target identification and minimize error. Many pilots had lost their lives by careful attention to avoiding what were classified as civilian areas and by following the rules. NVA antiaircraft fire didn't follow those rules. Setting up gun emplacements and camps in civilian communities was a sure way to avoid retaliation by the Americans. The greatest examples of this situation had been found in the skies over Hanoi, where the whims of unknowledgeable Americans led American pilots to their graves or to the shackles of prisons. As antiaircraft weapons were positioned, as the surface-to-air missiles were unloaded at the docks, we had been and still were denied the right to strike. With perhaps some good initial intentions, the government submerged the war in regulations and rules which prevented the campaign from being fought in any traditional sense. With our "rules" and openly broadcasted tactics, our presence there became a matter of postponing the inevitable. If we had declared war, then we would have had to engage in winning. Since that was apparently not the goal, there was no declaration of war, but great gobs of pomp and circumstance instead.

I finished the week of study and put the notes away, closed the last book, and walked from the building. What struck me most at that time was the matter-of-fact attitude. I had been given intelligence reports which simply related the facts. I was to draw my own conclusions. And, of course, I would go out and physically see for myself. One thing was quite clear: The Vietnam War, ominous in its own right, was even more than it appeared on the surface. The Communist movement was straightforward with all the techniques and apparatus inherent in its philosophy. The goal had never changed. It was still slavery and oppression, a complete denial of the value and freedom of the individual human being. But the American involvement was a real mystery, the techniques and methods employed giving question to our intent. The war in Laos was integral to Hanoi's plan to dominate all Indochina, and was perhaps as important as that in Vietnam for its many implications. The groundfire was heavier, and the traffic was heavier, and the movement of men and material was not solely into Vietnam. Cutting the Trail and North Vietnam's pipeline to other countries would be impossible with the rules and tactics of the United States. So what were we after?

I was firmly entrenched in the notion that we were fighting communism and its tenets. I thought that a righteous cause doesn't need lies and deception in order to succeed. If something is right and true, it will eventually prevail, no matter what. And fighting tyranny, removing the manacles of Communist bondage, was certainly a just cause. I couldn't figure out why our "secret war" had to be a secret from the world. The United States had never lacked support and morale for a just cause. In World War II men could hardly wait to volunteer for the battle. It was perhaps because they had an easily identifiable enemy who had aroused their ire. But now there was no clearly defined enemy threatening our shores. A philosophy, a method of deceit, was the enemy, perhaps already onshore. It was hard to ask men to fight such things as ideas. Thus the government forced the U.S. population to finance a project it didn't understand in places it never heard of, in a war we were apparently never supposed to win.

The van pulled up in a cloud of heavy dust, and I climbed in. The briefings were over. I had been fitted for my survival gear, had been issued a thirty-eight revolver, my helmet had been camouflaged, and I was on the schedule for the next day.

# FOUR

SINCE IT WAS TO BE my first combat flight, on June 5, 1969, I showed up early for the briefing. I selected an extra set of charts and studied the programmed target areas. The usual charts, in various scales, were covered with a clear plastic so that a pilot could mark on them and toss them about without much damage. They had even been mounted in booklet form so that a page could be selected and folded back to small proportions rather than having to grapple with a chart measuring some two by three feet. First flights were conducted in the A-1E, a two-seat version of the A-1, with an experienced combat pilot doing the flying. The neophyte was to study the operation and the terrain, and try to learn as much as possible about the area. Then there would be half a dozen training flights, followed by a check flight. Then came solo flights. The briefing was relatively quick. There was a time hack, a review of what had happened the night and day before, then a briefing on our target. The intelligence officer left and the pilot briefed me on the procedures we would be using. My pilot was Lt. Col. Dale Downing, a pleasant man who gave me every assistance. Quickly enough, we were standing by the airplane. It was the first time I had worn the bulky survival vest, and it felt as if a great handicap had been placed on me. It bulged with radios, ammunition, first-aid kit, and other items. I dragged my weight up onto the wing and climbed in. There seemed scarcely enough room to move, and after fastening all the straps and buckles and fitting my helmet and mask, I sat drenched in sweat from a one-hundred-degree day and comparable humidity. When the engine caught and the prop spun at a thousand RPM, it felt like someone had splashed me with cool water, the wind upon my wetness.

We taxied out, and I gave cursory glances at the tons of ordnance under the wings. It was the first time I had flown with the real thing out there, and it looked dark and threatening in olive-drab colors. The arming wires pierced small holes in the metal fuses so the wind wouldn't turn the vanes and arm the weapons. The arming crew made all the final adjustments, and we were quickly on the runway watching lead start his takeoff. Actual side-by-side formation takeoffs were no longer made since the A-1's immense torque could make for dangerous moments during the takeoff or abort when another airplane was inches away. And the brakes, adequate for maneuvering aboard a Navy carrier, were less than adequate if one elected to abort a takeoff with a full load. With lead some ten seconds down the runway, we started our takeoff roll.

"Get your maps out and follow along," the man said. I unfastened the little black bag of charts and unfolded one. Dale reached over and pointed to our position and said to watch for the prominent landmarks we would be crossing. Our flight was directed to the area of Laos code-named "Steel Tiger," the southern portion of the country. Since the rainy season was at its height, clouds covered much of the ground and it was difficult to get a true picture of the land below.

In the rainy season the sun could become a memory to those on the ground and something a pilot might occasionally see between clouds. We came to the Bangfai River and a peculiar winding part of it. "That's known as the 'limp dick,' for obvious reasons," he said. "You'll find that it's easier to learn the country by landmarks so you can get a quick mental picture of where you are, where you need to go, and where someone else is." The limestone land formations, known as karst, all seemed to take on strange shapes. We worked our way down the river for a few minutes. To the west of us stretched a long karst hill. "That's known as the 'rooster tail,'" he said. I eventually saw the "boot," the "three ships," the "duck," the "cathedral," and other appropriately named landmarks. Then we came to the target area. I had been impressed with the colossal beauty of the country, Laos being the greenest and most lush terrain I had ever seen. But where many bombings had taken place the foliage ended and it looked like a piece of the Great Sahara thrown down out of context. Our target was an NVA troop and supply concentration, or so the FAC said. He flew around the area in a Cessna O-2, a twin-engine light plane with one engine up front and one behind, normally referred to by us as a mixmaster. To me, the area below was an area of fairly dense growth, then bomb craters, and I saw nothing else. While Dale set his armament panel I began to feel that while the country was beautiful, it somehow looked deadly. At least it did at that moment. I even had a flashback to jungle survival school and hoped that we didn't have to walk around down there. Before I was ready we were rolling in and pressing down into the target area.

I felt the release of two five-hundred-pound bombs

and sank into the seat under a four-G pullout. I looked around for groundfire, even ducked just a little, but there was nothing to be seen. I didn't even know what groundfire looked like at that point anyway. "Notice how I'm setting the switches for the ordnance," Downing said indifferently. "Right," I said, not paying any attention whatsoever. I kept looking at the ground. Then we came around for a rocket pass. We made the same steep diving pass, but after the rockets had streaked out with their smooth-sounding "swoosh," I saw strange puffs of orange coming up from below, and we flew down through them. So this is what it's like to get shot at, I thought. I immediately lowered both of my protective helmet visors and sat rigid. We pulled off and climbed away, jinking slowly to spoil any gunner's aim. I had a tingling sensation across my shoulders and back, a reaction to danger, I thought.

"It sure is a strange sensation to watch groundfire for the first time," I said.

Dale turned his head quickly and looked at me. "What groundfire?" he asked seriously, all sport gone from his face.

"Those little puffs that exploded in front of us when we made that rocket pass," I explained.

He laughed. "That wasn't groundfire. We're using a special-type rocket that opens up after it gets out a ways. What you saw was just the explosive opening. We flew down through the smoke. Guess it did look like it was coming up at us, but it was just an illusion. Guess I should have explained about that." He laughed again, and I sat back kind of embarrassed and disappointed, yet relieved.

Just before we landed Dale said, "There's no need to rush things. When you really get some groundfire from some big guns you'll know it. You may never see the small-arms stuff, though. The muzzle flash is hard to see, particularly during the day. You'll often know it when it hits the airplane. Then again, you may take some small-arms hits and never know it until you get back. Depends on what you're doing at the time and where the airplane gets hit. Just hope they're all as easy as today."

It was several days later, after my checkride and while on my second solo flight, that I took a hit. After landing, I was postflighting the airplane and noticed a small hole where a bullet had penetrated the fuselage. I hadn't even known about it, had heard nothing, and never thought the area we had been flying in contained any groundfire. But someone firing a rifle had hit my airplane. I stared at the hole with an empty feeling, it suddenly striking me how precarious flying in combat was. When we got back to the hooch, lead said, "Rick took his first hit today." Someone said, "Big deal," and we all drank a beer, and no one seemed to think much about it. But I did.

With the dual flights out of the way, I had a little more time to take stock of where I was and what feelings I was having. The base itself looked like a wooden sculpture cut into the jungle. The flightline the heart of the place, was a scene from the museum of aviation history, with a collection of old airplane shaped by the old masters and sanctioned through admirable performance over time. I peered through the van's doors as we drove across the ramp to the airplanes. We rolled past the huge cowls of A-1s with their various names painted across the curved metal. Every pilot had an airplane assigned to him and he could name it as he wished, that name being painted on the nose. The pilot's name was stenciled along the cockpit. *Magnett Ass* sat alone, titled such due to its nature of collecting more than an average amount of antiaircraft fire. *Firebird* carried Ron Rounce's name, and Randy Bertrand's machine, *Blood, Sweat and Tears*, sat a few spaces down. Past *Iron Butterfly* and *The Crispy Criterer*, the *Midnight Cowboy* and *Peregrine*, we passed *Mafia Madness* and *The Wind's Song*, finally reaching a rather tired-looking "E" model which had *Yankee Clipper* on one side of the cowl. Jim Bender got out, and I drove on. The ramp didn't have a single machine of a design vintage more recent than 1949. The A-1s stemmed from 1944 concepts, and the old C-47 was the DC-3 of 1935. The C-123s were old Chase Aircraft inventions of 1949, and the old A-26 bombers were first seen in 1942. It was both satisfying and humorous to know that the great old designs still did the heavy work, and that few new machines were doing as well. Our antique assortment of airplanes became the basis for a cartoon in which two jet pilots were watching some biplanes off their wing, all piloted by mustached barons and representations of Snoopy with scarf in the wind. The one jet pilot was saying to the other, "There goes that outfit from Nakhon Phanom."

The base was Nakhon Phanom, NKP, sometimes referred to as "Naked Fanny," and often as "the end of the world." "Downtown" referred to the small town on the Mekong River where a forty-baht ride in a taxi driven down a half-dirt and half-concrete highway at the rate of Sterling Moss in a grand prix would take you in twenty to thirty minutes. The town had graduated from rice farming with water buffaloes to entertaining GIs with everything from questionable edibles to rare strains of venereal disease. The crudely constructed bars went on and off the restricted list, depending on which had the highest VD rate as presented by the flight surgeon at the commander's morning briefing. During one of my first days on base I sat listening to the radio, studying some manual, and realized that I was hearing a series of numbers on the radio. The announcer said, "Ok, guys, here's today's list!" And he just started calling numbers. I asked my roommate, John Flinn, what it meant. "Those girls downtown all have a number on them, on a little tag they wear. Those numbers on the radio are the ones with known VD."

The start of a combat mission was logged once a pilot was across the Mekong River, which meant Laos since that's where our war really was. The war was more precisely on the Trail, which looked like the moon from an altitude of a few thousand feet. It was cratered for mile after mile by thousands of bombs. And in what seemed like every few inches of it were heavy gun emplacements, guns which had not been used in Vietnam, guns which had been entrenched in Laos by the North Vietnamese. And at great expense and risk, pilots went out to the Trail in an effort to stop the flow of war materials. Whatever couldn't be put in trucks went on a bicycle, across the shoulders, on foot, by animal. And women and children often operated the guns along the routes. Our Western thought and tradition was out of place in dealing with such an enemy. Oriental thought was strange to us and it killed with unconventional methods. Words and thoughts were defined differently. "Killing" was what we did, but "liberation" was something the enemy performed. Where life was valuable to us, drudgery and death were commonplace and fully accepted in a fanatical cause. And so, once out into combat, we had to make certain our viewpoint matched that of our enemy so that we spoke the same language. Laos was a dark and mysterious place for us. We could sit at NKP only twenty minutes from the Trail by air and sip gin and tonics, or launch into the night sky and in that twenty minutes be immersed in devastating groundfire, giving one a sharp sense of the absurd, the incongruous. In a letter to a friend before we ever arrived in Southeast Asia, a pilot wrote to say that those who flew A-1s on the Trail had "brass balls." We were beginning to wish they really were.

# FIVE

THE ALARM CLOCK WAILED its normal dismal sound. I reached over slowly and shut it off. I had slept fitfully after dozing off while writing in my journal in an effort to record what my tour was like day by day. I was making slow adjustments to my new home, still having trouble with the damp and yellowed bedding, the putrid water, the cell-like room, the innumerable discomforts that went on ad nauseam to make life less than cheerful by former standards. I got up as if in great pain, which I wasn't, and looked through the little window in the door. It was a day which looked like cool San Francisco, with the promise of constant drizzle and perhaps fog later in the evening. The clouds looked frozen in pewter, the air cold. Not so. The opened door let in the eighty-five-degree morning and the moist oriental air managed to seep in like some apparition haunting me. The dope on my model airplane wing blushed and the wing warped. The climate wasn't conducive to anything I had in mind at that sleepy moment.

There was only cold water left in the shower, and even that was yellow. I tried to get used to it but was having less than complete success. My white towel changed to yellow-orange as I dried, and my toothbrush changed color shortly thereafter. My razor scraped my face into redness in the cold water. Our doctor said the water was safe, but I didn't like it even so. Standing before the little shaving mirror, I cursed my fate.

I traipsed back to my room, already hot and sweating. The calendar on my wall said it was June 28, 1969, a Saturday. It just wasn't a weekend sort of day. I dressed and headed for my briefing.

Our flight was directed to the Steel Tiger area again. It was the only area I had been to, so I knew parts of it fairly well. The lead aircraft was to be piloted by our operations officer, Lieutenant Colonel Neal, who had just returned from leave. Giving him a recurrency check as a matter of formality was Major Bagwell, who would fly in the right seat of the "E" model. I would be solo on their wing. The briefing was standard, right from the book, a carbon copy of the ones I had been through previously. Then, just as we were about to leave, the intelligence briefer came back to say that our mission had been changed and that we would be going north into the area designated as "Barrel Roll," the northern sector of Laos. The base at Muong Soui was about to be overrun, and refugees were being evacuated. The A-1s were needed to cover the helicopters during the withdrawal. I had never been to that territory except through the tales told in the hooch. The Hobos had flown mainly to Steel Tiger, and another squadron almost entirely covered the northern areas. Northern Laos was all high terrain, with ten-thousand-foot mountains and rugged ground everywhere. It was close to Hanoi and China and was described in foreboding and exotic terms. Colonel Neal said that even though I hadn't been up there, if I just followed him everything would be OK. He said he would point things out from the air. We grabbed a new

47

set of charts in a hurry, not having time to study them, and headed for the airplanes.

Flying combat missions was still fairly new to me; this was only my fourteenth solo mission. The survival vest was ponderous, and so was the heat. I was still a novice, and in no way did I consider myself really knowledgeable in the art of combat flying or one of the "old heads." The only thing I did with any skill was fly the airplane.

Someone had drawn a smiling face on the nose of the napalm container on the left stub. As I came to it on my preflight checklist, I read the little tag on the side. It said: "Napalm B, 475 pounds; Blu-32." As I got to the wing, the crew chief came up with my canteen of water. It was more than cold, it was frozen, a lump of ice with a plastic cover. I cranked the engine, checked the radios, and was airborne on lead's wingtip in short order. He requested a transponder check for his airplane, but we neglected my own.

Half an hour out we were at ten thousand feet and I was straining to maintain all of one hundred and forty knots level flight with the heavy load. We had nicknamed "E" models "fat faces," and I really knew why. The frontal area was larger than the single-seater, and there was simply more drag. The weather was already nasty, with thunderstorms and solid cloud cover. I didn't see the ground, and it was all I could do with the unwieldy machine to stay with lead, whose "E" was somehow faster than mine. I chased him through cumulus so big that I was awestruck with their size. They were the cleanest white I had ever seen, so pure as to be blinding. I lowered my colored helmet visor and flew on.

It wasn't long until I noticed that my TACAN set

wasn't working. I couldn't receive the base, nor could I tune in any other station. I called lead, who simply said to write it up in the maintenance forms when we returned. There weren't many radio stations anyway, and some of the ones we did have would go on and off the air depending upon who owned the particular portion of real estate where the transmitter was located. We could generally map-read with the ground in sight, or hold a heading for a predetermined time and be close to the designated area when the time was up. There was no map reading today, though, because the ground was obscured, so I set the charts aside and concentrated on the flying and my position on the lead aircraft. He would do the navigating. The cumulus was building and climbing, and I momentarily thought of us as two fish swimming in a sunken ship, negotiating its corridors and compartments. Actually, we were just that, metal fish in a sea of air. And just for an instant I saw another pair of metal fish heading in the opposite direction, swimming back to the cavern of more familiar things. They streaked from a large hole and disappeared into another. Then there was a deluge of rain which obscured my view. Presently I relocated lead and set about staying closer, wondering what the other pilots were thinking. I pictured the major smoking and eyeing the weather and the colonel hoping that I wouldn't do anything stupid.

It was both the curse and the fortune of the A-1 to have three different radios plus an ADF receiver. I monitored the cacophony of them all, with the helicopters making their rendezvous, the airborne controller attempting to direct the flow of traffic, and lead making periodic remarks. I still wasn't accustomed to the incessant chatter from so many directions. I had

49

been told that it didn't take long until one could even tell which radio was which by characteristic sounds, but so early in my combat life I only got frustrated trying to keep up with it all.

We flew from ragged cloud into a ragged clearing, and there was the immediate impression of emerald mountains bathed in white mist. It was stunning at the very least. Muong Soui was a mass of small buildings by a dirt landing strip, a few miles in front of us. It was a base frequently used by the civilian pilots and some of our FACs. Air America and Continental Air Services operated their short-takeoff-and-landing aircraft, as well as small transports, from the airfield, known as site 108 in their jargon where every little strip had a number as well as a name. (Both Air America and Continental Air Services were civilian companies under contract to the United States government—more precisely, the CIA.) Actually, Muong Soui was a 2,150-foot Laotian strip and could handle some of the smaller transports. To the north were long strings of people waiting for airlift. Apparently, the NVA was just down the road.

Several helicopters, mostly Air America machines, were ferrying refugees in shuttle fashion, passing each other going and coming. They looked like small green insects buzzing about the hills. We gave them a call and took up a circling pattern above, keeping track of individual helicopters and keeping an eye out for advancing troops and groundfire. But we circled for over two hours in relative calm. Rain moved in and out, with steel-colored clouds forcing us low to the hills. I scrunched around the seat, trying to keep halfway comfortable, but found it impossible. Flying a protective cover for so long just wasn't suited to either comfort or excitement. It was boring at best. Several flights of U.S. fighters moved into the area and were directed to strike various portions of the small base. The scheme was to deny the NVA use of whatever was left there, mostly American goods and supplies. There were numerous fires and explosions along the site as abandoned equipment was destroyed. It was a peculiar and frustrating feeling to be destroying our own materials, knowing that they obviously cost a fortune at the onset, not to mention the great waste of manpower involved. By the same token, if they were left intact, the enemy would be using them against us, a common tactic.

As we approached a lower fuel state, lead requested that we strike and that another flight of A-1s take over the cover job. We switched with a new flight and headed south to the FAC and the base itself. As far as we could discern, things were quiet and the strike would involve the fairly simple matter of hitting supplies in the open.

On command I moved back in loose trail formation as we picked up a circle around the abandoned airstrip. The FAC in a single-engine Cessna O-1 described our target as crates of supplies along the runway, and lead called with the familiar "Push 'em up and set 'em up," which was to say, increase power and set up the armament panel. I set the propeller to 2,600 RPM and moved the mixture lever to the "rich" position. Then I flipped the toggle switch to the left stub, the one holding the five-hundred-pound napalm with the smiling face. Lead rolled in, and I watched him commence his pass. His napalm dropped away and tumbled directly into the boxes and bins and containers. There was a gigantic ball of orange flame, and the A-1 pulled sharply away in a left turn. I called in and rolled on over into a fairly shallow pass to give me a long and smooth run over the target. Since there wasn't any groundfire it was much easier to come in low and set the ordnance on target chiefly by eyesight rather than by gunsight. I roared to the storage area, leveling around one hundred feet. The crates rushed into position, and I pressed the release button on the stick and started a four-G climb. Suddenly a steady stream of yellow-orange flashed by the right wingtip. There was no doubt that I was being shot at, but I was so surprised that it took a few seconds to register. My voice was broken as I hit the mike button and yelled, "There's groundfire!" That didn't tell anyone very much since I had been the only one to see it and my call gave little information. Lead came back, "Where from?" I wrenched my head around and jinked the airplane, but the gunners had stopped firing. Lead then suggested that we strike again but this time keep a lookout for gun positions. We had been so complacent before that it had been like a practice range. The FAC said he would stay high and scan the area. Everyone seemed rather nonplussed to me. I was tingling with anxiety and my heart was racing. Lead rolled in again, and this time the gun position was evident as the tracers spewed through the air. I set my gun switches quickly and volunteered to attack the emplacement.

In retrospect I considered this a fairly unintelligent move since a solo daylight duel with several anti-aircraft guns was a dubious pursuit. The aircraft was always visible, and I had no other fighter cover. And there was more than one gun to attend to. As I approached the small hill where the guns were entrenched, the tracers arced upwards, streaming past my wingtips. I felt a sort of cold numbness throughout my body as I rolled in on the muzzle flashes below. I was scared and breathing hard. I pushed the airplane into the dive quickly, putting the gunsight on the flashes below, and opened up with rockets and 20mm simultaneously. The tracers came up the way heavy hail comes down from a thunderstorm. It formed a tunnel of fire around the airplane as I continued down. The pass seemed like an hour, but only seconds passed until I was pulling up and jinking away. At this point everyone else was aware of the gun emplacements. The FAC yelled, "Wow, they're really hosing you down!"

I still hadn't taken any hits I was aware of, although the hot and cold flashes and the excitement had kept me well insulated from the hard facts. Lead called and said we would strike the position together for mutual protection. It was a good idea, although I wasn't much for going back through the agony again. But we did, coming in together from slightly different directions, guns firing together. The gunners were situated in circular fashion, with eight to ten muzzle flashes evident. As we fired I saw most of the guns stop shooting, but the couple remaining were dead accurate. I ran out of ordnance just before pulling out of my pass, the roar of my four guns suddenly stopping at the same moment. Lead initiated a hard left turn away, and I started to join on him. Suddenly a trail of white smoke began streaming from his right wing.

Colonel Neal abruptly called that he had taken hits, and I verified the smoke. The A-1 wing was relatively empty of anything that could be severely damaged by groundfire, the fuel being in the fuselage and in external tanks. There was only a thin hydraulic

53

line which ran through the aft section of the wing and served the aileron boost system. Apparently the hit had severed that line and the fluid was igniting. As I moved into closer formation to take a better look, the fire suddenly spread down the entire wing and enveloped the wingtip completely. I moved a few feet out and gave a call. "The wing's completely on fire. Get out while you can. I'll cover you." There was the possibility of the fire igniting remaining rounds from the wing guns, and the wing looked like it was going to burn off momentarily anyway. Major Bagwell called as I finished talking. "I'm getting out!"

The right canopy section blasted away from the aircraft and the slipstream carried it off. The spiraling rocket of the extraction system shot up with a thin flame, followed by the man's body. For a second the whole thing looked like one of the advertising films made by the seat company. The body looked like a mannequin, arms down, legs dangling. From my position just a few feet away, I watched the chute blossom and the body start its slow descent. The fiery A-1 was still going, Colonel Neal inside. I called the FAC and told him to stay with the first survivor and that I was going to keep track of the remaining pilot. They were already quite a distance apart. I had to move away from the burning aircraft again as its right aileron started ripping away from the wing, spinning away with the wind. The disabled machine started rolling, but the pilot wasn't out yet. But then we were down to no more than a thousand feet above the hills. There wasn't much time left. I moved to the other side of the airplane and, to my horror, saw Colonel Neal trying to get out over the side of the cockpit, which meant that his extraction seat had failed. My confidence in the seat went to hell in that instant. As the airplane rolled, his body was thrown about and the forces made his efforts herculean. Finally his body fell clear and the chute opened immediately, made one swing, and touched the ground. The airplane twisted itself into a ball of fire, then smashed into the ground. Its shrieking, mechanical death was ended in a second. A slender black column of smoke rose from the wreckage marking the pyre, and flame charred the ground around it.

I dropped down to about fifty feet and flew over the parachute and saw the pilot's body limp, hanging in some tall trees. He wasn't more than one hundred feet from the burning wreck, which was an obvious place for enemy troops to start looking. I wasn't able to tell if the body was moving or whether he had been too low when he got out and was crushed in the fall. I accepted the prospect that he was still alive.

Other strike aircraft were showing up, all A-1s from Nakhon Phanom. The FAC was directing them to the airfield area and gun positions, and one flight offered to lead me back to base. Since I had gone this far and knew where my last survivor was, I was determined to stay the course.

Then came another crucial moment as I spotted troops running down a small road to the pilot's position. I hadn't a single pound of ordnance left and felt completely ineffective. I was about to be a spectator. It was truly amazing how many things went through my mind during those moments. There were alternatives, possibilities, and above all some sort of action that had to happen immediately. I called for one of the evacuation helicopters to give us a hand and told him that the black smoke was a good position to head for.

I added that they ought to hurry—my survivor wouldn't be there if they waited too long.

It occurred to me that if I rolled in on the troops it might appear that I wasn't out of ammunition. So I tried it. I pushed the power up into the characteristic roar and dropped down to within a few feet of the ground, blasting down that road as if the airplane were about to swallow anything in its way. I wanted it to look as if a fire-breathing metal monster possessed of every oriental demon were about to annihilate every millimeter of flesh and blood in its way. It must have been an effective ploy; the troops jumped into ditches off the road and took cover. At least they stopped moving. I racked the airplane into a tight turn and came back. As I passed the line of men who had quickly decided not to proceed for another few seconds, I saw Colonel Neal trying to crawl away, moving in slow motion. At least he was alive. I turned back, thinking that perhaps the soldiers might be getting used to my antics. I decided to drop my empty centerline fuel tank if necessary. But the helicopter arrived shortly thereafter, and with great relief I watched the downed pilot being hoisted aboard and being lifted away. The FAC said that the other pilot had been rescued also, and that neither one of the survivors was badly hurt. I felt greatly soothed, turned into willowy nothingness. I slumped into the seat and whistled air through my teeth.

The situation was altered considerably when I realized that I had never been to that area before and remembered that I no longer had any operational navigational equipment. I had refused to leave the scene when other airplanes showed up, thinking that since I had been there when it started, I ought to finish and be certain my guys were safe. But now fuel was low. I would have done it in the same way again, but that didn't address my dwindling fuel quantity. The weather was the same, towering cumulus and lots of rain. I would have to get back through it the way I had come. I made another radio call to another flight of A-1s which had arrived on the scene during the rescue. "This is the Hobo wingman. I've never been to this area before, my TACAN is inoperative, and I'm not sure of the way back. I'd like to return with you if possible." The reply was quick and sounded reasonable at the time. "We're going to strike, so we're not going back yet. Just take up a heading of one-five-zero and you'll make it." I accepted the advice at face value and set out, promptly going on instruments inside some very wet clouds. I checked the compass and the time and held steady on my heading as best I could in the turbulence, flying with relief and attendant tumultuous rapture. It had been the most exciting bit of adventure I had ever been through. My adrenaline was so high that I had trouble fastening my oxygen mask as I climbed back to altitude, and my hands shook nervously. At least it was over, I thought. It was only a matter of time and distance on the southerly heading.

As a matter of course, I scanned the instruments and made the standard radio calls. The controller said he was unable to pick up my transponder and that my radio was weak. Very soon I lost all radio contact with the outside world. There was a good bit of turbulence, during which I noticed that my gyrocompass wasn't moving. It was stuck, showing a near southerly heading. I glanced up to the small standby magnetic compass which also showed roughly a south heading. It was at that time that I noticed another peculiar thing.

The mounting bracket for the little magnetic device had broken, and the unit was hanging such that the compass card wasn't free to turn. I raised the bracket, and the compass slowly turned to east.

For the very first time in my life I got that profound sense of loneliness that men have known in ships at sea, or fliers felt when they thought all was lost. I couldn't see the ground and had just discovered that my radios weren't working properly and the compass system wasn't usable. I was the fish that kept running into the aquarium glass, trying to get out, not knowing how. The clouds changed to a more ragged appearance, and I soon flew through patches of open air. Then I suddenly broke out of a wall of clouds, and before me stretched the ocean! There was no doubt about direction then. My wandering pilgrimage had taken me east into—and over—North Vietnam! I blinked several times, perhaps hoping it all might disappear. It didn't. I was over North Vietnam, almost out of fuel, no ammunition, and quite alone at one hundred and fifty knots airspeed. In the distance I could see roads, railroad tracks, and what appeared to be an airfield. It wasn't one of ours; it was in Vinh, a place where an American pilot was better than a soccer ball for fun and games. I shuddered and turned back to what was most assuredly southwest. I used the clouds for whatever cover I could, hoping interceptors wouldn't spot me. What sport it would be for a pair of MiG fighters to play with me! Considering the imported Russian electronics in the area, anything I might do could be futile.

Strange things came to mind, like my little wooden cup of pencils on my desk, and clean stationery and warm letters, fine writing sealed in envelopes, a bed

58

turned back and a good book beside it. Then my thoughts went from feeling sorry for myself to complete anger. I threw the map case to my side and even yelled for being so stupid. I cursed my plight and myself. I should have done any number of other things, like insisting to go back to base with the other aircraft when they asked. But I hadn't. What I had done was not simply get lost. I had followed what would be normal procedure in normal circumstances without the knowledge that I was already in trouble. I was no longer lost. I knew precisely where I was. The situation had developed in a matter of perhaps fifteen minutes. It was amazing what one could do in so short a time. Fifteen minutes in one direction meant safety; another direction meant one's possible destruction, or imprisonment at the very least. In a sense, it was all unavoidable with the conditions set up as they were. Given the same weather, the same broken instruments, the same high-adrenaline situation, and the same lack of experience, most airmen would end up in the same place. The question was, what was I going to do about it? There was still a flyable airplane and apparently some fuel left. The story wouldn't be over until I went down, wherever it would be, and I went about seeing to it that at least I got as far as possible. I pulled the power back to the minimum and jettisoned my empty fuel tank to decrease aerodynamic drag. The best I could do was apply everything I had ever learned about flying and survival. It was all I could do. I would need every bit of that skill; anger and despair wouldn't help. Only some composure would. But I was very scared once again. For some moments I felt helpless, empty, and I fought the vision of going down and being captured.

59

My earphones were filled with static that sounded like jamming. I had heard it before. Although it was late in the day, I couldn't follow the sun to a westerly position because of the heavy clouds and storms. There were a few moments when I thought about the importance of little things, such as the lines on the fuel gauge. The needle was resting on the "empty" line. I wondered if it was accurate. Presently I went about putting my charts in a neat pile and fixing the cockpit for my bailout. I didn't see how I would make home base with an empty gas tank and many miles left to go. So as not to give up I tried the radios again. I went through two of them and a number of different frequencies, then got a response on the third. There was a weak reply from a Sandy, then some voices from the command post. The A-1 Skyraider rescue pilots went by the call sign "Sandy," and they were revered for flying against all odds to protect and rescue downed pilots. I was elated for a second, then obsessed with the notion that talking to those people wasn't the same as being there with them. At least they would know I was still airborne and alive. I came into more familiar terrain as I passed several places that I had seen during my first orientation flights. Then there was a most beautiful sight. Two A-1s, Sandy One and Two, came roaring up from the west. Lead called, and I recognized the voice of my roommate, John Flinn. It was a damned fine sight. They swung around and gave me cover, planning to escort me until I had to get out of the airplane. In a few minutes I could see the airfield across the Mekong. The engine kept running, somehow. I stayed at altitude, hoping that I could glide if the engine quit. After a ragged eternity the three of us arrived over the field and I started a forced landing pattern,

60

alerting the tower and other traffic. I came around at idle power, high on final, and once it was certain that I could land even if the engine quit, I slipped away some altitude and landed. As the wheels rumbled on the ground I moved the yellow canopy lever and let in some fresh air, as I thought I might not breathe anymore. It was cool on my dripping body. The airplane and I came to the end of the runway and pulled off into the dearming area with the sound of the tailwheel locking lever snapping into the "unlocked" position. As I put on the brakes the engine made some coughing sounds. The deputy commander for operations, Colonel Fallon, jumped onto the wing, gave the fuel gauge a disbelieving glance, then said to shut it down. I later learned I had scarcely a couple of gallons left—not much for an engine that consumes about one hundred gallons an hour!

A jeep picked me up and drove to the helicopter which had just landed with Colonel Neal and Major Bagwell. The squadron was out in force to welcome back two of its pilots. Bagwell had a few scratches and bruises and his flight suit was torn. Neal was about the same, with bandages on his forehead. They both greeted me warmly and thanked me for being there. John Flinn came over with a bottle of champagne and poured it for us. He gave me a wink and said, "Welcome back, roommate. We were wondering if you were going to make it. Here, you probably need this. You look like you do."

I sipped the icy liquid. "I can't tell you how happy I am to be here," I said faintly. It was a tremendous understatement.

Hindsight has been a natural talent for most people and was devastating in the hands of some "career-minded" officials. I went to the intelligence debriefing amid questions and suggestions of what I might have done and so forth. The debriefers were interested in the gun emplacements at Muong Soui. One officer mentioned that there had been several surface-to-air missile firings while I was in the north over Vinh. I remarked that I hadn't seen any, although I had mainly been in the clouds. If they had come close I hadn't known it. I began to realize that I was in a mild shock; I was shaking somewhat and was having trouble talking well as my voice was being taped. After trying to re-create the episode I left the room in a trance. At the end of the long corridor stood my squadron commander, hands on hips. He said, "Do you realize how this reflects on me? DO YOU KNOW HOW THIS REFLECTS ON *ME?*"

I frowned, trying to make some sort of sense of what the man was saying. I thought he might be waiting to shake my hand or welcome me back. But he went on.

"How will I explain this to *my* commander? One of my pilots getting lost—and how could you, as a former Air Force navigator, get lost?"

I slumped against the wall and said, "First, I was never a rated Air Force navigator. Where in the hell you got that idea I don't know."

He rubbed his chin, then said, "Well, I thought you were. You should know better anyway."

"And second," I went on, "there is a lot more to this story than simply getting lost."

He shook his head and went on about how the affair would reflect on him and his leadership. He was really saying that on his way to the top, he had no place for anything that might appear to reflect badly on him, this situation looking that way to him. It would have been far easier for him to explain a combat loss if I had gone down under fire than to explain a living and breathing pilot who came home, by whatever circuitous route. A battle loss happens in the course of war—but this? I explained about the airplane and the nonfunctioning equipment and my lack of experience in the area, but he said it was all an excuse. He ordered maintenance to check the airplane completely. If he could rest some blame on my shoulders he could breathe easier, his record unblemished. But I couldn't figure what "blame" had to do with anything. Two pilots had been successfully rescued and I had returned with the airplane, even though little of it worked. I was bitter and hurt, somewhat dazed and shaken. My survival gear felt like a ton, and the sound of the engine was still in my head, the voices on the radio still yelling, the picture of North Vietnam still etched clearly in my mind. I repressed the urge to strike the man and, with what little energy I had left, turned and walked off.

I went back to my little room and dropped onto my bunk. I was angry at myself for letting such a man bother me. Like anything of such a nature, you do what you must when alone, no one to point the way. You make your decision alone and act accordingly. I was the only one up there in a beat-up airplane trying to rescue two pilots and get back home. I resolved to pay less attention to what others thought and more to experiencing my own life and standing up for my own beliefs. At least I had learned one thing well. I opened my journal and wrote, "Unless you've walked in another's shoes, be quiet." It was an old adage, but I had learned precisely what it meant. Then I turned to the wall calendar and circled June 28. Beside that date I wrote: "What a hell of a weekend!"

A few weeks later, in the truly distorted way of life I was experiencing, I received my final verbal reprimand from the squadron commander. Then he changed personalities and went on to say that it was a fine mission, that what I had said about the airplane's mechanical problems was true after all, but that I needed more experience. He showed me a paper which he had written to his commander showing how he had instigated new and more effective procedures to eliminate the sort of situation I had encountered. It also said that I had been briefed on my errors, including an improper engine-out pattern, and had learned my lesson. Then I went to the large briefing room and was presented with the Distinguished Flying Cross for heroism.

# SIX

JOHN FLINN SAT IN OUR ROOM listening to the radio. I was working on a model P-47 Thunderbolt, and he was smoking his pipe, watching.

"You really ought to smoke a pipe," he said. "With that blond mustache you'd look like something right from England. Here, I'll give you this one." He handed it to me along with a small tin of tobacco.

The aroma snaked from the can, carrying visions of old libraries and scenes from old movies, Sherlock Holmes and all that. We were soon sitting in swirls of smoke, the radio again blaring the numbers of the girls downtown. My P-47 was taking shape across a small plywood workboard.

"About time to hit the sack," John said, cleaning his pipe, turning off the radio, drawing the room into solitude. He slid into bed and put his head back on folded arms. "So you're keeping notes on all this for a book," he said.

"Yeah, I'm working at it, trying to record what we're doing, the real flying, what we think about it all, maybe trying to make some sense of it. There's no doubt that some of the greatest and most dangerous flying ever done is right here in the old A-1."

"Sounds good," he said. "Have anything I can read now?"

I tossed him some pages in a binder. "This is about all I have in any sort of readable form."

He opened the cover and began to read. I put the cap on the tube of glue and turned out the work lamp. I sat on the edge of my bunk about three feet away from John. He was turning the pages slowly, reading intently.

"I like what you have so far," he said, "and I know that once you get into the rescue business you'll have some real thrills to write about. You've had your share already, but wait until you hit the Trail in broad daylight! A rescue can be the wildest, most exciting thing you can imagine." He reached for the top of the dresser and picked up the little shoulder patch which said SANDY ONE. "This rescue business is the best, most rewarding operation in the entire war. And if nothing else does, getting a man out makes sense. It's really great to actually pluck a guy from the enemy after he's been shot down. It's a great feeling; sensational!"

John explained something about the operation, which had been the subject of many stories, the gallantry and heroism of the rescue pilots held in the highest esteem. The rescue force was nicknamed the Sandys, and they sat on alert, flew rescue orbits daily, and went straight into the hell of any groundfire to rescue downed airmen. All this in one-hundred-and-fifty-mile-an-hour airplanes! Each A-1 squadron selected its most experienced and competent pilots to serve in the force a few times each month. Every day there were six Sandy pilots on alert, Sandy One being the head man, on down the line through two other leads and wingmen. Every day the numbers changed so that through a three-day alert every lead would have moved up from Sandy Five to Three and finally to

Sandy One. When any launch was in effect, Sandy One was the man to organize the tactics and proceed into the area first. Many battle-scarred airplanes attested to the ferocity of that sort of combat work.

John put the patch back on the dresser and went back to reading. I got into bed and wrote a quick letter. Finally John closed the binder and tossed it back over to me.

"Good stuff," he said, "but of course I don't like to read anything about death. You've got to laugh around here. You'll notice there's more laughter than anything else, except drinking. They kind of go together when someone's trying to kill you every day. You'd better laugh, or you'll end up crying. Your outlook changes when someone you know gets killed over here."

I thought about it for a minute. "That may be true, but I've always thought that although we may be sad for a while, we never have lost a friend if they are truly our friends. I mean, what is really the person never can die, if that makes any sense to you." I was into another area where my lack of experience allowed me great latitude in speculation, such as what the Air Force was all about when I was much younger, what the war was about before I was in it, and now, what death was really all about without ever having faced it when someone very close died.

John smiled. "Great words, and maybe you're right. No one I know about ever came back and told me what the truth of it really is. Houdini said he would, but I don't recall him showing up yet. It does appear awfully final when it happens. Anyway, I'm too short here to worry about it anymore. I've got about three months left to go, which includes an R and R to Hong

Kong. And then again, I've been doing this a long time now, and you learn what to do after a while. And you can tell who's going to get it. The minute the new guys walk in you know which ones will survive and which will stay over forever. You get a feel for it."

"How about me?" I asked.

John turned out the light and said, "You'll make it."

John headed north the next morning, climbing into clean air where little dots of cumulus were punctuating the sky. He turned across the Mekong and disappeared into the miles of daylight. I went into the squadron building and sighed at the heap of papers which had to be typed and read and edited so as to increase the sensationalism of an already exciting existence. The office work was drab at best. I sat with the whir of the air conditioner, an hour to go before my own briefing time.

Ken Ohr, one of the squadron pilots, jerked to a halt outside the door. I looked up. He was in his flight suit, sweating, looking as if anguish had been permanently branded into his body. "John's down," he said, staring at me.

The words hit me like a bomb.

Neither of us moved.

"Did you hear me?" he asked. "John's been shot down at Muong Soui. No chute. No beeper." That meant no one had seen him get out and there was no emergency transmission from his survival radio. Ken turned and stomped off down the hall, and I followed, trying to believe that John was OK, that he would be rescued. We went to the command post but couldn't get any more information. Then it was time for my own briefing, and we were directed to Muong Soui, where the battle was raging savagely.

We headed north, winding through massive clouds, which had erected themselves along the path. It was a long forty-five-minute flight which lapsed, seemingly, into hours of reflection. Then we were there, under the clouds, near the abandoned airstrip, near John. Smoke filled the air and climbed into the cloud bases. The FAC circled below in an O-1, keeping his distance from the groundfire. There was a small village below consisting of perhaps a dozen hooches.

"The NVA took over that village," the FAC said. "They've got the hooches loaded with ammo. Matter of fact, these are the guys that shot down one of your A-1s a little while ago." I searched the hills for a sign of the wreckage but couldn't see any. The ground was covered with splotches of black and small fires.

"Have at the area, and watch out for heavy groundfire," the FAC said, leaving us and going to observe from a distance.

"Let's make random passes," lead called out, "and let's cover each other. I'm in!" I moved the switches, flipped the arming toggles, and set the gunsight. As lead got halfway down his dive pass, I rolled in, the pipper a symbol of death tatooed in the gunsight. Tiny streams of red groundfire shot up but didn't seem significant. The hooches got larger and larger, my thumb rested on the release button, and when I reached the right point I pressed the button and pulled off. The napalm struck a hooch, which erupted like a volcano. Projectiles blasted from the area as the intense heat set off stored ammunition. Lead pounded another hooch with a five-hundred-pound bomb, and I saw a black-clad figure come flying from the trees like a rag doll, arms and legs spread like a child's pencil sketch of the human figure. It was the first time I had seen anything like it. Then we started strafing into the fires, setting off explosions which climbed back into the air with us. I armed all four guns and flew down through the fire and smoke, between the hooches, spraying 20mm, like water with a hose. The radio chatter was quick and abrupt. "Lead's in, watch that gun to the south; off, turning west." The FAC: "Great! They're all on fire now, every one of them! Hey! Watch that new gun position from the hilltop north!"

The air was churning with the heat of a dozen burning structures, the careening of unaimed ammunition, the smoke of powder and flesh. My tracers raced out ahead of me, the pinkish dots puncturing the rolling flames, sending wood and bamboo splintering up into the air around the aircraft. My oxygen mask was filled with my own sweat, and the cockpit was steaming hot. Then we finally ran out of ammunition, both aircraft maneuvering easily with the fresh, unladen agility. The clouds above had changed from white to dirty gray, and the ground looked like a bleeding open wound. I rolled the airplane over again and again trying to find John, but there were only fires and a hundred possible gravesites, each one sending up a thin stream of black smoke. The old airfield at Muong Soui was a shambles, with craters in the runway, the buildings crushed and burning, the ground open and stained. Our target was obliterated. There wasn't anything left but dark smudges on the earth where hooches once stood. It was about the same place where I had fought guns for the first time, where two pilots had bailed out, where I had tasted my first real battle. Now it had claimed John.

I joined the wingtip of lead's aircraft, still breathing heavily and still fired with the sights and sensations of the last few hours. I was wrenched by emotions, buried in thought, racked by the situation that had killed my roommate and fellow pilot. We climbed through the darkening clouds and found clear air at eleven thousand feet. The ground was finally obscured with cloud cover, which was refreshing, as if the ground were the war, the evil. The sun reddened in its descent, and the sky changed color with it. I broke off from formation long enough to make a long and easy barrel roll around the ball of red sun, making it an airman's salute to a lost buddy, a toast to John. Then the night came fast and clothed the earth and sky in hard black. Flooded rice paddies turned to mirrors in the moonlight, and there was a hint of approaching rain.

I walked into the room but left with a quick turn. I didn't want to be there yet. Rain came later, beating the dirt and the wooden buildings unmercifully, pounding every roof and hut. The main hooch wasn't full of the usual laughter. There was a determined silence and grim faces. I walked in the rain for a while, feeling bathed by leaving the day's perspiration and horror in the mud, the reddish brown slime that gurgled underfoot and covered my boots. And there was wind.

The flier's world was so different from that of the ground troops. When a pilot didn't come back, that was it. There was no mutilated body, no remains other than a small room of physical objects. The man just wasn't there anymore, as if vanished into intergalactic space, plucked from us and turned into invisibility. But our room was filled with conversations bouncing from every wall, from every object. My pipe rested on the desk; John had taken his with him. *Once in a while I like to smoke it when things get slow,* he had said. *It puts a nice smell in the cockpit too.* The can of tobacco rested under a wingtip of my model. The air conditioner kept spinning with the same clatter, and the spiders were weaving their webs above the door in the wet. Time didn't make any sense. I didn't know what day it was, nor was it of importance. What counted were my thoughts, my ideas of what was real and true and what I would think about John and that experience in the spectrum of living to come. I wondered what thoughts had devoured John in the last moments, but I realized they would be final secrets kept forever. For me, it was the first time that death had been so close, so violent, so hard hitting. It was the test for my thoughts. OK, buddy, I thought, you said something about what death is and is not, so let's see how you come out of this now. *Great words,* John had said. Death was there in the room with me and I was trying to fight it, knowing that what was really John couldn't die. I sat in the darkness on the edge of my bed. It rained all night.

A numb cloud of swirling haze covered my head as I walked from the room into the heat of another day. The hooch maids were already sorting out the laundry, polishing row after row of combat boots, and several airplanes filled the visible sky. It was morning, awful, hot, damp, noisy morning. Giggles came over carrying a load of underwear and socks.

"Where John?" she asked.

I didn't know what to say to her. She understood so little English. "John no come back," I tried in simple words.

She looked back, not making sense of me, frowning, then smiling. "No come back?" she repeated.

I nodded and walked off to the shower. When I came out she was still there.

"John *never* come back?" she asked.

I nodded again. How could I talk philosophy or say what I thought when we weren't even in the same language? Giggles sniffled and ran. I went inside the room and put on my flight suit returning to the walkway in a few minutes. It was a scathing-hot day. Giggles stood there staring at the small garden beside the hooch.

"John put flowers into ground long time ago, I help him. Now I look at flowers and see John."

How eloquent, I thought. "Yes," I said, "and I see John in the sky and in the airplanes and in the room."

She smiled and went off with the laundry, and I went to fly.

It wasn't long until the mission was behind and I was sitting alone in the officers' club, a plate of cold food pushed to one side, my hand holding an empty can of beer. Colonel Fallon walked in, saw me, and came over.

"Mind if I sit down for a minute?" he asked. He pulled the chair out and dropped into it. He too had flown that day. His silver-white hair picked up light like a magnet, covering his head like a glow. "I thought we ought to talk about John for a minute. He was a friend of mine too. I know how hard it hit you when he went down and I know how something like this can feel, but I wanted to say that we can't let it get to us. We have to take the good from those who leave us and not stay in the dumps. We have to keep going. John was a hell of a guy, and let's not forget it. His death wasn't the big thing—his life was." He looked down, jiggling the silverware.

"Yes, I know," I said. "I'll be just fine. Thank you."

"Good," he said, standing. We shook hands, and he walked off into the night. I went back to the empty room and to bed.

I took off the next day looking forward to a new sky, fresh clouds, the paean made by the sound and feel of the airplane. The experience was short-lived. Detached radio voices announced that another A-1 had gone down. It was the Plaine des Jarres area again, and we turned north to help if possible. The new radio frequency was full of rescue talk, A-1 pilots covering the area and the survivor just now coming up on the radio. It was Colonel Fallon! There was a pounding in my chest and I strained to hear every word, but the distance and other radio chatter made it difficult. As we came closer I knew it was a tense situation. We could hear small-arms fire over the survival radio when he talked. And then the excited words, "They're coming down the hill at me!" There was the sound of what we took to be his .38 Smith and Wesson, a minor instrument pitted against an army. Then he was hit, struggling to move away. He finally yelled, "They're here now. They're almost on me! Bomb my position and you'll get them! Bomb me!" And his words ended forever. The airplanes made every attempt to strafe and stop the advancing troops, but to no avail. There was finally silence as we all realized that another pilot, another man, had been plucked from us, taken from the sky. There was no more left to do. The groundfire ceased, and there was no longer a single trace of the valor which had existed on the surface moments past. Once again, a bunch of battle-worn planes and pilots turned homeward.

With both my roommate and Colonel Fallon lost in action, it was felt that I ought to have some time off. I was promptly ushered to Bangkok for CTO, compensatory time off. At the Don Muang terminal I hailed a taxi, which was difficult since a staggering number of drivers, promoters, pimps, and children versed in advanced pilferage swirled around me, making forward progress onerous at best. The driver changed the shape of my luggage, giving it the form of his Lilliputian car trunk. We screeched around the airport and finally settled on the main highway where serenity was broken only by occasional collisions, honking, fully applied brakes and accelerators, high-G-force lane changing, and other routine features of Bangkok existence.

We finally maneuvered down Petchburi Road, changed to Rajadamri Road, onto Rama 1 Road, and into the Siam Intercontinental Hotel. And then, with about one gallon of Singha beer, I sat by the pool trying to relax, to think about anything but the war and combat. But I couldn't do it. I kept wondering what was going on up there, how the battle was going, if anyone else had gone down. The man lying next to me said that the war was extraordinarily good for his business and he could now afford to visit places like Bangkok, that the war was a just and good thing also, against communism and all that. He later mentioned that he had managed to get his son into the personnel field in the States and that he wouldn't be going to Vietnam. I plunged into the pool to mentally cleanse myself, or at least to cool off from what I was thinking.

75

But it was all the same, the clattering of dishes, people finally able to afford the luxury of travel but too old to enjoy it, voices of finance and traffic. I got the impression of people simply trying to fill the hours, to make something of a huge void, checking off squares, marking time. For what? And I found that I had nothing in common with those people. I had come from a place where every day was drama and violence, the roar of aircraft engines, fighting weather, fighting an enemy. The people there were immensely alive, bigger than life. Even those we knew as "dead" were more alive than those on a hot Bangkok day around a pool. I couldn't talk with them. How does one communicate with *real* dead people?

I jumped into the night mirage that is Bangkok after dark. Kobe steak sautéed in burgundy flambé with cognac at Nick's Number One, a taxi to the President Hotel and a quick walk downstairs to the Cat's Eye for more illusion. Another taxi down Silom Road and a stop at Club 99, saying hello to girl number two, and off again to the Montien Hotel and a winding walk downstairs to the An-An club, drinking under strobe lights and leaving for a stop at Max's Place on Patpong Road, street of broken dreams, watching the girls, talking with the Air America pilots, taking another taxi to the Balcony and walking around the corner to the Garden Café, dancing and listening to the band play songs of the day. "Yesterday ... when I was young ..." The music wove a collage of thoughts across my subconscious: night flying, friends dying, books in the sun, guns firing, my empty room. The band played on with my nodding head. "Yesterday when I was young ..." My God! I was still in my twenties! But I felt ancient. And I also knew that I wanted to go back north and fly those airplanes again, that I needed to be there, that it made sense for me when little else did.

I took a C-130 back to Nakhon Phanom and plodded once again through the red dust that was home. It was good to see and hear the formations roaring overhead and the sputter of smoke from old radial engines. Back at the hooch, Maj. Loren Alfred was working on another model airplane, sanding and gluing, still in his flight suit, his pipe gone out long ago, his Beethoven records playing under a plastic dustcover. There was the scent of balsa and paints. And it would be just the same if one wandered by at three in the morning after night flying. Al would still be covered with balsa pieces and sawdust and his hands would have model paint on them and his pipe would have gone out some time ago. And his beautiful, flawless models that took so many hours to build—hours of release from combat flying—would be given to the first smiling child he saw. He didn't care. Loren Alfred was a man who had found happiness. I began to understand what it was that lured me, drew me back to the airplanes, the engines, the men who shared this life. It was the very substance of life, real life, everyone doing what was natural, things having true meaning as they never did before. It was perhaps that we could lose it in the next hour, tomorrow, next week. And for once we honestly began to think about things, to find the beauty in life, to see and feel and touch as if for the first time.

"Gosh, Rick," Al said, "my wife really didn't understand how important all this was until I took her to a model-airplane contest. She watched me with the little planes and saw me helping the kids with theirs,

77

and when the day was over I could see that she finally saw what it was all about. She finally realized that my life revolved around four things—lift, thrust, weight, and drag."

We went down to the main hooch were Bill Miller was dragging in from a tough mission, lots of shooting, a rescue attempt that he had been called into. He popped open a beer and said, "I want to tell you—going to one of those rescues is like going to see the executioner himself. The shooting is something fierce!" He downed most of the beer. "And a funny thing happened when we got back. We went to the club for something to eat, and it was like I was more alive than before. Know what I mean? It was like the first time I had ever eaten or touched something. Like I was sitting there *feeling* the white tablecloth. And the food tasted good. And I finally realized that it was because I was alive. A few hours ago I wasn't sure. Boy, you really start seeing things when you might not be around much longer. You know, I think we're in the best position, as pilots I mean, to understand this sort of thing."

Bill had expressed what I had been thinking for some time.

Al said, "Well, it's a good point to reach because you can start doing what's really important to you and you don't care much for what anyone else thinks. You become who you are, so to speak. I think most people's lives are hopeless. They never have any real loves, they think of status and possessions and maturity. But you come here, to a crazy war where you can get killed anytime, and you start seeing the basics. You suddenly stop letting other people live your life for you. You create your own world by what you value. And in the middle of war you're happy. Crazy, isn't it? You know,

78

I hear that a lot of people think I'm pretty strange. When I get those five days off to go to Bangkok I usually stay here and build my models and read. It's quiet and nice and not particularly strange. Besides, that Bangkok thing gets old. Rick, you just came back. How was it? What did you do?"

I thought a second and said, "I really can't remember."

# SEVEN

**M**OST OF THE TALES of terror in our air war were told about either search-and-rescue operations or night combat. As the time came for my first night rides, in early August of 1969, I began to listen intently to the stories, most of them grossly exaggerated, I hoped. Because the A-1 was low-flying, relatively slow, and therefore highly vulnerable to groundfire, it went to the heavily defended areas mainly at night, unless there was a rescue attempt. Then it was anything goes. At night the airplane was less visible and therefore, it was thought, we could maintain better survivability. But it was impossible to muffle the roar of an R-3350 engine, and the gunners knew well in advance when we were coming. They also knew that we were around ten thousand feet, usually lower, which put us right in the midst of the concentrated groundfire. Added to this was the fact that if a pilot were shot down at night, he would have to wait until morning for any rescue attempt—there was never a night effort. Thus the risk of capture was great.

Since night operations were in the vicinity of the Trail, there was certain groundfire from the big guns, at least 23mm and 37mm. One hit from one of those guns could well mean the end. I saw a 37mm shell sitting in the squadron building one day, foreboding in its brass color with Russian markings, a cold metal cylinder over a foot long, with a silver head. It was heavy, and I set it back on the table with a great amount of awe.

The procedure at night was to dive-bomb in the dark, to a target perhaps marked by a small light, a marker dropped by a FAC from above, into unknown terrain, while the guns blasted away from below, bracketing the airplane as it descended. It sounded like some sort of madness when described, and, once experienced, it was, for certain, one of the wildest sensations ever imagined by a pilot. I couldn't even speculate on what it would be like to roll in, watch the altimeter unwind with the plunge into the depths of black, and somehow evade the groundfire while attempting to track a target and release ordnance! My training back at Hurlburt Field had been done over well-known terrain with the city lights of Fort Walton and Destin Beach to keep us company. And no one shot at us.

I was also treated to some pictures of A-1s that had been hit at night. Twisted chunks of metal had been peeled from the airplane structures with incredible force. Flaps had been completely severed from wings. Wingtips were missing. One plane had a hole in the wing so large that several people were standing in it, posing for the picture. Quite often when I would be going to an early-morning briefing, the night fliers who had returned were to be found in our bar, vocally and physically describing the night's activities. They were knights who had fought the dragon, an experience heretofore unknown to me but waiting on the scheduling officer's clipboard.

It was with apprehension that I climbed into the cockpit on a dark night, with my night combat instruc-

81

tor, Maj. Walt Davis, snapping the buckles and fittings into the seat extraction system. I settled myself into the aircraft commander's left seat, and Walt adjusted himself into the right seat of our side-by-side A-1E. I was particularly attentive to the survival equipment, thinking about possibly having to make use of it at night. I was excited, yet there was fear nagging away at me. It was the fact that night was a great equalizer. It covered things familiar, made the ordinary sinister, kept safe landing places a secret, and hid the enemy who waited for us. Even the airplane seemed different. The camouflage was a somber charcoal in the night. Exhaust flame licked around the fuselage before me; instruments which had been familiar daytime friends were now strange in red lighting. There were no comforting lights on the horizon, no city in Florida to keep me company. It was a lethal feeling, as if night clearly defined our purpose in darkness.

The lead aircraft finally took off, and I had a sense of a ship slipping out of harbor, its lights swinging to the east. We took off with me flying but really an observer on the first flight, and as the runway lights raced behind us we suddenly came into complete black and I felt like a tiny molecule of life suspended in some endless black void. We were on instruments the moment we left the runway. Then we cruised through thick cloud for thirty minutes on a heading prearranged to take us to an FAC and a target. I was comforted somewhat by the briefing, which had stated that since we were still in the rainy season we could expect little, if any, groundfire on this flight. There was some turbulence during which we were tossed against each other in our fat-face airplane and once thrown up into the canopy, both our helmets crashing into the plex-iglass.

Walt Davis, my intrepid instructor, reached into a little pocket and brought out a cigarette which he lit, the swirling smoke momentarily caught in the light of his match. He pushed the intercom button and said, "I sure hope you don't think I'm going to do this sort of thing night after night. It's bad enough when you're alone and can fly the way you want. If you take a hit or go down, then it's your own problem. But riding along trying to give instruction at night when they're shooting isn't what I like to do best. So unless you crash or something, you're going to pass this check-ride. Just thought I'd let you know."

"I appreciate your deep concern for me," I said.

"Think nothing of it. Some night you'll be riding over here with a student, and you won't like it either."

He was correct. Solo combat flying was the only way to go. That way the pilot was free to handle the aircraft as he felt necessary. With a student it was a different story. Being new to the situation, the pupil took longer to perceive what was happening. When the guns were firing one didn't need to linger over decisions. And so, sitting in the right seat giving an instructional flight meant there was a greater danger than ever. There was a minimum number of dual flights before the new man went solo, and Walt wasn't plan-ning on taking one minute more than necessary. "By the way," he said, "if there's any groundfire tonight I'd appreciate it if you'd miss running into it." I looked over, and he gave a determined nod and a wink.

We were in such thick cloud that the fuselage position light lit the outside world in a ghostly white. The rotating beacon blinked red across that white like a psychedelic dream. It was so distracting that I turned the lights out, something we would do momentarily anyway near the target area. We flew from the clouds and eventually made contact with the FAC. There was a white marker visible through a wispy cloud bank; I watched the strike below as lead expended his ordnance. There wasn't a single round of groundfire. We finally switched altitudes, and I made four passes into the dark and pulled off out of ordnance. It was somewhat like training back at Hurlburt but without all the aids of those city lights and the psychological advantage of knowing most of the natives were friendly. I breathed harder as the plane went into the dive, and there were a few moments when my eyes searched a dozen places simultaneously, scanning for groundfire, surveying the flight instruments, the target, and the gunsight, flying and thinking and talking and concentrating on staying alive. Other than that it was relatively simple.

We finally headed back home. The same clouds hung about the route back, several veins of lightning darting about as if conducting a secret business of their own. The weather was a nefarious combination of wet and electricity. There was an unusual silence, Walt not saying anything, me keeping the ship level in the foggy cosmos outside the canopy. Walt took out another cigarette. The match lit the underside of the plexiglass into a million spiderwebs where it had been rubbed and scratched year after year. The turbulence caught us like a single leaf in a tempest.

"I wouldn't mind if you'd detour a bit around some of this stuff," Walt said with a snicker. We couldn't see with our eyes and were relying on information presented by the instruments, the visual data of daylight represented by numbers, needles, and colors. Unfortunately, none of them said one thing about a serene path through the perils of thunderstorms. It was like flowing through waterfalls of India ink in a clear bubble.

"I'll say one thing about the right seat," Walt went on. "It'll make anyone a devout coward. It's pure torture over here." He laughed again and blew smoke through the cockpit; I put my oxygen mask back on. "A guy could get to be a paralytic sitting over here," he was saying. "You'll find out. The sooner we can get you checked out and the sooner you fly some night missions, the sooner we can make you an instructor. And then I won't have to come out here so often."

We pressed on until crossing the Mekong in a descent, entered the GCA pattern, and bumped to a touchdown. "Great, just great," Walt yelled. "You pass. We didn't crash!" He started to laugh but coughed instead, hacking away for half a minute or so.

Turning off the runway, I said, "Walt, who do you think's going to win? The gunners or the cigarettes?"

He coughed again, then said, "Rick, if you fly at night on the Trail for a living, it doesn't make much difference if you smoke or not."

Keeping Walt's words in mind, I prepared for my first night-combat solo. It was a damp August night with the remnants of thunderstorms hanging about in the dark, lurking like titanic clumps of energy. I wasn't particularly tense about the flying itself, since I had hundreds of night hours in other aircraft, but the thought of combat over hostile areas at night did run through my mind several times, mainly because of the possibility of capture. I tried to put that from my mind; I knew it could get obsessive and out of hand. Some people got to worrying so much that they just couldn't fly anymore. What their minds and stomachs were going through I could easily understand. In any event, I was wide awake and ready for my first flirt with solo night combat.

Hank Lavender was leading, and the two of us went about the usual antics of the last cup of coffee, the trek to personal equipment for our gear, and the rattling drive across the pierced steel planking ramp to the aircraft. I had an "H" model, which I liked, and Hank had an "E" model, which he hated. That empty right seat made it difficult to see on that side, and one always wanted to see anything that might be coming up, particularly groundfire. I made a flashlight check of the airplane and climbed into the cockpit for the start and radio check-in. Everything was normal, there was a slight breeze, and I was anticipating the accomplishment of returning from the flight. Hank called, we checked all three radios, got the altimeter setting and runway advisory. I waited for Hank to roll past, then followed in trail to the run-up area. Long flashlight wands guided us into run-up position, and I closed the canopy for the engine check. There was negligible drop on either magneto, so I closed the throttle, opened the canopy, and set my hands up on the canopy rail. That was the signal that my hands were not touching the switches and that the arming crew could arm the weapons without my setting something off as they worked. I looked over to Hank, who was visibly perturbed. Then he called on the radio. "Damn mag drop is something else. I'm going back and take the spare." He wheeled past me and headed for the flight line. I sat alone and let my arms fall outside the cockpit, the wind flailing them about in a delicious coolness generated by the propeller. I let my head fall back against the headrest and peered up into the night. It was a mildly euphoric sensation.

After five minutes Hank called again. "They think they can fix it, so I'll be there in ten minutes or so. Sit tight." I sat. It was amusing to consider the fact that a modern era still clung to the old to do a job and do it well. We were flying anachronisms, piloting Spads through a supersonic world, tasting thunderstorms at eight thousand feet when an SR-71 was hitting three times the speed of sound above seventy thousand feet. It was a ludicrous situation but one I applauded. I wouldn't have missed the Skyraider for anything. Ten minutes went by and nothing happened, so I took out a paperback book and started reading, steadying the pages against the wind and vibration.

Hank appeared in fifteen minutes, driving smartly beside my wingtip and jerking to a halt in front of the arming crew. The power went in again, the exhaust flame jutting back from the large stacks, and he checked the mags once more. This time there was a backfire which rolled across the parking area like a cannon blast.

"I don't believe this thing," he said, continuing with a tirade of cursing, ending with: "This is it. Either the spare or we call it a night. Hang loose."

He jabbed in the power and swiveled around the left main gear, finally roaring back down the taxi strip and into the parking area. I went back to my book, wondering if we would ever get off. Hank came back again in another fifteen minutes with a new airplane.

"Hope all this wasn't designed to tell us something," he said.

In short order we were ready for takeoff. As his power went in I saw the weight come off the tail and the tailwheel strut extend. Brakes released, Hank started forward, and his airplane soon changed from a black shape to a set of lights which eventually lifted from the earth and climbed into the scud off the end of the runway. I lingered a second, then followed suit. It was down the runway, night, keep control and centered, check the torque pressure, check up and down, inside and out, in a single, perfectly directed glance; airspeed, the feel of the machine, the load transferring to the wings, the wings sensing their reason, and my hand knowing with pressure on the stick, lighter on the wheels until we made the simple and unique transition from a ground machine to a creature of the sky. There was that final moment when I left the world of chromatic colors, that instant when the runway lights blazed by, then suddenly quit, ending my dependence on the ground and putting me in a world of black and white. Night was exciting, even in solid ebony, when there wasn't too far to go. I reached out and touched the levers and switches without looking at them. My hand knew where they were. We were united, and I was succinctly and irrevocably part of the machine. It felt good.

We drifted in and out of clouds all the way to the target, which was Tchepone in southern Laos, not a very hospitable location on the Ho Chi Minh Trail. In the light of day the area was once again like the cratered moon. I saw it all in my head as we approached the area.

Hank turned off his position lights some fifty miles out and I was visually alone, darting through clouds without natural horizon, generally on instruments. It was a forty-minute flight that ended at a large clearing in the weather. The target was a truck park in Tchepone, defined once again in terms of distance and heading from a faint white ground marker dropped by an FAC. Hank made his passes while I held overhead, the usual procedure. There was no groundfire. I felt better since I would be able to devote more attention to making an accurate pass and doing well on this first night solo. Yet I recalled the reminders about flying at all times as if someone were going to shoot. I scanned everywhere as it came my turn to make the attack.

We traded altitudes, Hank going to nine thousand, me dropping to eighty-five hundred. I made last cockpit preparations for dive-bombing down into the dark, then called in. I flipped the master arm switch on simultaneously with the roll in, but nothing happened. The gunsight was cold and dull. The pipper wasn't there! I jerked the toggle lever up and down as I penetrated the dark below. Still nothing; not even the alternate light switch for the sight did any good. I punched the mike button to say that I couldn't release anything but heard a break in the static and a lifeless transmitter. The cockpit lights which I had already dimmed went out entirely. Pulling out of the dive on indistinct instruments, I tried to communicate, but the radio was lifeless. Obviously there was some sort of electrical failure, but it wasn't revealing itself with any clarity. Then the generator warning light came on bright red. I attempted to reset the generator, but that also failed.

I recalled the words from all night briefings: "If you have a problem, just use the manual release handles and jettison everything. The explosions will let everyone know you are in trouble." I flew over the target area and pulled both the outer and inner wing station handles and felt everything drop away. I looked into the dark, but there were no explosions. Nothing went off. There wasn't a second's gleam of light. My adrenaline and heartbeat went up, something that was becoming routine for me in such a short period of time. With the trim set in a down position for dive-bombing, the aircraft had entered a violent dive when I pulled the manual release handles. I yanked the stick aft and climbed back to my prescribed altitude. It was no time to run into other airplanes by being at the wrong place. I was nervous enough when the cockpit started filling with smoke and the instrument panel was nearly obscured. The propeller began to surge, and sparks poured from the exhaust stacks. I ran through procedures for the generator while trying to make sense of what was happening. Something inside me very objectively and detachedly said, "Well, Richard, you're going to spend the night down there, at *least* one night."

I pulled down my clear visor to cover my eyes and tightened my straps for the exit. Fighting the nose-down trim and the smoke, I thought about being captured once again, the vision of being lashed to a tree and skinned alive that many of our companions had faced before. I had so much adrenaline in my system that I was shaking and truly scared. Another voice, one I liked much better than the first, said, "Not yet, don't give up yet." I was still flying in a ragged sense of the word, and there was no reason to give up when I could at least get further away from Tchepone. As if to comfort me, the propeller stopped surging and the sparks went away. But the smoke was still there. It was stinging my eyes and smelled like a real electrical calamity had taken place. I unzipped my flightsuit pocket, took out my little flashlight, held it between my teeth, and attempted to fly with what was left. The only thing that appeared workable for navigation was the magnetic compass, the one we referred to as the standby compass. It sat atop the instrument panel and pointed roughly west. I swung to the right and attempted to set out northwest. The attitude indicator started turning upside down, toppling without power, and I used every ounce of determination to avoid looking at it, to keep from believing I was really turning upside down. The heavy stick began to hurt my arm since all that down trim created a great deal of pressure. I went through a series of oscillations which carried me roughly a thousand feet either side of the altitude I was trying to maintain. Figuring I might have to vacate the airplane, I got out my chart and looked over the best place to bail out. I selected the highest ground and tried to fly over it on a return course to the base. The Rooster Tail was my choice. It occurred to me that perhaps my survival radio would work, and I unzipped it from the little pocket in my vest and opened the canopy enough to stick out the extended aerial, which was something like the whip antenna on portable radios. Alternating between voice and the emergency beeper, I received nothing.

Stuffing the radio back into its pocket, I closed the canopy, tried to regain my altitude, and changed hands on the stick. As I ended the procedures for generator failure, the smoke began to filter from the cockpit, and after a short time I was once again able to breathe clear air. The magnetic compass still showed northwest, and I kept it in that direction. We had flown southeast to the target for some forty mintues, which had been partially in a departure pattern; so, figuring that a three-mile-a-minute airplane would do around ninety miles in half an hour, I tossed in the forecast winds and derived thirty-two minutes on my heading. It should put the airplane directly over the base. I calmed down a bit, changing from stark terror into a more relaxed frame of mind. With facts and figures and something constructive to do, I found it easier to keep from worrying about nightmarelike eventualities. The weather was still there, and I tried to keep the airplane upright using the standby compass and its fluid level. It was rather an impossible task, and fortunately I would break out of cloud decks in time to accurately determine aircraft attitude, which was usually a matter of being in a steep bank. It was tiring and hard work, but it was taking me home, I hoped. It was really a matter of keeping from panicking and applying some rational thought, something easier said than done in such a situation. I thought Vinh had taught me a lesson with my infamous episode from the Plaine des Jarres into North Vietnam. I was still shaking.

For thirty-two minutes I kept the machine going, flying with less than precision but with brute force and physical endurance and great amounts of willpower. In that moment of time I was over a thin layer of cloud through which I saw lights, bright lights. I reduced the power and descended through the misty white and broke out directly over the town of Nakhon Phanom. The field lights twinkled in the distance under some low clouds. I smiled, I laughed, I sat back weary yet delighted.

Skimming the cloud bottoms, I flew by the tower flashing my flashlight and moving the throttle to get some attention. I had no idea if people thought I had gone down or not. As it was, I was flying a phantom ghost ship across the runway, lights out. I saw no return light, so I continued down the field until the boundary, where I made a sort of teardrop-shaped reversal and came back for a landing. The flaps wouldn't go down, nor would indicators indicate, since the electrical system was out, but I leaned out the open canopy and watched the gear move forward into position, the knee-caps on the struts showing that I had wheels down. Blessed are the basics of aviation where a pilot can stick his head out and see things. The wind felt good and cool. Cloud drifted across the end of the runway, and light drizzle sprayed the cockpit. I took the flash-light and placed it in my left hand, which also held the throttle. With quick flashes I was able to see the airspeed indicator. Over the threshold I turned out the light and made a blackout landing on the wet runway.

I walked into the hooch well after midnight. Hank was sitting there waiting, drink in hand, the room otherwise empty. He smiled and shook my hand. I knew he was drinking alone to either a man gone down or one hopefully returning through the storm in a disabled airplane. But I also knew that he wouldn't tell me which one.

"Welcome back," he said. "How about a drink?" We clanked our mugs together, and Hank said, "I sure hope it's just that you are having all your emergencies in the first part of your tour. You've already had your share. It ought to be clear sailing from here on out."

He finally left to sleep, and I sat alone pondering what had happened. It was truly an incongruous world we were living in. It was hard to believe that I had gone off into night combat over Laos, fought the weather, waged battle over enemy territory, had the emergency, almost panicked, made it back, and was sitting with a beer in a rather quiet room listening to a record playing. It was like a dream, except that I was in my sweaty flight suit and the sound of the engine was still in my head. And it had seemed so big and important that I might well die, that I might not come back, yet I was having a beer as if it were now nothing at all. I was still sitting alone when the sun came up.

The next night I was in a good mood. Hoping that my emergencies were in fact things of the past, I whistled and hummed, dressing for the flight. It wasn't that I was completely relaxed about things, just that I felt things somehow had to ease up. Indeed, flying at night over Laos wasn't something to take lightly. One's imagination didn't help either. At night, the mind was an insatiable dynamo which went a thousand directions and could picture anything. Across the Mekong, city lights behind, it wasn't difficult to hear a different engine sound, to sense that the prop was surging, that the exhaust flame was different. If there was weather, aircraft attitude could become questionable; perhaps the instruments were wrong, not likely, but possible. Was it groundfire below, a muzzle flash, or the moon's reflection briefly bouncing from a rain-sodden rice paddy? The pilot sat relatively motionless, hands on the controls, while the mind engaged gears faster and faster. And you just had to keep it under control, organize a direction, concentrate, and, if anything, dream about something pleasant.

And so, as a gunner's moon poured cold light on the base like stars on snow, a hard and clear night where the enemy would have a view of black shapes against the sky, I dressed for the flight. While I imagined people donning a suit and tie and stepping out for dinnner back home, I slipped on my sage-green flight suit, wings and name sewn in black along with my captain's bars. They were in black so they wouldn't show in case I had to go down at night. I took the pleasure of soft white socks, then zipped up my jungle boots. Dog tags hung coldly around my neck, finally warming against my skin. The switchblade survival knife went into one pocket, the rechargeable flashlight into another. Into a small plastic wallet went my Geneva Convention card, my USAF ID card, and some small change. A pilot didn't want to get captured with much else. You didn't want to give away everything about yourself. No rings, no mementos, no photos, just the basics. Two number two pencils and a paperback book completed my preliminary apparel. I caught the blue van outside the hooch and headed for the briefing. The only significant thing was that we would be going to Mu Gia Pass, perhaps the area of most intense groundfire in the dry season.

Individual equipment issue was a storehouse of pilots' gear, survival vests, guns, ammunition, helmets, and like assorted paraphernalia. I reached into bin 383 and grabbed my survival vest, tossed it over my right arm, then swung it around my back and slipped my other arm into it. The vest was heavy since it contained so many things. In an inside pocket were special documents placed in a waterproof pouch. The package included plasticized survival maps and a "pointee-talkie" book which included words and phrases in several languages. The idea was to point to American words and phrases. There beside would be the same words in various languages. There was also a "blood chit," designed to hopefully secure a downed pilot's freedom with pledges and promises of reward for helping the man make his escape. These statements were made under a full-color American flag. Two survival radios went into pockets on the vest front, and there were individual pockets for a compass, flares, first-aid kit, and a revolver. I had sewn two bandoliers down the front which held a dozen or so rounds of .38-caliber ammunition each. There was also a fifteen-inch survival knife down the back. I put on the harness that buckled to the extraction seat, grabbed my helmet, and walked to the storeroom. I handed over my gun card and received my Smith and Wesson .38, butt number 398. The ammunition bin was full of shiny brass bullets, and I filled the gun, snapped the cylinder shut, and inserted the weapon into my vest holster. I momentarily recalled standing there one day with Ken Ohr, one of the squadron pilots. As he loaded his gun he had said, "Oh, I almost forgot. If I go down, *you* kill me, not them." And I just looked at him, wondering if I really could do that. "Don't look at me that way," he had said. "I'd do the same for you."

Stepping out into the night and walking to the airplane across the ramp, I was having the same fascination with night and airports, the same thoughts I had as a child. I used to sit in the lounge at the old Lockheed-Burbank Airport with an airplane magazine and watch the takeoffs and landings and the way night settled on the airport, the way the place took on a mystical, spellbinding quality. It was the same as I walked between these parked aircraft so many years later, the A-1s sitting nose-high with a multitude of spotlights shining on them, their white-and-black undersurfaces gleaming, the drab camouflage dark and lifeless. The airplanes had no stencil of the Air Force. The Stars and Stripes were gone in most cases. There were only numbers, names of the pilots along the canopy rails, and the names on the cowls. It was all a secret. Rotating beacons flashed red every few seconds and position lights blinked codes of colors. Some cowls were open and the spotlights probed the inner sanctum of fittings, tubing and ducts and blocks of metal, nuts and bolts, and the wet bodies of mechanics with no shirts, sweating in the tropical night, covering themselves with grease and oil, trying to make all the pieces work, yelling through the wind and roar of churning engines. In a nostalgic way it was as if Lindy ("Slim" to his friends) would come out of a little hangar door and inquire about the weather and the airplane for a first-light takeoff. Or Antoine de Saint-Exupéry would be there leaning against the prop of his P-38, showing me a card trick as he would before a recon flight, patting me on the back. And the many others, as if they too were standing amongst the airplanes, waving, saying, OK, it's your turn, but we're watching, a part of you. And we were the Lindys and the pioneers, carrying on the traditions. We were doing it by flying prop-driven A-1 Skyraiders in the night of August 1969. The airport lights were the same that danced across my eyes when I was a boy. Climbing onto the wing of my airplane, I wondered if that little upstairs room at Burbank Airport still had that glass case of model airplanes where I left a seven-year-old's fingerprints.

We were a little early, so I waited in the cockpit as a trace of a breeze swirled through. I rather absentmindedly turned on the ADF radio and twisted the knob, which rotated the dial and caused a series of shrieks and rasping sounds as my earphones filled with static. Then there was a pause, followed by the Armed

Forces Radio station. The slick announcer gave an introduction of a hundred words in about five seconds, in the same tone as the raucous sounds that followed. The proponents of discord and electronic braying had invaded the night.

I eliminated the entire episode with a single flick of the toggle switch. As I sat gravely pondering what I had just heard, I turned on the position lights which flashed from the wingtips, fuselage, and tail. There came a gentle click, click, as the solenoid opened and closed on the flasher mechanism. Click. Click. The music of my medium, I thought. Click. Click. A prelude for my own music. The long chain of nights and days in combat was trying to rob me of my perspective again. An entire orchestra at my disposal, and I was turning on the commercial radio station. I played the game. "Let's start 'em up" was the radio call. I raised my baton and motioned for a soft but lucid prelude. Click. Click. The inverter switches snapped precisely to the "on" position. There was an immediate whir of the inverters sending AC power through the system. Another silver toggle switch linked me to the fuel boost pump. Snap. Hummmmmmmmm. A swinging needle, pointing to twenty-four pounds of fuel pressure, kept time to the music. Brakes set. Crunch. I reached for the black starter button. I pressed it down and started the propeller blades rotating, sixteen times around before start. Grind, grind, grind, with the high-pitched whine of the starter to accompany the swing of the prop. There were rising and falling trills as the movement gained momentum. Then came the inaudible movement of the mag switch to the "both" position. The building score shaped itself towards the climax of twenty-seven hundred horsepower belching and

98

coughing into life with the final rhythm of a melodic beat. It was harmony personified as the fluids rushed through miles of tubing, and electricity flowed to all the right places exactly on time, and the orchestra played in perfect accord. With a final series of hand signals designed to terminate all further connection with the mundane, the machine rested on its own merits, the concert being memorable, the conductor satisfied. There had always been a symphony at my fingertips, but I just hadn't been listening.

Sitting mere inches behind my twenty-seven hundred horsepower, I taxied into the arming area, checked the mags and the propeller, and pulled the throttle back into idle. With my hands on the canopy rail, the signal to arm the ordnance, the arming crew approached to set the switches that would allow me to release the weapons and set fire to the night. The men had lights mounted to their heads, and they took on the guise of a group of doctors, specialists to be exact. And they were, professionals with the tools of destruction, carrying on their own tradition dating from the time when men sharpened weapons for battle and knights fought in body armor. They swarmed around the airplane through the beam of my taxi light which shone on the immense propeller lest anyone walk into its whirling blades. The light turned the giant prop into a huge, very solid, and very noisy platinum disk. The bodies ran under the wing, behind the fuselage, and to the starboard wing. And as that crew worked in the heat and noise, I studied the gauges and many needles glowing in soft red light. What I would have given as a child to sit in the cockpit and monitor the heart of an airplane. I was doing it years later for pay, not really for money but for myself, for the love of flying, for personal ideals, and because, once in the air, men tended to be real and alive and beautiful, something the ground seemed to take away. The arming crew ran back to the leading edge of the wing and made a thumbs-up signal indicating that the machine was ready. I returned the gesture and brought my hands back inside the cockpit. The crew then ran to the other airplane which had pulled up alongside. I moved the throttle and added enough power to turn to the runway. Radio frequencies were changed. "Channel Two," the voice said and I chanted it back. "Hobos ready for takeoff, tower." "Cleared on the runway, Hobos." We rolled into position and centered between the long row of runway lights. We turned our lights off and sat in darkness, the instruments dim before me. The canopy slid shut with its "Whir . . . clunk." In a matter of seconds, that seven-year-old boy transformed into me, set out solo into the night, seventeen years later.

We launched to find a man in the dark, a man in the mountains of northern Laos with a squad of men. Like all men of his sort, his real name wasn't known to us. One night he was Lulu, another night Pogo, or White Rose, or Kingpin, or others, several taken from the names of bars and bordellos in Vientiane. To find our man we had a set of coordinates and little more. And so, once again, we were like the aviators of old using the very basics of flying, the primary tools of the trade, time and distance, a little wind, and some sort of intuition of where the heading led or what the area would be like. This bygone era of dead reckoning wasn't dead yet. It was alive for perhaps one of the last times, along with the relics of prop fighters. Looking over the maps in the single-seat cockpit with my light, alone, in the dim red light of the instrument glow, I realized that I was supremely happy. I had been able to time-travel back to an era in aviation that made sense. I wouldn't have to go about saying I was born twenty years too late.

The needles of the modern navigation systems wandered around their dials because the signals were too weak in the distance, and across high mountains they were unreliable at best. The bearing pointer aimed circularly to nowhere, useless. The only thing of value was fundamental aviation, dead reckoning, time and distance. It was beautifully simple, a trade known to the early airmail pilots, to those who flew the mountains of Spain for the Latecoere Company, to Skyraider pilots in Indochina. There is a heading, perhaps drawn on the pilot's map. If there is no wind, he can take that heading and fly at a known rate over the measured distance. He simply waits until the time is up and he is there, at least within a matter of several miles. If there is a wind, he adjusts accordingly, his intuition adding a few degrees into the wind to compensate for drift. To those trained solely in electronic navigation, riding the invisible beams of airways, all this seems folly, inaccurate, ancient. Yet it works when nothing else does. And it offers a sense of true satisfaction. To fly at night, through the weather, to a point in the mountains hundreds of miles away, and then wage battle, then to return by the same method, is a supremely satisfying experience. It is sum and substance for a pilot.

Because of the ancient method, we arrived at the right place. We called our man, and he answered, saying he could hear our engines overhead. How beautiful, I thought. It was midnight, the cockpit was hot, and the exhaust flame lashed back beside the cockpit below my bubble cover. We had flown three miles a minute over the heading and distance, and now the man could hear our engines overhead. In typical native manner, he said, "Have many, many bad guy all around. You drop bomb three hundred meter north from my light." There was a brief flash of light below, then darkness. It reminded me of the tales of blackouts in London. One man lit a match and it became a veritable beacon. Lulu's light was gone and we had but a memory to aim by.

We decided to drop our own indicator, so lead rolled in and dropped a flare marker. We then took turns striking into the dark, each time Lulu offering his corrections and telling us how well we were doing. I often thought that all they really wanted was some company, and we were it. I couldn't blame them. I didn't want to be crawling around the mountains of northern Laos at night either. Again and again we rolled in, missing the mountains, seeing the dark summits pass as we descended into the crevices below, until our ordnance had been completely transformed from cold metal into the blazing fire below. We then bid adieu to the jungle and men below. As quickly as ever, the man called and said we had killed one hundred bad guys, his way of saying something to make us feel good—and that he had absolutely no intention of wandering over to see exactly what had happened. Killing one hundred was his reward to us for coming all the way, for staying out well past midnight. It, of course, wasn't real.

At that time of year, we could put the stars to use as well as time and distance. Orion's Belt at ten o'clock would take us home every time. Three miles a minute and we could finally see the lights ahead, the little jewels of human habitation on the ground, the haven for airplanes when they rested on the tarmac between flights. There was a gentle screech of tires on concrete, and the open canopy let in what felt like cold air, although it was still about eighty degrees. We were wet with perspiration. I unlocked the tailwheel and turned off the runway, noticing lead's position lights in the de-arming area. We had changed worlds again, back to earth.

I rolled back to the parking spot, the crew chief waving his lighted wands to indicate direction. I slid the mixture lever to cutoff and the roar ceased, the propeller slowing from a solid disk to individual blades, then stopping completely. There were the metallic sounds of cooling airplane parts creaking, contracting, like a living thing coming to rest. Oil smoke drifted back into the cockpit, and the chief climbed onto the wing and stood beside me.

He took my helmet and asked, "Switch off, sir?"

I smiled and said that it was off. I smiled because those words were being phased out of aviation for us. No more mag switches, no more mixture, no more propellers for that matter. The jet engines had little of such character. It was like savoring old and vintage wine that will be no more, so make the very most of it and enjoy it while it lasts. The ground was a hard and foreign place compared to the warm and revered cockpit. I was wet with sweat, and there was a pain in my back from the hard cushion. And my fanny was sore.

We went to the club, where the waitresses were asleep but cold beer waited. Other pilots drifted in, some waking up to fly, some coming back. There were the bodies belonging to the voices we heard in the sky.

103

We felt complete, part of a little exercise in the noble art of tailwheel, prop-fighter flying. It meant so much to us and probably so very little to anyone else. No matter. We wanted it that way; we savored our vintage wine.

Voices in the night are a figment of the imagination. They are not real. It does not happen. A pilot cannot go about believing in ghosts and voices. Anyone knows that. But the next night I was to know a voice for an instant and it would save my life.

I launched into the dark behind the lights of Ron Rounce's airplane, which was turning east beyond the runway's end. "Sure is black," came Ron's detached voice over the radio. "Yep," I said. It was. There wasn't a moon, no lights, no fires, nothing. The airfield lights faded into the distance and there was only the white fuselage light out ahead which blended into the stars when I could see stars. It was an elegant analogy, that my leader had vanished amongst the stars. The instrument lights turned down, I sat in a dim red hue. It was a matter of sitting in a metal bubble of life flowing through space and time. Then we came to the target.

"I've got two trucks on the road," the FAC said from his Cessna 0-2 Skymaster. "My mark is the red one between the two whites."

I picked out the red mark and oriented myself to the cardinal points of the compass. The number of markers on the ground was amusing since the entire Trail was littered with markers from various strikes. One night we had made contact with the FAC and thought we were in the area. He described the ground markers, which we finally made out, and cleared us in. After the first few passes, the FAC said he couldn't see any ordnance going off. And after further discussion, we decided that we weren't even in the same portion of real estate. We had been out bombing on some other marks left from a previous strike. But this time we were in the right place. Ron called in and his napalm splashed like a waterfall in slow motion.

Aside from the strike fires there was only black night, no groundfire, and silence beyond the engine. Ron continued his strike, then finished, called for me to come on down, and I began mine. I planned on four to five passes and started in with a forty-degree dive for the first. The fires below were bright and made it easy to locate the target area. No one shot, no one said anything. All in all, it was uneventful.

Now, if you ask a pilot to do a roll, chances are he will do it to the left. It's easier to move the stick that direction for right-handed people. So most turns, rolls, or whatever go left just as a natural move. So I made four left turns from my four passes. It was a routine that was made easier when there wasn't any groundfire. Then there was dive number five. The pipper glowed pink in the gunsight, and through the glass I could see the roaring fires below. I hit the release button and started to climb. And then it happened. A tiny voice, one that didn't belong to anyone I knew, but clear and distinct, said, "Turn right, not left." I did. I yanked the stick violently right and watched a stream of tracers streak by my left just a matter of feet away, just where I would have been, usually. There wasn't a word until it happened, then Ron said, "Hey, they're shooting from behind!" And that was all. There was that single stream of fire, perhaps ten rounds of hot and hard metal a few feet away. Then I turned, and we went back home. There were no more voices.

We sat at the bar. "Fairly simple night, huh?" Ron mused.

"Yeah, I guess so," I said, not sure of it. "Say, do you ever hear voices in the cockpit, I mean when something's wrong or they're shooting?" I finally asked.

"You're kidding." Ron laughed. "That's a lot of baloney."

I didn't go right to sleep. I lay there thinking, not convinced. And finally I knew I was wrong. Voices in the night don't happen. They're not real. All that mysticism is a sham. There is no logical explanation. I turned out the light and thought some more, trying to approach sleep. Then it hit me. I sat up and snapped on the gray table lamp. Just because we can't touch something doesn't mean it's not real. Of course! I turned right instead of left, and that was real. I wasn't blasted from the sky, and that was real too. I looked around the room. There was a half-finished model airplane, stacks of books, papers, writing pencils, the remnants of my physical existence. I was there too. My flight suit hung damp from the locker door, A-1 oil across one leg, my gloves dangling wet from a leg pocket. Real is a lot of things, I reflected. And then, out loud I said, "Thank you, little voice, whoever you are." I turned the light off and went to sleep.

There being no month, no day, no year, no particular differentiation of time flow except day and night, it was just another night. Jim Kelly and I were again relegated to the role decribed as "truck killing." We gave our mission this title as if the trucks themselves had life. In actuality, they carried life for guns, ammunition mainly and whatever other supplies could be carried. The trucks kept the jungle soldiers going, fed the guns, and mainly led to killing the round-eyed Americans. And whatever didn't come from those trucks, whatever didn't come from the harbor at Haiphong, came from the United States by way of theft and capture from the scavenger hunt of Southeast Asia where our goods had been scattered at random. So we killed trucks when they dared to run and we could find them.

This night we would run into another rule of the big Southeast Asian war game. As we went near Mu Gia, a FAC called and reported some dozen or more trucks, all with lights on, coming down the Trail! It would be a fantastic target, and we altered course to meet the FAC accordingly. In the interim, the FAC was calling in the target to a higher headquarters. The call was not to report what we were about to do, but rather to request permission. As we all waited, the FAC's navigator mentioned that on close checking, the trucks were still actually in North Vietnam, which was why they had their headlights on. The game was played such that we told our adversary where we would fight the war and with what weapons. Thus the enemy was free to use whatever countries and areas he wanted at will, such as driving with their lights on to the imaginary line we had drawn, then turning them off and moving on one at a time. That, of course, made it more difficult, often quite impossible, for pilots to locate and destroy the vehicles. It was also astoundingly more expensive. Where the same ordnance could be used for the larger target, it was now used on a single truck. Shortly, the higher headquarters called back with a request to verify the coordinates. As we watched the trucks in line, Jim and I set up for a strike and the FAC called in the best escape headings, best routes to take should we take hits and have to bail out. Deciding that fighting an enemy meant taking the battle to wherever he was, we proceeded to roll in and eventually destroy every last truck in the convoy. It was a veritable field day, ammunition exploding and trucks burning. A lot of guns would want for ammunition due to this strike, and perhaps a few lives would be spared. And as we turned away, the FAC said that they would confirm the coordinates as well within the legitimate battle area.

"Did you ever get the idea that we're not in this to win?" I asked Jim on the radio as we cruised back to Nakhon Phanom.

"Yeah," he said, "but the flying's sure great."

And, of course, that was one answer for us, great flying and the dedication to ideals that we carried with us. It was almost as if we not only had to fight an enemy army but the mysterious ways of the U.S. government as well. The more I thought about it the more angry I got. I began to take it out on the airplane, swearing at the aged "E" model that was painfully slow, the maintenance items that hadn't been fixed, bad radios, and so on. I didn't need to practice my speech to the crew chief as I figured it would flow effortlessly just as soon as the engine stopped.

Pulling into the parking spot, I grabbed the mixture lever and coasted to a stop as the prop came to a halt, the oil smoke fading away. I was climbing out of the cockpit as the crew chief came up to the wing.

"How'd it go, sir?" he asked.

I threw him my helmet. "Terrible," I snarled. "Not only is this a crazy dumb war, but the airplane's a

108

piece of junk. Don't you bother to check it before it goes out?"

"Yes, sir," he said, trying to stay calm. "It's just that we don't always get time to do things properly."

I fumed out of the cockpit. Standing on the wing, I turned back into the oven of a hole in which I had sat for the last few hours and checked that the switch was off. Then I turned to the chief and, grabbing my helmet, said, "I'm going to write this airplane up right on down to the dirt on the floor."

Clutching my gear, I turned, slipped on the oily wingwalk, and slid all the way down the wing to crash onto the metal ramp. I sat up wide-eyed from the long fall and sudden drop off the trailing edge. The A-1 sits so high that people had broken ankles and legs from the very same maneuver. Lying there on the ramp, I looked up at the chief, who was still standing beside the cockpit. At first resisting the impulse to laugh, he suddenly broke into a roar, doubled over, lost his balance, and slid down the wing to the ramp beside me, smashing into it with a loud clank. I looked over at him, our eyes meeting head on. There was a brief silence as we both sat on the ground, then there was an avalanche of laughter.

"Well, it's one way to get a new outlook on our problems," I said.

The chief raised himself on one oil-covered arm and laughed again. We lay back and laughed into the dark hot air. The pickup van rattled across the ramp to where we were sprawled out beside the airplane.

The Thai driver leaned out. "You OK, sah?"

I raised myself from the ramp, signed the form with my name only, carried my gear into the truck, and waved to the chief.

109

"See you tomorrow night," he said.

I thanked him for putting up with a frustrated combat pilot and trundled off across the ramp to the bar.

That next mission was to be number one hundred for me, one hundred combat missions in the A-1, occasion to sew on the little patch that had an A-1 firing its gun in the night over the "one hundred missions on the Trail" wording. Ron Rounce was the lead, and I liked that. He reminded me of J-3 Cubs because as a kid he had a bright yellow Cub with the black lightning bolt painted down the side, a real airplane. Every kid knows about Piper Cubs.

It was a late briefing, 0100 hours, an hour after midnight. We hit the sack at nine, up at midnight. "Hey, Ron, you up yet?" I called into the dark of his room.

The small lamp on his desk lit the wall of airplane pictures taped at random. Ron was still in bed. "Hm? Oh, yeah. Yeah, OK."

I waited outside, looking at the stars on a mirror-smooth night. It was cool for that place, and I had my collar up and wore the white silk scarf Richard Bach gave me once in July in Iowa. The end stuck out of my flight suit, and faded ink said, *For Rick, from Dick, July '68*. And I momentarily recalled the grass fields, the aerobatics and biplanes of that summer, and the wonderful aviation books Bach had written, as well as the philosophy that would ultimately become the best-selling book *Jonathan Livingston Seagull*.

His jacket on, hands in his pockets, Ron emerged from his cubicle of sleep. We strolled off to the officers' club not saying much. "I'm tired," he said, yawning. And I was too.

110

The briefing was normal. The big guns were coming up stronger than ever with the dry season and the trucks were running in larger numbers than before. The roads were more solid as the rains went away. The briefers finished and left. "Any questions?" Ron asked. "Nope." We had flown together for so long that we knew the numbers and figures and our methods like clockwork.

We had about fifteen minutes before we had to get our vests and helmets and to go the airplanes. Ron took out his paperback, a worn copy of Ernest K. Gann's *Fate Is the Hunter,* and I took out my *Dandelion Wine* by Ray Bradbury. There was a silence as we read.

We went to personal equipment still not saying a word, put our books away at the same time, and got our equipment, the clanking of buckles and the plastic sounds of our swaying helmets common to us as we carried the gear from the bins out the door. We sat in an open truck and passed through the sentry gate on the way to the ramp. The sentry was asleep, his head lying on folded arms.

I had #734 again, the same as the night before. It ran well. I walked by Ron's bird across the ramp to nine, the crew chief said hello, and I felt mildly good. was in the mood to fly. There was a full, marble gunner's moon and plenty of stars.

I started up and checked the gauges, the flaps, and adjusted the volume on the radio. Then I sat and listened to that beautiful engine. I looked across the ramp to Ron, who hadn't started yet. Then his prop started rotating and the engine caught. I imagined the movements inside the cockpit, the starter depressed, the primer on, the belch of smoke. Ah, ha! There was

111

a gigantic backfire. Ice-blue spurts of flame shot back from the engine, lashing out at the night and the cockpit as if shouting anger at the creature who dared to wake the sleeping dragon. The engine failed to start. Ron tried again. The prop turned, the engine caught, spurted flame, quit. As I watched this contest between man and cold machinery, I realized that this was the stu of my life. Leave, home, dinners atop pinnacles modern architecture over blinking lights, a handful mere possessions, all like the fun of last summer' memories, something that happened once, long ago and not very important.

Aircraft #511 wouldn't start, and Ron's voice on the radio showed his mood. "Can't get the damned thing to start. Guess I'll have to take the spare." sympathized with him. An airplane that wouldn't star was a real pain, like thread that wouldn't go through the needle's eye, like a leak in the roof over your bed.

"OK, I'll be waiting on this frequency," I said to him. With time to wait I sat back and let the night soothe me with its wind and its mythical deities who ran amongst the stars. The slipstream whipped the sleeves of my flight suit, the night was right.

There was a tap on my left shoulder—huh? lifted the edge of my helmet and the chief yelled un derneath, fighting the engine noise and wind at 1,000 RPM. "Weather hold," he shouted. I got that sinking feeling, like not getting to play in the game when really wanted to. A radio call confirmed it. The targe had bad weather, and someone was smart enough t put us on a weather hold. Switches off, little knob rotated, toggle switches clicked, mixture off, the en gine died. The last of the exhaust smoke drifted awa across the ramp, and the crew chief took my helmet

112

the map case, and I unclipped the strap buckles and stepped overboard and down onto the wing. I walked over to Ron's plane, which was covered with mechanics who couldn't start it either. One explained that the primer wasn't working right. Another offered the suggestion that a regulator wasn't opening and closing properly. Soon Ron drove up from his trip to the spare airplane. He shook his head, and I smiled.

We waited back in the big briefing room. We took off our survival vests and piled our things in heaps on chairs. Our books came out again. With our feet up on chairs there was only the well-oiled whir of the air conditioner, a silent black telephone, the wisp of pages turning in Ron's book, an American flag, and a very official-looking map of the war with multicolors, numbers, and lines. And someone had drawn a chalk sketch of Snoopy on the black board with the caption as he faced his interrogator: "Snoopy Brown, U.S. Army Air Corps. 102-10-3107." It was then 3:30 A.M.

"Sure like the way this guy writes," Ron said.

I nodded. "Yeah, great pilot's book."

3:45 A.M., and the voice of a colonel from the command post. "Canceled. You boys are canceled. Weather over the target was impossible, so you can go on back to bed."

I turned and went back to where Ron was still reading, stretched out across two chairs. "Yeah, I heard," he said. "But I really don't feel like going back yet, do you?" He was enjoying the book and the hour and what we were doing. "No, not really. Still want to fly," I said. "What a letdown," he went on. "Won't get to see the sunrise from the air either. How about we read for half an hour more before we go?" he asked. "Yeah, fine with me."

We walked to the officers' club and had two cups of tea, woke up the waitress to pay the bill, and sauntered back to our rooms. Sunrise was starting and the ground was still. We looked to the horizon and listened as if there were to be a great sound to accompany a great sunrise. "You know," Ron said, "it looks like a big painting, and those stars look like pinpricks in a huge blue paper with a light behind it." The description was perfect.

Strolling down the walk in front of the rooms I said, "We ought to stay up awhile and watch the sunrise." We stopped in front of our numbered doors, old wooden doors with our names on them, changed from whoever had them before. "Well, I think I'll go to bed," Ron said. "I want to get up and read in the sun before we have to brief again." He opened his door and disappeared.

In my undershorts I walked back outside a few minutes later for a last look at the start of a new day. Ron had changed his mind and was lying in his hammock strung up with parachute cord. He didn't turn, knew it was me, and in that morning's delicious silence, looking at the waking world, started spinning that web of nostalgia which was our true love.

"You know," he said, "I'd almost forgotten how good this is. Reminds me of the times I spent in the field waiting for the dawn so we could start cropdusting. That was in Montana, and the morning was like getting a present with the sun and the clear air and the airplane."

I thought about that image, the biplane nestled in the grass, the guys in overalls with coffee looking at the first glow of a new day. Ron was letting me taste some of his vintage wine. It was good to me, too. I went back inside, and when I returned Ron was gone. The sun was up, the wine had been consumed, and it was time for sleep. Mission number one hundred wasn't flown that morning, but what took its place was perfect, like iced lemonade in the hot sun, quite nice indeed.

Trying it again a night later, I was assigned with Maj. Lowry Martin. We sat in the club before the flight, asking for trouble by ordering the day's special. Lowry sent his plate back to the kitchen twice, then changed his order to something more standard. To fully appreciate this predicament, one had to realize that even though it was an American club, it was essentially a Thai base and run by Thais. We just paid the bills for the privilege of operating from that location. Thus, the waitresses and cooks were Thai and had very little conception of the American taste in food and drink. And, while their ways often were peculiar to us, ours were equally absurd to them. Communication was difficult. If we ordered dinner, they would ask what sort of dessert we wanted also. And so, all at once, everything arrived, including the ice cream, which melted swiftly in the heat. And so on.

The base van pulled up outside, and we got up and left. The club was in true form that night, but as the van squealed around corners we finally began to laugh about it all. The driver, Thai, of course, turned the gears into a grinding machine as if meat were being prepared for market. Clouds of dust blew in the front door and through the open doors at the rear. We laughed all the way to the briefing.

Lowry briefed, and we took off into a bright sky, the moon not quite full. The airborne controller didn't have any spectacular targets and there hadn't been any

115

reports of big truck movements along the Trail. The controller was another innovation of our war in which the FACs, out on their own, called in their respective targets to the controller. There, in a four-engine C-130 transport, the information was organized, and when flights like ours called in, we could then be directed to whichever FAC had the most worthy target for our equipment. We would then be given the FAC's call sign and location with his appropriate frequency. The controllers were naturally given call signs and, being night oriented, were known to us as "Moonbeam" and "Alleycat."

"We've got lots of reported groundfire," Alleycat said, "but nothing worth your time yet. How about holding for a while?" Lowry consented, and we held in a ten-mile-wide orbit about fifty miles from the base. About an hour went by while we listened to reports of intense groundfire, but still no word of good targets.

Then I heard Lowry make a call to the controller. "Hey, why don't we go on over and fight them guns?"

The controller might have choked on his coffee, as I almost did. Then he replied, "OK, Hobo, be our guest. We have a Candle FAC in a good area for you." He gave us a strike frequency which we used to contact the C-123 that went by the "Candle" call sign. The FAC had moved well to the side of the area and was holding high above. A multitude of guns was spraying the sky, the explosions of 37mm antiaircraft fire flashing across the horizon. Our little patch of sky was marked with precision.

Although we had three radios aboard, VHF, UHF, and FM we assumed that our enemy could hear some of our conversations. Even though we had been admonished not to use titles of rank or even acknowl-

116

edgments by "sir," slang and jest often filled the airwaves. I imagined the NVA shrugging their shoulders and shaking their heads at this night's repartee.

"We're in the area," Lowry said the FAC ."Wonderful," the man said. "We could tell." The guns had opened up at our engine sounds. "We've got some marks down there, and the road runs roughly north and south between the two white ones. We had some trucks earlier, but lost them. There's a lot of groundfire, and if it's guns you want, take your pick." The markes were easy to spot for a change, and I checked the map with my flashlight and got a good idea where we were. It wasn't a particularly nice location for night fighting. It was like the abandoned house in a lonely field that scares children. The child wouldn't be quite certain if the monsters actually haunted the place, but we knew for sure. "If I'm cleared I'll go on and roll in," Lowry said. "I think I see where that one gunner is."

The FAC said it would be just super for us to do as we liked with the guns, and he then moved posthaste to a further corner of the area and climbed even higher for good measure. It was possible for him to take hits as the gunners fanned the sky for us and missed.

"I'm in," Lowry declared, starting from the north. I couldn't see him because we were blacked out, but I could picture his path down a forty-degree plane from seventy-five hundred feet. "I'm off," he called, "and breaking to the east." I put the ship up on the left wingtip waiting for a gun to follow the sound of Lowry's airplane. One did. I called in.

It took a good bit of mental gymnastics to keep the picture straight in my head of where everyone was and what we were doing relative to each other in the dark. The muzzle flashed as clips of 37mm streaked up and arced away to the east after Lowry. With the other plane well clear but still drawing gunfire, I stared dropping my cluster-bomb units over the gun position. With the gunners still absorbed in following Lowry, my CBU went off, drawing a sparkling line right across the gun. It stopped firing. "Hey, good work, Rick. Look out! Another gun off to the south!" I barely had time to notice before the tracers from yet another 37MM position were driving up an accurate line towards me. I banked steeply, and the pinkish tracers swept by the belly.

"OK, I've got one spotted," Lowry called out. "I'll be east turning back to the north," I yelled back. "Have at him." I jinked again, just enough so that another clip of tracer fire darted across my wing rather than into it. Then I pulled a constant four Gs as I twisted and turned to clear the area. Lowry rolled back in, and I saw his four 20mm guns blazing away like sparklers coming down from the heavens. His bullets struck the ground around the gun firing, but two more positions opened up. They were all firing at the sounds of our engines while we maneuvered, and when we got the moon behind us they shot at the black silhouette of ghost airplanes. The tracers came closer, and I made the comment that they were pretty good gunners.

Lowry said, "Yeah, there's one over here that's damn good. There's one way south that's not very good, though. We can leave him alone. But look out for this one way up north." How blasé, I thought. I'm scared half to death out here, but we're rating the enemy gunners as if it were a simple contest at a gallery. Some of the gunners were really terrible, not coming anywhere close. We sometimes figured that

118

they might perhaps not have their hearts in their work, content to aim wide so as to avoid our retaliation. If that was their intent, it worked.

The FAC was keeping count of everything from his front-row seat, and it came across the radio like a newscast. "OK, there are seven guns firing now. There's another one from the north! Now there's a twenty-three millimeter from the middle of the target area!" It was hard to tell who was saying what as the tracers fanned the sky and everyone was yelling. I cranked my head around as if it were mounted on a full swivel. Everywhere there was tracer fire and the white flashing of exploding metal. It was an odd sensation to watch the explosions from the cockpit. The engine sounds generally suffocated the hard explosive concussions, so there were the tracer lines coming up, a second of dark as the tracer burnt out, then a silver-white burst of energy as the warhead exploded. It was the Fourth of July extravaganza without the festive mood. Before I really had time to reflect on the proceedings I was rolling in again. I keyed the transmitter: "Roger, Hobo four zero, I've got you off to the west, and I'll be in from the north." Lowry's napalm went off, splashing north to south. The gunners irrigated the sky as one might a lawn on a summer's afternoon. They followed the airplanes as if they could see them. There were so many guns firing that I couldn't pick one out to shoot at. I opened up with the 20mm, which made blinding flashes on the wings and a deafening sound in the cockpit. Kicking the rudder pedals, I yawned the airplane, spraying armor-piercing incendiaries over two close gun positions. The ground lit up where the bullets were hitting, and hundreds of minute white flashes blinked across the ground like sparks of electricity

119

gone mad in a mass of tangled and shorted wiring. Some guns stopped shooting. Others started from new positions. I pushed the throttle forward and saw the hot exhaust flame shoot up alongside the cockpit. A shooting star fell through the sky in its silent journey. Flinching, I twitched the stick and jerked the airplane to avoid what I thought was more groundfire.

It seemed like hours that we were in battle. Still there were 23mm and 37mm guns sending round after round into the sky in rapid succession. They were like little volcanos erupting at random. A 23mm was belt-fed, unlike the 37mm, and the rounds pumped up as long as the gunners could keep their triggers down. How the barrels kept from melting was a mystery. The 37mm sent up clips, usually seven in a group, and we would usually dodge them if given sufficient warning. Unlike the jets, we never flew high enough or fast enough to get out of range. There was so much metal exploding in the sky and falling on Laos, we also wondered if the magnetic properties of the earth might be changed from Laos alone.

Pulling off my last pass, I called in out of ammo and said, "I'm off the west, Winchester." That was the call sign for no more ammunition aboard.

Lowry was ready to roll in. "Roger, four one, I'm in for one more run on 'em." The guns fired at each other, 37s at Lowry and his 20mm back. "Wow, they're really good tonight! I'm off west. What's your altitude, four one?" Lowry asked, laughing.

"I'm back at eight point five," I answered, "and all switches off and safe. Fuel is fifteen hundred pounds."

The guns followed Lowry's climb while he said, "OK, Rick, I'll be at eight."

The FAC called to tell the score, which was slightly fantastic. It was incredible. He said that we were there for twenty minutes, not the two hours it felt like. "You guys really got them angry. You took about one thousand rounds! You got two thirty-seven-millimeter guns destroyed and a probable on another. And we're getting out of the area. Sorry we haven't further BDA, but all you wanted was the guns anyway." Bomb-damage assessment, shortened to BDA, was the name of the game passed on to the higher headquarters in the game of tons and sorties. My personal assessment was that I was happy to be headed home.

I pulled the throttle back to cruise power and slid the prop lever back until the tachometer registered 2,200 RPM. "That's OK, Candle," Lowry said. "I had a good time anyway." Lowry, with his west Texas drawl, his infectious smile, and his penchant for dueling with antiaircraft guns, was a real piece of work. While most of us could be scared at getting killed, Lowry would be making quick time back home from the guns so that he could hear a fiddle player in a country-and-western band at the club. Amazing!

The calm was shattering, as if we had leaped from a roaring inferno into the solitude of an English moor. I settled back, and Lowry probably did too, except that he was most probably smiling. About five seconds of breath came out as I melted into the crevices and nooks around the hard seat and the impossible array of straps and wires behind me. We were on our way home. I whistled another lungful of breath through my lips. Everything was in one piece, still.

The LF radio was inviting, and after twenty minutes I turned it on. There was a news broadcast. "And the first men to walk the moon are back, folks! Listen

121

to those cheers! They're boarding the ship right this minute. What a day! What a moment in history! Imagine—the first men on the moon!"

I wondered if they had noticed the heavy ground-fire across our little portion of the earth, the moon giving us away to enemy gunners while astronauts stepped on its surface for the first time in the history of our world. The cheers filled my earphones, and I took a quick glance at the moon which hung like a big ornament in a black sky. "They're waving at us now," the announcer shouted. "Imagine, back from the moon!" It was so incongruous that I just sat idle, staring back at the moon. Lowry had his radio on also. "Feature that," he said. "Here we are slugging it out in these old birds, and those guys are walking on the moon. Makes you feel funny."

Not only did it make me feel funny, antiquated, lost in the Dark Ages, but it also made me realize that if we could walk on the moon, we could certainly settle this mundane little war. But we were obviously serious about going to the moon. And, of course, dealing with those whose terms of reference could be summarized by the muzzle of a gun and rice paddies and water buffalo was far different from the purity of a scientific endeavor like spaceflight. After men had blasted themselves into space at speeds over eighteen thousand miles an hour, Lowry and I droned on to the base in our old warbirds at something less than two hundred miles an hour. The moon, with its new significance, hung over the battlefield as new flights passed us on their way to fight on the Trail.

Studying the BDA reports the next night, it was obvious that the ground guides, known as forward air guides, shortened to FAGs, were sending out grossly

122

inflated reports as a reward to the night fliers. It was our experience that after a strike in the night, the FAG would immediately tell the flight how many had been killed or what had been destroyed. It would have been impossible to get such an accurate report before daylight, when the squad could actually talk over and see what had happened. But their inflated tidings went into official records and became a joke to the pilots. The FAGs, mainly native soldiers, often laughed as they gave the report. The Saigon generals thought it was impressive.

One night a pilot coming home from a strike in another place called one of the FAGs and asked if there was any BDA for him. The pilot hadn't even worked with the fellow. The man called back and said, "You kill one hundred bad guy." And so it went into the reports.

Shortly thereafter, however, we noticed a change in the wording from those voices below. We suspected that someone had mentioned that people were not believing them when they went about night after night giving the same old "you kill one hundred" routine. Col. George Miller, commander of the 22d Special Operations Squadron, was out on one of those nights of the new policy. After his strike and the fires had subsided and everyone had gained his composure, George asked for the BDA.

"You kill ninety-eight bad guy," came the serious voice.

"Oh, come on, Pogo," George said. "Whatdya mean, ninety-eight?"

There was a moment of silence, then the voice returned. "OK, you kill one hundred and two."

\* \* \*

Lying in the sun, resting before another night, someone mentioned that Christmas was coming.

"You sure?" I asked.

"Yep, I think it's in a few days."

That was one of our little odd pleasures, the total forgetting of time and dates. If you were the sort who felt that a fighter pilot had to own a Seiko or Rolex watch, then you could tell Sundays at least because Sundays always turned up in red on the little calendar. But one day was as good or bad as another, and such comforts as holidays, weekends, and regular time off were relatively unheard of. Some of the ground pounders had "office hours" and all that, but the combat troops weren't given to such schedules. "Christmas, huh?" I mused. That used to be a time for the scent of trees indoors and hanging loads of sparkly color all over them and not sleeping the night before when you were a kid. I wasn't sleeping the nights well as it was, but for other reasons.

About three nights before Christmas, the giant scheduling officer in the sky turned over his very analytical mind and pointed pencil and decided that I should be kept on the night-flying line. I was informed of that fact while sprawled in the sun, hurling obscenities at everything making noise. My aching head. I had escaped yet another night of the enemy's cunning attempts at grabbing my young body, and had celebrated in the usual nocturnal method thereafter. The schedule was posted. "DRURY: 2200 TAKEOFF." It was axiomatic that one complained about the schedule. Partly, I suppose, because it made one feel as if he could change it. But it didn't change. Unless some colonel decided to see firsthand what the war was about, or someone got shot down, we went. If we were

124

below the rank of major, and sometimes even then, we were the pawns of whoever didn't want to fly, those who felt we weren't doing our fair share, or, occasionally, someone too scared to go himself. The schedule stood in all its imperfectly printed glory.

We launched into the night in our expedition to northern Laos. My wingman pushed in his power seconds after I started rolling and was off somewhere around the four-thousand-foot mark utilizing the A-1 pilot's usual fancy footwork and agility. It was as black as dreamless sleep. Once away from the base, we were over jungle, and either we made the transition to instruments or hoped that the powers that be would lift us to cruising altitude. Sometimes they didn't.

"Climb check," I muttered into my mask. The A-1s had been running terribly, their engines being a conglomeration of remanufactured parts, and night flying was a test of one's fortitude. What would ordinarily be an almost imperceptible vibration during day flight was easily construed to be a major structural crisis at night. The air was dingy with the smoke of burning rice crops, making the flier's world a little less than magnificent below eight or nine thousand feet. Los Angeles smog was about half as bad. While the legitimate farmers were just doing their time-honored jobs, Charlie was picking up the idea to make the visibility worse. In the rice-burning season, Laos itself was almost invisible, and a pilot could easily run into it in a dive. At night we could see the muzzle flashes of the bigger guns, telling us that there was ground down there somewhere. Other than that, we were on instruments, sometimes even during the day due to the haze. The smoky film did make for some extravagantly red, burning sunsets, also like Los Angeles in the late afternoon of a smog alert. Our night wasn't in the middle of the season, though; it was the beginning really, and we were quickly on top and in the moonlight. "I'm level. Back to cruise power," I said to my wingman, who was now just a voice on the radio and lost to sight.

My old Wright R-3350 pumped away without as much as a tremor, not a chance to abort and go home. It was one of those nights when I knew we were going all the way. Besides, it was nice up there in the rarity of clear air with the stars.

We had been assigned to work with a Laotian FAG known as Kingpin. It so happened that Kingpin was situated in some lofty mountains nearly two hours away. At least that was where he was reported to be. We had a set of coordinates and were doing our night time-and-distance flying once again. Time about up, I attempted radio contact in the idiot English we had developed. I twirled the knobs of the VHF radio and gave it a go.

"Hello, Kingpin. This is Hobo. You hear me?"

Silence. A 37mm airburst miles away. The sound of the engine.

"Kingpin; Hobo. How you hear?" Checking the map with my Japanese rechargeable flashlight, I decided that we were somewhere over where he ought to be. Heading and time was all we had. "Kingpin, damn it. You hear Hobo?"

There was a crackling of the radio static. Then a very distant voice: "Hobo. Kingpin. You come help Kingpin?"

That, I thought, was just brilliant. No, Kingpin, we just happen to be about four hundred miles from home and were wondering what you were doing tonight. But we had to be nice. After all, the poor fellow was down there in the night and someone was trying to kill him. "Yes, Kingpin, Hobo come help you. You have bad guys?" We had also developed the "good guy" and "bad guy" nomenclature to make things easier. It was all very wild West drama.

"Rager, rager, Hobo. Have many, many bad guy. They all around. They shoot big gun at me."

Maybe it was so. No muzzle flashes could be seen, though, and perhaps the fight in question was strictly a small-arms affair. But the "big gun" wording made me think it might be a mortar. If there was small-arms return fire, then it made things easier. It could even be interesting. It sounded like rain on tin and put those little holes in the airplane. Usually that was about all it did. The big guns were different.

"OK, Kingpin. You give us coordinates where you are. We come help you." I flipped the flashlight on and got ready to copy his numbers.

"Hobo, Kingpin. I have coordinate..."

I copied them and checked the map. Then I called my wingman. "Hey, you copy that? Either the guy doesn't know where he is, or he's a hundred miles from here." Sometimes the "find me puzzle in the sky" was normal with a FAG, like hide-and-seek. Then again, we sometimes got voices that gave a position to hit and, on checking, found the location to be on designated areas of friendly troops. One of the enemy had a radio and was trying to get us to bomb the friendlies. Then we would hurl obscenities at each other.

We went back to the basic. "Kingpin, this is Hobo. You hear my airplane?" It usually worked.

"You stand by, Hobo. I go listen."

Silence. The little man was climbing out of his

127

hole and peering into the night sky. He was soon back. I was still in a left-hand orbit.

"Hobo, Kingpin. I hear your airplane. You come nort maybe two mile."

Swell. We drove on nort for a minute or so. "Hey, Kingpin. You hear my airplane now?" By that time I was looking over the fuel supply. With some unusual forethought someone had ordered a full centerline tank, so we still had enough 115/145-grade fuel for another hour of playtime, as it was called.

"Rager, rager, Hobo. You over my position now."

We had finally narrowed our position down to within a few miles of dark ground. The mountains were high, and a cruising altitude of 9,500′ didn't put us all that far over them. There was an immensely deep valley below. "Kingpin; Hobo see big valley. Where are you?"

"Rager, Hobo. Bad guy in valley. You put bomb in middle of valley." With such a pinpoint target there was obviously no hesitation. A few five-hundred-pound bombs spread around in the night would be perfectly harmless.

"Look here, Kingpin, I want to know where *you* are." It wasn't in the rules to bomb Kingpin himself.

"Hobo, Kingpin on top of the mountain. You bomb bad guy."

That was some better. "OK, Hobo drop bomb in valley."

The depths of that valley were as black as could be. The moon lit the tops and spread dim light a ways down into it, but that was about all. Setting the wing station selector to the left stub, which held a five-hundred-pound napalm, I peered into the murk

and hit the mike button. "I'm in hot from the west."
I left a single fuselage light on so that my wingman
would be able to see where I was going. If I was
lucky, I might even be in the right valley. I wasn't
too worried about antiaircraft fire from that location;
not hitting the ground was foremost on my mind.
Rolling over partly on instruments, partly by moonlight, I stabilized near a forty-degree dive and looked
through the gunsight to the valley below. I was closing rapidly and I promptly descended below the tops
of the mountains. My unhesitating bravery was running thinner as the altimeter unwound, and I immediately thought, now, look here old boy. If he's
up there and I'm down here, then what the heck? I
won't be dropping anything on him, so why press
this attack? I hit the release button, felt the loss of
five hundred pounds, and grunted under a three-G
pull-up. The nape splashed like one giant flashbulb
in my rearview mirrors and made the sky like a bowl
of milk. Back to instruments. Kingpin let us know
that he was enjoying the show from his position
above.

"HOBO! You have number one bomb! Ver-ry
good. You do same same again."

Hell of a way to spend the last couple of nights
before Christmas, I thought. "OK, Kingpin, we'll put
it right there."

I did, and after swapping altitudes, my wingman
did too. The valley wasn't dark any longer. It was a
mess of little fires and splotches of sparkling 20mm
hits. Kingpin thought the whole thing was delightful,
and, if nothing else, we kept him company for a while
on an otherwise lonely night. As we climbed back to
altitude I think it was entirely without precedent that

129

Kingpin said, "And to you, Hobo, a good night." Ah, the Christmas spirit.

After level-off, all was quiet except the engine. We had come to sometimes discount that, and "all was quiet" didn't have anything to do with the engine's bellow. There wasn't a sound on the radio. I computed a heading and time home, and we set out in trail, a two-man tribe across the desert following a magnetic compass to the oasis. There wasn't a bump in the air either, and it was just a matter of cruising to Nakhon Phanom, no more shooting, no more vicious lunging at the earth at night, just smooth, homeward flying. I was infinitely relaxed. Funny thing, I thought, how I had come to love being alone in my airplane! I was the man in an old novel I had read, who discussed religion with a minister. The man was thought to have no religion whatsoever, barbaric in some ways, ideas bordering on paganism. Attending a physical, concrete and wood church, the man said he never felt further from God than in one of those places. But he said he was in chapel with a good sunset or with the stars, or clouds, the wind. And I was in concert with those thoughts. My church, my place of worship—the sky. Not war, not the insane confusion of what man has allowed on earth. But the quiet elegance of being up here, a place that does not ask favors or court the superficial. For survival, it demands understanding and courage, determination and true religion. For reward, it offers the substance of joy, love, and freedom. I had found the place where I could talk with myself and, if only for an hour or so, be alone with myself and taste the fruits that had nothing to do with money or power or possession. Controlling my destiny, with my life in my own hands, miles above the earth, I had come to see more than flesh and bones. My Christmas present was the best of all, a little communication with the divine and a bit of joie de vivre at prayer in my church.

I tuned in Radio Saigon on the LF radio. It worked perfectly; Al Hirt was playing an up-tempo version of "Winter Wonderland." Then I saw it. The snow, the most expansive ocean of snow I had ever seen. Limitless white snow, a truer winter wonderland than I had ever seen, bathed in the ethereal moonlight of a pilot's night far above the earth, miles above anything. Billowing white snow clouds. Sliding across the crown of it, I descended lower, and soon it was flowing across the wings as if I were never to touch the earth again, as if I were destined to play angel there forever. It was the finest Christmas snow ever. I rolled on through the mythical night as a leprechaun in the forests.

Eventually descending through my snow clouds, I lit a cigarette and crushed the package back into the zippered pocket on my sleeve. I was really a nonsmoker, and I soon managed to drop the silly thing in the cockpit. I couldn't find it and was soon almost inverted trying to figure out where it had gone. Sometimes I liked the taste of a smoke, particularly on a night flight, but this was ridiculous and dangerous. Then the creature gave itself away by emitting smoke from the base of the control stick. Even a little Christmas fire to keep me warm. It was most likely fatigue that made me simply open the canteen and empty its contents on the smoke. The smoke stopped, and I figured that the next guy to fly that airplane would take an unexpected bath when he rolled it upside down.

Then I argued about flying Christmas Eve, which, as I said, really didn't make sense because one day was like any other anyway. But it was the principle. Lt. Dale Townsend and I sat in the briefing room, Christmas Eve, 1969. I kept calling him Peter because Peter Townsend was a Spitfire pilot in the Battle of Britain and I just got into the habit of calling Dale by that name. "Well, Pete, what's it going to be?" Like there was really some choice.

"Well, why not try for a gun? If we've got to go out there, let's go gun hunting."

This meant that we would let the 23s and 37s have a go at us and thereby disclose their positions by their muzzle flashes, as I had done with Lowry Martin a few nights before. We were to gallantly roll in and shoot back. It was very exciting, but most of the advantage belonged to the gunners. They were deeply entrenched in caves or barricaded well enough that only our direct hits would stop them. For this stunt, we were visible against the gunner's moon, and our engines gave our positions away. "OK, Pete, if that's what you really want, let's have at it."

Dale had just checked out at night and was still motivated for such things. And like every night before, we were out there once again. It wasn't long before the gunners welcomed us to Christmas Eve. Their greetings of pyrotechnic cheer were airbursting somewhere around nine or ten thousand feet all around us. Overhead, another couple of thousand feet higher, the twin-engine C-123 was orbiting, calling out two trucks which were on the Trail. Dale thought he would try for them, and I could see where the guns were when they opened up. That was considerate of him, since it meant he would be the main gunner's target and not me.

Lights off, he called in. His napalm splashed, and a 37mm opened up with a volley of tracers. "I'm off breaking west!" Dale yelled out, leaving me in position and ready.

Gun switches charged, I called, "Roger that; I'm in on the gun." Mentally figuring where Dale would be with his lights off, I rolled in and put the pipper on the muzzle flash of the 37mm gun below. Then I squeezed the trigger on the stick and gave a longer-than-regulation burst, like four or five seconds. The big gun was still firing at Dale's engine sound as my 20mm shells hit it. There was a sudden explosion, which was most likely stored ammunition next to the gun, and then a steady fire. The gun stopped firing.

"You got the gun!" someone yelled through the night. But I had angered someone else as a 23mm chased me back to altitude. I was jinking on instruments, blinded by the muzzle flashes of my four 20mm guns. Dale rolled in on him, and the night went on that way for an hour or so.

When it was over, not because we had won the war at that point on the Trail, but rather because we were out of ordnance and just a little scared, the observer gave us our tally. "You guys got one thirty-seven-millimeter gun destroyed, one twenty-three-millimeter gun silenced, two trucks destroyed, one medium secondary fire, and you picked up three hundred and fifty rounds of Christmas cheer from twenty-three- and thirty-seven-millimeter guns. Have a happy!"

Dale and I drove back through the warm night

133

air until our target was a dot of fire receding in the distance behind us. Once in a while there was a spasm of explosions which shimmered through the ebony dark. Then it was far behind. I tried to conjure up some sort of holiday expression, some sense of understanding for humanity. It wasn't easy.

As the lights of the field blinked reluctantly through many miles of polluted air, I did a slow, slow roll around them. It was soft and buoyant in the night. I let the nose drop, then pulled up into a loop into the brimming cold light of the moon. And then Dale and I descended into the GCA pattern. He pulled up alongside in the de-arming area, and we taxied back in formation. It was after midnight; it was Christmas. Calling the command post, Dale was still excited from the strenuous melee. "Two of Santa's finest on the deck logging two hours each. Merry Christmas."

Our total earth celebration amounted to a cold beer and a rather dubious breakfast.

A few days later I was having breakfast in Bangkok with Lt. Col. Ruben Ware, a man who had already fought in Indochina long ago with A-20s and A-26s He had even flown to and from Hanoi back then. He' seen it all before, and he acted as though it were jus another chapter in the long book of his life. I mentioned my thoughts about flying on Christmas and how it was strange to contrast our life there with the holiday season at home. Escaping unscathed was my Christmas; at home it was buying presents, trying to be cheery, and usually missing the flavor of what the event was supposed to be. We missed it in spite of saying the appropriate words and phrases and acting in accor

134

dance with the social rules of the season. Old Rube smiled his deceptive smile. Behind the exterior of a lieutenant colonel with that combat history was a man intent on someday writing a historical novel, a man with some beautiful thoughts and a most elusive nature unless one listened carefully. He told me a Christmas story over breakfast. It brought together some of the things that had been evading me through many of those nights.

"I remember a particular Christmas Eve, years ago. I had one of the first B-57s and was on a cross-country. That was in Europe, and my family wasn't with me. So it was really a lonely time, like it is perhaps for you now. My wife had sent a letter, and in it she had mentioned that one of the children had been told that there wasn't any Santa Claus. He was upset about it. Well, this particular flight was a beauty, with lots of lousy weather and thunderstorms. I still had that letter in my flight suit and was still thinking about it in the back of my mind. It was like someone had taken a part of me away.

"The darned storms were fierce, and it wasn't long before I realized that I'd never make it to Brussels. So I got another clearance and climbed. I finally popped out on top, around forty thousand feet. It was then only a matter of flying on to the alternate destination. I sat back and thought about what my son had begun to think. The plane was going smooth as silk, and I scrunched down into the seat, relaxed. And, you know, I was suddenly awestruck by what I saw. The stars were twice as bright as I'd ever seen them before, the vicissitudes of the weather were taking place below with opalescent streaks of lightning deep inside the cells, and a comet even went its way before me, de-

135

scribing a fantastic arc across the sky. I was young myself and could look down sometimes all the way to the ground and the lights of towns. I could see all the sky, total geography was mine. It could only happen in a flier's world, as you know. Everything began to make sense. It all fit. All the people, all the places, all the events—being alive! In a nebula of an instant of time I realized that I would have to communicate all this with my boy. I would have to tell him that he was wrong, that there really was a Santa Claus. It was real.

"After I landed, I checked into the BOQ and sat to write him a letter. It took a couple hours and was only one page long. It was a single page that had to be just right. I mailed it hoping it would mean something to him and that he would understand. I got a letter back saying that the boy was really happy, that he finally knew for certain there was a Santa, and that the two other kids had said to him, 'See, there really is a Santa Claus. We knew it all the time!' And you know, Rick, that was one of the happiest Christmases I have ever had."

Mostly to myself and unintentionally understating what I felt, I said, "That's nice, Rube. That's really nice."

He smiled at me once again. "You know something else? It's amazing what parts of our culture we leave over here. We don't always leave the good, the real meanings of American life, the philosophy. We leave a lot that just isn't true. We don't even bring Christmas here." He got up to go.

"What are you going to do today, Rube?" I asked.

"Well, I've been here before and I was young, like you. So all that playing is behind. Think I'll have a nap and soak up some sun later. Remember, I'm an old man now. I can guess the sort of things you'll be doing. Have fun. And Happy New Year."

He sauntered out the door with the morning *Bangkok Post* under his arm. His back to me and not turning, he offered a wave of his hand.

"Yeah, see ya, Rube. Happy New Year."

# EIGHT

**M**ANY OF MY OLD DOUBTS and suspicions about what the Air Force was really like were surfacing again. The old fictions and dreams that I carried with me into the Air Force had been promptly shattered during my first assignment, pilot training. Reality wasn't quite as good as the great old aviation movies and the many books I had collected. I wanted a career in the Air Force as a pilot and considered changing my mind only a few months after I had started the training program. Although we were all officers, and the days of the cadet hazing syllabus were supposed to be history, we were still treated like incorrigible dunces. Rather than having seasoned veterans to respect and learn from, we were faced with numerous second lieutenant instructors with a couple hundred hours' total time in airplanes. In most cases we were expected to run and jump at their arrivals and departures. The only thing they could teach was what they had read in the manuals. It was impossible to maintain any sort of respect for them as pilots. One of them even went so far as to show me how to roll in and drop ordnance, fire guns, and evade antiaircraft fire. That was all well and good except that he had never been further than the confines of a pilot training base and had never been closer to a fighter than touching one at an airshow display.

y A-1H, #257, with *Sopwith Camel* on the cowl, later
anged to *Midnight Cowboy* after frequent night flying. A
ge airplane, it sat some twelve feet high, with wings span-
g fifty feet and a propeller diameter of fourteen feet. Not
hing of beauty to some, its dripping oil and fragrance of
rn leather were the essence of true aviation to me.

A pilot's Southeast Asian survival vest was a ponderous affair. Sprouting survival radio, first aid kits, ammunition, pistol, survival knife, and assorted documents, it was very awkward.

Groundcrewmen loading ordnance on an A-1E. A fuse extender is being installed on an MK-82 bomb.

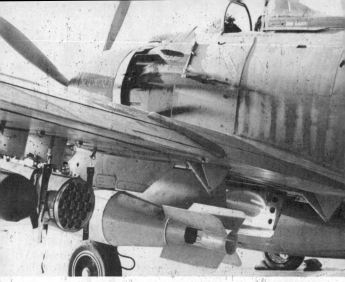

Rearview of wing-mounted ordnance on my A-1H showing why the Skyraider often looked like a huge magnet flying over a junkyard.

Even though the R-3350 pumped out a lot of horsepower, the heavy load we carried and high drag it produced kept our A-1s from achieving very high performance. Notice the great amount of frontal area on the underwing ordnance in this photo, a typical rescue load of CBU, rockets, 7.62 millimeter miniguns, and 20 millimeter in the wings.

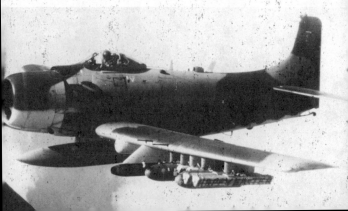

On November 28, 1969, Lowry Martin (in A-1H #608) and I met an AC-119K "Stinger" gunship over southern Laos to see if A-1s could provide escort cover for gunship operations. The AC-119K had the addition of two J-85 jet engines in wing pods. Its added arsenal was impressive: two M61A1 20 millimeter gatling guns, AN/AAD-4 forward-looking infrared sensor, and Texas Instruments AN/APQ-136 search radar with moving-target-indicator mode. The bulbous protrusion forward of the door is a Motorola AN/APQ-133 side-looking beacon-tracking radar.

The North American OV-10, a fine Forward Air Controller (FAC) aircraft; flown from Nakhon Phanom, they were known by the "Nail" callsign.

The "Jolly Green Giant" rescue helicopter. Capable of air-to-air refueling from an HC-130, the giant Sikorsky was the backbone of the search and rescue recovery force.

An A-1E Skyraider on a dive bomb pass over "Steel Tiger," the southern part of Laos where the terrain was generally flat in comparison with northern Laos, which was code-named "Barrel Roll."

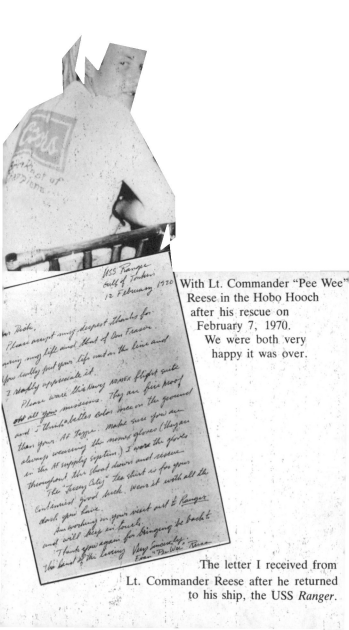

With Lt. Commander "Pee Wee" Reese in the Hobo Hooch after his rescue on February 7, 1970. We were both very happy it was over.

USS Ranger
Gulf of Tonkin
12 February 1970

Dear Rick,

Please accept my deepest thanks for saving my life and that of Don Fraser. You really put your life out on the line and I really appreciate it.

Please wear this Navy NOMEX flight suit on all your missions. They are fire proof and I think a better color than your Air Force. Make sure you are always wearing the nomex gloves (they are in the AF supply system.) I wore the gloves throughout the shoot down and rescue.

The "Jersey City" tee shirt is for your confinement, good luck. Wear it with all the dash you have.

Am working on your visit out to Ranger and will keep in touch.

Thank you again for bringing me back to the land of the living. Very sincerely,

Evan "Pee Wee" Reese

The letter I received from Lt. Commander Reese after he returned to his ship, the USS *Ranger*.

Battle damage was the A-1's forte. This spectacular damage was taken during a SAR. Note the left wing, holes in the fuselage, ripped away right wing root sections, and flap section completely shot away.

John Flinn standing in the gaping hole of the above aircraft where 37 millimeter nt through the wing.

On the ramp at Nakhon Phanom drinking champagne after my last A-1 combat flight on May 6, 1970. It was both a happy and sad moment; I would miss the airplane but not the antiaircraft gunners.

People said to me, "Things will be different out there in the *real* Air Force." But they weren't. There was more game playing, all backed up with the threat of what our effectiveness reports might say. I found that only when I was alone in a single-seat airplane in combat was there any "real" Air Force, and that was mainly a matter of what was in my mind and how I pictured things. A lot of people didn't even like that and went off to other jobs less dangerous, content to shuffle papers and game-play again. All my celluloid pilot heroes and paper knights didn't really exist except for a few people who also fought the system. And that appeared to be a heck of a way to have to live one's life. It happens to be the only way, though, for those who must be themselves. Once again, the Air Force was trying to illustrate graphically why I ought to get out and not make it a career. I was too interested in aviation and a little too hung up on the notion of fighting totalitarianism and championing freedom. People might be inclined to think those items are what the Air Force is all about. It may have been, but it didn't appear to be anymore. Of course, it can be said that military doctrine only reflects civilian direction.

And so the squadron commander heard that I had written some things for the aviation magazines and made me the awards and decorations officer. Since his initial lecture on what constitutes right and wrong, I had been apprehensive of him. My doubts were well founded. We returned from a mission during which I had been subjected to the most trying formation flying I'd ever experienced. I spent nearly two hours bitterly repressing the urge to punch the mike button and tell the man what I thought. It wouldn't have mattered. He heard what he wanted and saw only what he thought would fit his version of reality. The only thing to his credit was that he flew the airplane well, alone. Some said it was good experience to fly with him because one learned about restraint as well as how to change three radio frequencies while in a sixty-degree bank in tight formation. Wingman consideration wasn't in the man's repertory, so anyone trying to maintain some semblance of formation truly had his hands full. At least the man was consistent in his eccentricity which allowed everyone to know that some sort of insanity would most likely happen next. I was happy to land and forget the whole flight. The words of a friend kept ringing true: "How come the wrong people fly the right airplanes?"

We walked into the squadron building and I threw my hat on the counter, simultaneously dropping into a chair. The colonel walked into the room and called my name. I thought I might be scrunched down far enough in the chair to be invisible, but I wasn't. "Drury, I want you to get into the office there and write up our mission for the DFC."

I thought I surely must have missed something during the mission. "What for?" I asked.

"Well, report all the hooches destroyed and the supplies we set on fire. Put in the weather and whatever else you remember."

I couldn't recall anything worth more than a cold beer after the flight.

"You're the awards and decorations officer for this squadron, so get in there and write the narrative. I want to see it as soon as you get it finished. Triple space so I can edit." He turned and walked off.

I went into a small office and sat at a large gray desk. The lined notepad stayed empty, my pencil resting on top. There was really nothing to write unless I created some sort of fiction, which wasn't the reason for the awards system. I had always thought of the Distinguished Flying Cross as a real measure of a pilot, about what the man was really like in a combat airplane under fire. It was part of a great tradition, and a man ought to wear the medal with great pride. And here I felt I was being asked to make up a story so someone could get one for doing virtually nothing at all. The system helped promote that sort of thing also. If a man wants to get advanced in rank and position, he needs to have awards and decorations in his record. And since they were being given out like popcorn, not having any citations of valor or whatever began to look as though the man must have been well below average. He obviously wasn't "performing."

I read the regulations which detailed the form and construction of awards and outlined what they were given for and looked over the examples. Nothing came close to what we had done, which had been a fairly routine flight in some rainy weather where we had bombed and strafed some obscure target mostly hidden by dense jungle. I had personally seen no groundfire, and none had been reported. I picked up the yellow Venus number two and scribbled some thoughts and finally typed a page which was a factual account of the mission. I even tried to make the weather sound foreboding. I took it to the commander's office and stood while he read it.

*"No! No! No!* This isn't what I want! There isn't one word about the groundfire we took, and you won't get approval for anything unless you put in the groundfire hazards."

I tried to be calm. "Sir, as I recall, there wasn't

any groundfire. I didn't see a thing, and I was there with you."

He looked away to some pictures he had made of a truck burning under a napalm fire. "Nonsense. There's always groundfire, even if you can't see it. They're always shooting at you. So put it in your reports. How do you expect us to get awards?"

There was a crashing reductio ad absurdum comeback which I resisted. Although the American flag stood in the corner of the room and words about patriotism were etched in brass, the truth of the matter was buried in promotions and awards and the unwritten requirement that a "combat command" was necessary for promotion to the grade our commander was looking at. Medals would look nice across a desk in a peacetime United States. At home, only a very few people would know if they were real or fiction.

The colonel leaned on the desk and drilled his stare into me. "Now get back in there and rewrite this. I want it triple spaced again so I can make corrections for the final typing."

I turned and left, walking down the corridor and back into the dismal office. I sat with the page of type staring at me from the desktop. I didn't see how I would give in to his military solipsism. It wasn't just the squadron commander; it was common to many of the higher-ranking officers who had grown into their own worlds, leaving their "inferiors" behind. It was the old story of the politician who, enamored with his lofty position, forgets easily why he is there. He is no longer affected with the basic and necessities of life or those "under" him. The results were apparent in the war we were fighting. Bomber commanders directed policy for fighter operations, tank commanders directed overall policy for the entire war, and uninformed and oblivious civilians, living in idealistic fantasies, swayed tactical wisdom. Instead of saving lives or shortening the war, it just enslaved more people. I looked back at the notepad and decided that I wouldn't give up. I turned off the light and walked out.

I sat in the big chair in the operations room the next day. One of the squadron pilots, Lt. Jim Kelly, was erasing names and inserting others on the large manpower board. He turned when he got to my name.

"I thought you were a great author," he said with a smile.

"I have trouble with fiction," I replied.

"Well, you can have just the facts from now on. You've been fired. You are now the squadron historical officer." My name was smeared from black print and finally wiped away with the cloth.

"That calls for a celebration," I said. "It feels like a monkey off my back. A beer for all."

Jim finished with the names on the board, and then we put our hats on and left, marching down the long corridor past the office with the American flag and the engraved words of inspiration. I opened the door, and a blast of clear air filled my lungs. It was a great relief.

In keeping up appearances, the wing staff flew with each of the A-1 squadrons sometimes during the week. Since they said they had more important things to do than fly in combat, they were assigned to the easier missions and, of course, seldom if ever flew at night. There were exceptions, but not many. Flying with most of them was not like flying with the regular guys. One didn't feel inclined to chat on the radio,

143

nor was there much in the way of aerobatics on the way home. It was a chore to be tolerated rather than a flight to be enjoyed. And so it was with combined anger and astonishment that I listened to the words of the squadron commander. I had been called after a night of flying and was to report to the squadron as soon as possible. I stood before him wondering if I would yell or exercise self-control in the most trying moments.

"I'm really tired of having to find out where you are all the time, Drury. Even though I've told you about it before, you still don't show up around the squadron enough. I'm just about ready to make this an eight-to-five duty day for you and make you report in, every day, seven days a week."

I stood like marble. Internally, all the guns on Uncle Ho's Trail were firing a year's supply of ammunition. "I flew last night, sir," I said.

He shuffled some papers on his desk. "That's just an excuse you guys use so you won't have to come in here. Just like you think that Sandy alert is an excuse for not coming down to the squadron building and doing the additional duties. Well, you're all wrong. I'm going to have all that changed."

It wasn't worth the time to argue, nor was it worth provoking the creation of official paperwork explaining what a dumb lot we were and declaring us all incompetents. True or false, that would tag along with us forever, imprinted on every personal form like the plague. It was sort of a military blackmail where the threat of unkind words on our forms would keep us in line.

The commander went on. "Now, the wing commander is having his last flight next week. I am assigning you to take care of the preparations and see to it that things are done right. I want a big cake baked and lots of champagne."

That he would select me for such a dubious honor I put in the category of torture for past events. He must have known the abhorrence I felt for the madness of the system I was witnessing.

"We don't bake cakes for our own pilots, and they fly every day," I said. My words were as a single match struck against the force of the sun.

"He's the wing commander, *my* commander," he said.

I understood. Damn the guys, damn the men who did the real dirty work of the war, to hell with reason. Where there was that officer efficiency report, there was dirty pool, and the road to full colonel was going to be paved with toilet paper for this man. I didn't want any part of it. "Sir, isn't this going to be a bit much? Why not the usual champagne and hosing down with the fire truck?" He yelled, pounding on his desk, "Because, damn it, this is *my commander!*"

Another thought came over me, a mild gambit. Perhaps if all that nonsense were actually done it would be so obvious that it would reverse the intended outcome. The man would look so silly that even he would see it. I made a few phone calls and it was arranged. I winced from the very thought of it all; this particular wing commander wasn't a bad sort. On the other hand, his deeds hardly warranted such a big reception.

The day came, and we all made the trek to the ramp. There was a large empty spot on the ramp where the colonel's aircraft would be parked. Our trucks pulled up and a table was set, complete with tablecloth. Then the cake. It had a sketch of an A-1 on the top with the words, *Last Flight*. All in all, it was disgusting. Several bottles of champagne were cooling along with the glasses. Someone got the best-looking WAF available to make the presentations, which meant that a miniskirted female in a blond wig stood amongst the machinery of war, laughing and carrying on as if the whole Southeast Asian conflict had been designed in her honor. She and the event complemented each other thoroughly.

I wandered to a far corner, where my embarrassment wouldn't be quite so obvious, and watched as the colonel and his wingman came by in a high-speed pass, very low, and pulled up into the downwind leg for landing. I watched as the beautiful machine turned into its resting spot and the magnificent propeller quit turning. What a disgrace to such a fine machine, I thought. The fire truck stopped and our squadron commander turned the handle and awarded the presentation of cold water to the pilot who had survived a year of combat flying, or at least that was the significance of the event for everyone else. It didn't signify all that much this time. The WAF trundled over to the colonel and planted a kiss and served a glass of champagne. I turned my back, feeling a disgust I had never known before. There was an airplane in the hangar; its exposed engine was far more interesting. And then the event sort of came to an end with our commander snapping to attention and saluting as the colonel drove away. As the procession was falling apart and the glasses and bottles were being tucked away, there was the sudden realization that one of our squadron pilots, Ken Ohr, was also coming back on his last flight. There was a flurry of words about the availability of more champagne and glasses. It was all in the realm of a second thought that one of the actual combat pilots was also through with a year, a *real* year of combat made up of lots of dark nights and thousands of rounds of groundfire. Then again, he wasn't writing an OER on a high-ranking officer, so it wasn't of equal importance. Ken came back, and there was that last pass, that long and sad swoop down the runway for the last time, and the last landing. It was always a combination of happy-sadness. Ken wheeled into the chocks and got the cold water, the glass of champagne, wore the same big smile as pilots do when it's over, and drove off in his wet flight suit. It really wasn't a right ending. The songs had been sung previously, for the wrong man. The melody was swept into the distance and the sound of jeeps on the metal ramp clanked away in procession.

Possibly only one of very few so angered by the episode, I was the only one not to attend the farewell party for the colonel. I stood at the little bar in the hooch in my flight suit and refused to be a part of something so meaningless. My life of always giving in, going along with people, had ended abruptly. The room was empty except for me and the furniture. And then the group came back. "You missed the party," someone said. "I hope so," I said in return. "Well, the commander is thinking about reprimanding you or something. He said it was obvious you didn't go." It was interesting that I had become so important. But it wasn't anyone's importance involved in the issue. It was the same old nonsense about whoever doesn't fit into the mold is wrong or bad, different, and not to be tolerated. I wasn't fitting. Indeed, I was living in disgust at most of the fawning, vacuous regimen of

147

the system as propounded by our so-called leaders. The colonel came in, and I left.

It is a sad world, I thought. Once again, the military was visibly rewarding its "yes-men," its least deserving. It wasn't much longer afterwards that one night the door crashed open with such force that the window fell open on its hinges with the sound of splintering wood. I woke from a sound sleep as the light went on and two figures walked across the room. "Hey, you guys, get up!" The voices repeated themselves until they were standing beside our bunks. The deputy commander for operations and our squadron commander stood there, both in pajamas and robes. It was the first time our squadron commander had been in anyone's room, and it was strange to see him standing there, particularly in *my* room. "Guess what?" the DCO asked.

Joe, my new roommate, and I looked at him with a completely blank stare, apparently sufficiently empty to ask the question without words. "Your commander has just been promoted to *full colonel!*"

I wasn't trying to be cute or anything of the sort, but I immediately said, "You've got to be kidding!"

It wasn't taken the way I meant it. "No, no, it's true. Imagine, full colonel!"

I leaned on one elbow, silent, still a little heavy from my former sleep, yet sharp enough to wonder at a system that would allow such things to happen. "Come on to the hooch. We're having a little party to celebrate." The two turned and walked out, the window again banging against the door on its hinges.

"I guess we'd better go," Joe said. We dressed silently and walked out. It was around midnight.

The hooch was filled with sound as usual, and

there were a few shaking heads and winks as we walked in. I held a beer and drank reluctantly, not really interested and very disappointed. The colonel smiled and held up his drink, an unusual sight since he had never had a drink in public to my knowledge. There was a toast, and we silently drank to it. Then he came to where I was standing and softly said, "You know, Rick, I never thought I'd make it." I resisted the first impulse to say that no one else did either. And then I was suddenly overcome with sadness for the man. His entire world revolved around medals and rank, and his was an impossible existence. I couldn't see him as ever being content or happy. There was a definite element of sadness to his situation, and as he stood there drinking he seemed so pathetic I couldn't look anymore.

As I turned away, one of the pilots from another A-1 squadron walked over. "Are you ready for another blow?" he asked.

"What now?"

He set down his glass and gave me a look as if the most unbelievable thing in the world had just happened. "Do you know our squadron commander at all?" he asked.

"No, I've hardly ever seen him," I replied.

"Well, our squadron was first organized as the only night A-1 outfit. We actually flew only at night and still have most of the night missions. Well, this guy has *never* flown at night and refuses to go. He says he has to attend morning briefings, so he can't be out flying at night. Of course, he also gets to miss the groundfire on the Trail and all that. He flies the nice missions in the day when he feels like it." He took another long drink.

"There are a few who attend those morning briefings and still fly at night," I said.

"You bet they do," he went on. "Well, I'll tell you what is amazing. He was on the same promotion list as your commander, and he's over at our hooch celebrating making full colonel too!" He emptied the glass to the bottom and poured another tall Scotch. There was not the benefit of a mixer.

"That's pretty amazing," I said. "I wonder if any of the good guys ever make it? All we see is the worst examples getting ahead. I'd like to think that every once in a while a good man makes it too. By the way, what are you doing over here if there's a party at your place?"

He smiled. "Get this. He's over there smashed and telling everyone what a great pilot he is and how to fly fighters, and I was sure someone was going to punch him in the mouth. I just had to leave because it might have been me that did it."

"The view isn't that much better over here," I said.

"No, not really. At least he's not telling us how great he is, not yet anyway. He might after a few more drinks. He's probably too stunned right now. The thing that's getting a lot of us younger guys is the fact that once these characters get back home they'll be full colonels with a chestful of medals. They'll be running things, and no one will know the truth. How can others compete with romanticized reports and the things that cover the forms that go to the boards for promotions? It's like unless you're a phony you're no one at all."

I laughed. "That's not restricted to this organization. You'll find it everywhere. We're just disappointed in the good old Air Force."

He took a final gulp from his glass, which finished his second drink of straight Scotch. "Just think," he said, "when they leave here no one will ever know the truth."

"They will themselves," I said. "And sometime it will catch up to them. It just has to come back in one way or another."

He turned and headed for the door. "Yeah, guess that's true. At least I hope so. I'll just have to play my life for myself. I'm not a good enough actor to play all those other parts. But over here, it makes me mad as hell. This is supposed to be a war, and we're out there getting the bullets and they're here taking it easy and getting promoted. That does get to a guy."

He walked out the door, and I was left with our colonel and empty glasses. The hour got on and I left with the others, the colonel climbing into his jeep and disappearing down the street in his pajamas and robe, a full colonel.

The phone call came quite early, or at least I thought it was early because I had put up with the new colonel's celebration, finding my bed and sleep again at four A.M. I looked at my watch as I picked up the receiver. It was nine in the morning. The heat was smothering and damp. "Yeah," I said.

"Say, the squadron commander wants to know why you're not down here doing your additional duties this morning," the voice said. The man had obviously not mellowed with his new rank. The dreaded words, "additional duties," rang in my ears again. Being a pilot was taken for granted, everyone was supposed to fly. But it was the gigantic reams of senseless paperwork that the inspectors saw, that got a colonel to the "top." It made a lot of young officers see their futures as a grim span of time spent over meaningless papers that usually just repeated what some other paper said.

I faded into a dream in the heat, tired and melting in the torrid kiln of Thailand. It was a legal nightmare; I was being tried for not doing the job of information officer or historical officer or not seeing that some colonel who never had anything to do with the guys had a sensational farewell party. The opposition was sitting there, every man looking identical to the next with their hair cut so short they all looked bald, every man with hate in his eyes for the man who had deviated from their prison rules, the man who had said, "No, I will not be like every other man here. I will not embroider reports so you can get promoted or get another medal."

The prosecution presented its case in great detail with a grand flourish, even naming the numbers of forms: 1098s, form 90s, 229s, sections, paragraphs, codes, pointing fingers at me and smiling because they knew that books of numbers and things were Almighty law. And they thought that special arrangements and agreements each had made with each other on their climb to power would hold me like a limp doll. The only person there who was open was the judge, a fellow with a certain unmistakable look in his eye. I felt that I knew the man well, remembered his biplanes in the grass, yellow wings over emerald fields, the worth of a man crazy in love with life who knew that a man isn't worth anything unless he is himself with his loves and can express them, that every new idea, every discoverer, every artist, every man worth the name of Man had stood against the forces of mass disapproval in his time. I knew the judge understood those things and wasn't worried about the end. We are often wont to despair while a full chorus of angels sings behind us.

The time came for me to stand and say whatever I thought necessary. My speech wasn't prepared because there had never been any reason why the truth should be justified. I spoke as I wanted to live. "I won't give in to you because I have the most golden opportunity here, a chance for real learning and finding. I have brought myself here not because any computer system or design of military rotation has deigned it to be, but because I fought every rule and regulation and overcame all the so-called impossible obstacles of the organization. I didn't have the right amount of time in the forms, or the right forms themselves, and I went on writing letters and calling and writing. And it all worked because *I had* to be here and fly *this* airplane, so that I could better express what I am, so that I could do what is *right*. I did *not* volunteer to be an administrative cog. Never, never. That is *wrong* for me. If others can do all the deskwork and bootlicking and charade-playing, then feel good about it, let them. But it doesn't make them any more responsible or me any less."

I could see the uniformed group staring at the ceiling, shaking their heads, wondering how to effectively get rid of me in a "professional" manner. But I went on.

"If one does what is right for himself without interfering with anyone else, then he is being responsible in the only true way, regardless of the words of others. Conformity is *not* a virtue. It will kill your system because you won't get fresh ideas. You will have to see that. I fought the system to get to this

153

point, and I refuse to let anyone take it away. You can't, anyway. Tell me how stupid it is, how irresponsible, how wrong, but as long as I value my dream, then it is right and I will not let anyone spoil it for me. Shame on you for trying. I refuse to listen to the voice of the destroyer. Tell me how the things I love are gone, that we are stuck with a rather uninteresting demise, that I must come down from my lofty perch and face what you call 'reality,' tell me that and I must laugh. I must live according to the highest truth I know, not the lowest. I must expect that higher truth as my normal level of life. If illusion is your way, then that is too bad. Your false beliefs have become *your* reality, not mine. I choose freedom. I choose learning and perfection, not the cowering down and ridiculous bowing to someone because he might condescend to help you in your stupid rise to nothing in particular. Make it because you are right and honest and capable, not because you are not. I will win because truth always does. The Air Force can be a great place for one to live his truth. Look at your medium: the sky, flight, wind and stars. How can you want to dishonor that? And so, Your Honor, the defense rests."

That's what I should have said, there, on that hot section of wooden planking, the telephone in my hand. But I didn't. I simply said, "If they ever make flying an additional duty, then I'll really have it made." Then I hung up and went back to bed.

The next day's schedule stood in black ink, and I hated it. For some reason unknown to me, I had been delegated the unpleasant task of flying lead with the new wing commander as my wingman. I protested. The scheduling officer laughed. Someone had to do it, and I was the victim. At least the time of day was nice. It was known as "commander's hours," about ten in the morning.

Sitting in the small briefing room, I checked over the targets and chatted with the intelligence officer. "You'll be going north," he said. "The weather has been so bad that most everyone has just been dumping their ordnance in the same spot rather than coming back and landing with it. It's in the corner of the Plaine here." He walked to a large wall map and pointed to the area. "It's easy to find and there's nothing in it. So if you have to dump the stuff somewhere, that's as good a place as any." The Plaine des Jarres, known in our jargon as the PDJ, had very little of anything left on it anywhere. It had become something of a huge dump zone in itself.

The door opened and the wing commander came in. I stood. He didn't notice, turned, and went back out for something. He came back with a new pencil and sat down.

The briefing started with the weather, followed by latest information from the operations people. Then the intelligence officer launched into an erudite discussion of the war, which was knowledgeable and refreshing. I presumed it was so complete because the commander didn't know very much about what was going on out there. He had his own world, and most of us didn't know where it was. The door to the room opened and the deputy commander for operations came in, greeted the commander, and made small talk about nothing in particular, including dinner plans. And then he said, "We just came back from the PDJ and found a good target." He walked to the map and pointed to the terrain just defined to me as a "dump" area in case we needed one. "We put everything we had in there!

155

Really gave it to 'em." I looked at the intelligence officer, who tried like hell not to laugh, then glanced back at the wing commander, who brought the situation to the apogee of insanity.

"Yeah, we're really pounding them where it hurts," he said. "What we're doing is stopping their advance, spreading them out, and stopping their ability to re-group, reorganize, and launch another attack." He had really worked himself up and was nodding with obvious satisfaction at his little speech. Then he finished with, "We'll probably hit the same spot." Although I was the flight lead in name, I figured it wasn't for real.

The intelligence officer left the room with a furtive wink at me, and I was left with the commander. "Well, sir," I started, "after takeoff come on up into formation and we'll check each other for the usual things, leaks, ordnance, and so on. Then, on my signal, move out to tactical formation and we'll fly that way to the target area." He was doodling on the briefing card while I talked. There really wasn't much reason to continue when he sat through the briefing as a mere formality anyway. So I concluded by asking if there were any questions, which there weren't, and we left.

We didn't take the usual faded blue van trolley trip because the commander had his very own, highly polished, blue staff car. It even had air-conditioning. I hadn't been in a car in so long that it was a novel experience. I said, "So this is what cars look like inside." There was no response. It hadn't a wooden seat or the normal bone-shattering ride, nor was it filled with the dirt and scum which coated other vehicles on the base. Rank does have its privileges, as they say.

156

I turned out of the pattern and watched his airplane start on a regular formation join-up. The usual procedure was to stop just off the wingtip where each plane would be readily visible to the other pilot. This wasn't a regular join-up. His aircraft kept coming until it passed underneath mine, finally moving completely out of sight without stopping. "Everything looks good to me," his voice said on the radio. All I could tell was that his airplane was flying. "Thank you," I said, wondering why I had even bothered to brief him in the first place. I could have demanded proper procedures since I was technically the lead, but knew the repercussions that would follow if I did.

I intercepted the 330-degree radial of the Nakhon Phanom TACAN, as always, as I had brief, but I was essentially flying solo into combat.

"Where are you?" came the commander's voice.

"Uh, I'm on the three-hundred-thirty-degree radial, level at sixty-five hundred feet, on the standard departure," I replied to my wingman, who had disappeared.

"OK, you just stay there and I'll find you," he said.

Getting misplaced on the departure was a bit much. The commander's airplane appeared on the distant horizon and finally passed under me, swinging from my left to right where he stopped, perhaps a mile or so away. For the next forty-five minutes he stayed there in what he considered formation. The man appeared to be totally unknowledgeable about fighter integrity in a formation or the tactics of flying fighters in a combat zone. For a moment I wondered how he could have passed the training, then realized that with his rank and position he would always pass. As men of that ilk came to a checkride, they generally always got through because no one would dare to flunk them. Yet most of them would be better off doing anything besides flying in combat, including commanding such an organization. And once into his position, the man had written "law" about how we could conduct our operations. His rules were outrageous, like no overhead patterns (the traditional method of making a visual approach), or instrument approaches rather than normal time- and fuel-saving visual approaches. His way of avoiding incidents was to approach the point at which no one would even take off. That was his concept of safety.

The haze got worse and worse until the ground was barely visible. "I can't see the ground," he said.

"That's OK," I replied. "I know where we are." Having flown around Laos almost every day and night, we could generally tell where we were by the prominent landmarks, the mountains that stuck out of the haze, and had an idea of where we were by how long we had been flying and in what direction. The commander hadn't flown enough to get the departure down yet. I made some radio transmissions so he could home in on the signal, which worked after fifteen minutes of such frustrating nonsense. In the meantime I got in touch with a FAC and, rather than dumping in the fresh bomb craters of the other strikes, we proceeded to his location. With a combination of pilotage on mountain peaks and ADF procedures on the FAC's transmissions, I reached the target in fairly good time.

"I don't have you, lead," came the commander's voice, again.

"Tell you what, sir," I said. "I'll strike and you'll

see the bombs going off. Shouldn't be any problem."
I couldn't see his airplane anywhere.

"Good idea," he said.

The FAC and I discussed the target, supplies on
and beside a road, the escape routes in case we went
down or got shot up, then he cleared me on target. I
rolled in through the haze and covered the road with
CBU and rockets. The CBU looked like huge sparks
going off in the murk, thousands of them glittering
like small strobe lights. I finished the strike and
called my wingman in to take over.

"I don't see your strike," he said. There was a
second or two of flushing anger as I sucked in some
breath and jerked the airplane up on top of the haze.
Then he said, "Oh . . . I see it now." The FAC cleared
him in and he called, "I'm in . . . now!" I watched the
ground but didn't see him. "I'm off heading south,"
he said. I kept looking. "How's that, FAC?" he asked.
The FAC said, "I wouldn't know. I can't see anything,
and I'm right over the target. Sure you dropped anything?" I saw an airplane in the distance a couple of
miles away which turned to the south. "Yep," he announced, "I dropped it all in one pass."

Applauding him silently for his extreme interest
in the situation and his obvious accuracy, I turned and
chased the fleeting dot of an airplane. The FAC said
good-bye, and I changed radio frequencies. We had
flown over an hour to a target and wasted every ounce
of gas, oil, and ordnance the man had used. I was
outraged.

I caught up with my wingman within half an hour,
at which time we could see the Mekong River. We
started a letdown. I called the radar controller and
requested an instrument approach, to please the Al-

mighty book of rules my wingman had made. I was cleared for a radar-controlled approach, a GCA. Then I got an amusing radio call. "I'm going to break it off now," the colonel said. "I want to go look at something over to the west. See you later." The commander turned away and once again disappeared in the distance.

I canceled my request for an instrument approach and made an overhead break and regular landing. The ordeal was over. I was highly discouraged.

There was a note in my pigeonhole box that said to get the monthly historical report to wing headquarters. I took the paperwork and solemnly strolled to the big building. That batch of papers I had nicknamed the "Hysterical Report," another piece of administrative officer material which was being written by the combat pilots. I slapped pages onto a gray desk and walked out. I passed a sign which was tacked to the wall outside the wing commander's office and stopped after a second look. Considering the source, it was ironic, there in bold letters: *Our mission is to fly and fight and don't you forget it!* I walked out and slammed the door.

The word spread and it was law within seconds. There was to be a commander's call held at the officers' club, and everyone was ordered to attend. The date and time were printed on official-sized paper that was tacked to walls; a few found their way into the latrines as well. Commander's call was traditionally the time when the wing commander informed his men on what was happening, how things stood in light of the "big picture," and offered a chance for discussion and fresh ideas. I could think of perhaps a dozen items that needed to be discussed and solutions found in the not-too-distant future, from the rusty water and lousy food in the club to the stupid way pilots were being treated and the absurd thoughts which had been legislated into regulations by one or two men. It was indeed time to have such a meeting.

The club was filled to capacity, many of us standing along the walls and on chairs. The colonel walked in, we all stood as was the custom, and he marched to the podium which rested before a pitcher of water and some papers. We sat on his command, also custom, and watched the man drink a glass of water. It was thrilling. Then he spoke. "Ah . . . the general's visit." He sipped more water. We thought perhaps he had malaria. "Ah . . . he was impressed. It was fine work, men." A concurrent yawn went around the room. "I think credit belongs to those who deserve it. But we can't afford to let down. Watch that appearance, those mustaches and haircuts. One thing I have to tell you is that the officers' club has been losing money, so we have decided to raise the costs a little." A little rumble crept through the air. In a combat zone, the club wasn't primarily in business to "make" money. It was foremost to serve its members. Good service would bring about increased participation. But that had been discounted. A captive audience didn't have any options. I also wouldn't have been surprised to discover that we had lost a lot due to corruption among some of the people who operated the base and the club. I'm fairly certain that the Thai commander got his piece of the action to include slot machines which were clattering away in a room set aside for them. Some Thai officers had even been found tampering with the machines, taking money from them, but nothing ever happened to them. It was, after all, their country.

161

"Everything is going well. I'm happy with the service here and the food is much better than before. I can see that with everyone trying hard and together as an instrument of the unit's policy we can get the job done."

He drank more water while we all looked at each other in astonishment. The man hadn't said anything, yet he was talking. He was right. *His* service and *his* food were better. He had even constructed his own private dining room where he could be away from the rest of us.

Then, to show that he had mastered one of the basic techniques of prisoner-of-war camp operation and psychological warfare, he made a remarkable edict. "I've had a long debate about the tables here in the club. It appears that the flying squadrons have moved several tables together so that they may sit as a group. Well, we just can't have that sort of thing anymore. So from now on, all tables will be separated, except mine, of course."

The technique was classic. It was a demoralizing move which took the common bond of combat flying and tried to break it. The pressure had come from the ground-pounders who didn't have such camaraderie, and the commander had given in to it. With our hooches also under pressure from the nonflying people and the club going to hell, we weren't given to a very charitable disposition.

Then, as if to say to us, "And to show you what a good guy I really am, there's free beer and snacks in the other room," he said that if there was nothing further we were dismissed for refreshments. The whole meeting was such a joke that most of us were laughing.

I sat with Col. George Miller, who smiled in

embarrassment. He was a career man, a sound thinker, and an effective leader. Every time he tried to point out the good in the organization, we would be faced with such an empty affair as the "commander's call." I felt sorry for George because he didn't have anything to point to and say, "See, there are some really sharp people in here." He said that for some reason, the truly intelligent and even brilliant military men were isolated in jobs where we seldom saw them. He said that we ought not to base our final judgments on what we were seeing at the moment. But then I had to ask, "What else did we have to go on?"

We finally left arm in arm, past the commander, past wilting figures trying desperately to get that "combat tour" and good words on their forms, and past the large A-1 model which Loren Alfred had built, perhaps the only worthwhile item in the club at the moment.

As if the commander's call wasn't enough, the bulletin board said there was a "pilot meeting" to be held at the squadron at 1500 hours. I originally thought it would be a good time to talk over some flying details but had also learned differently about that. Leaving the hooch in a flourish of empty beer cans and Martini olives, we jumped on the trucks and drove to the building. Someone unlocked the door and we filed in.

"Room—*atten-shun!*" There was the shuffling of feet, a silence, then the "leaders" marching solemnly to the platform. "Be seated," the colonel said. There was a drawn-out clearing of his throat. I looked around. There were some twenty pilots there. Obviously it would be a good place to talk about flying. Then the colonel: "Ahem. Ah ... I have noticed that some of the troops have mustaches growing beyond the corners of their mouths. Now, you all know the regulations.

Nothing beyond the corner of the mouth. Obey those rules. It shows good discipline. Now. Haircuts. I shouldn't have to even mention them. But you all know the regulation on them, yet you persist on letting them grow long. I don't want to see any of those new styles." He faced us with his hands on his hips. "I've also noticed that there are certain of you that do not show up around the squadron very much. I've stated it before and I'll say it again. *Everyone* flies airplanes. *Everyone* flies in combat. *That* isn't the important thing."

I looked at the fellow next to me. He frowned and whispered, "That's really strange. I thought flying in combat was the important thing."

The colonel went on. "The important thing is to perform your additional duties. You've all been assigned various duties: information officer, historical officer, disaster control officer, and so on. These are the important things. You've got to do them well, for me and the squadron. That's the way to get ahead. When it comes time to turn in your efficency reports, those are the things that will count. What else will there be to rate you by? So let's see you down here. Do those additional duties. OK. If there are no further questions, that will be all." He looked at someone in the front row, who yelled, "*Atten-shun!*" We all stood up, and the "leaders" departed. The guys filed out of the room, but I didn't leave yet. I didn't because I really couldn't believe it all. The commander's call was a farce, and now a so-called pilots' meeting had turned into another joke. Nothing of any significance was said except that flying wasn't very important. The pilots were fighting a tough war, yet the main concern was mustaches, hair length, and the never-ending quest for medals and rank.

164

Shortly, an unusual mission came down to the A-1 squadrons. A North Vietnamese surface-to-air-missile site had been located, but repeated attempts by jet flights to destroy it had been unsuccessful. Someone got the idea that A-1s with their greater accuracy might be able to do the job. It meant that some highly vulnerable aircraft were going to set sail on a hazardous journey, to say the least. A SAM site wasn't to be treated lightly. It was bad enough for fast and high-flying jets but could be disaster for a flight of A-1s unless everything went just right and every man did his job with great expertise.

A six-ship flight was selected, but when we heard the details there was a roar from the amazed pilots. The wing commander was going to lead the entire flight, by his own order. I leaned on Ron. "I flew with him a short time ago. He couldn't even find the target, not to mention getting lost in formation." Ron shook his head. The same thoughts were being echoed around the room. The obvious facts were that it involved a chance for that extra something in the man's effectiveness report and an opportunity to get a medal of some sort. But it also meant he was jeopardizing everyone in the flight. With some sound thinking, at least, the man had been given a wingman who was experienced and could take over if necessary. He would undoubtedly be leading the flight silently.

The flight launched and headed north. It was immediately apparent that the commander's wingman was running the show. "You're doing just fine, sir. Just a few more degrees left. Fine, sir."

As had been the case when I had flown with the commander earlier, he couldn't find the target, even passed it, and when he was told about it, started turning

165

about trying to locate it. "Just look there to your left, sir," his wingman said. He described the target and practically led the man into it. The colonel rolled in, dropped everything in one pass, and pulled out, heading smartly for home. The rest of the flight went to work pounding the site, destroying the Russian equipment. One missile ignited and went scurrying across the ground, blowing up when it finally hit a small hill. With multiple passes, the position was turned to ashes. The mission was accomplished, the flight did well, and everyone came back. That was a monumental deed in itself.

Sitting in the squadron building thereafter, I saw one of the pilots walk past, angry, slapping the wall as he went into his office. "What's the matter?" Jim Kelly asked. The man looked up gravely. "That son of a bitch," he scowled. "Who?" we asked. He held up a small paper. "This is a directive to write a recommendation for the Silver Star for the wing commander. He wants one for leading that mission to get the missile site." There wasn't much to say. The man didn't hold a monopoly on such behavior. It was something that would be inked onto his personnel record and become official. And even if he didn't get the Star, he stood a good chance of getting at least the Distinguished Flying Cross. After all, to be a "leader" one had to have all that in the record. A lot of good men didn't have such a record, and they'd never get to the exalted throne. And, after all, if you played that sort of game, that's where you wanted to go.

There was yet another "pilot meeting." There was the same theatrical entrance, the same clearing of throats, the same lingering over empty detail while the substance escaped untouched. There was immediate discussion of the "additional duty" assignments and how in general we were all a motley lot which, thanks to our enlightened commander who watched out for us, barely scraped by. The decision had been made that those who had such duties, and that meant everyone, would prepare a folder on the duties, responsibilities, history, future, progress, evaluation, and finally suggestions as to the particular job. It reminded me of the busywork handed out in school when there was in fact nothing else to do. Empty time intervals scare lots of people because they haven't the personal resources to make them worthwhile. So they had to be filled with kindergarten finger painting and mature seventh-grade chart construction. The colonel felt just terrible if he had idle troops; idle, that is, when not flying in combat. He felt that he was an effective leader if his men were always doing something, no matter how absurd the task was. He felt he was dealing with grammar school mentality, certainly not thinking, reasoning adult people, so he pursued the only course he knew. He sidestepped the fact that each pilot came equipped with a mind. I opened my paperback and read, adequately hidden in the last row of the room.

Talk about flying was rare, and when I heard it I looked up just to be sure the meeting hadn't ended and something worthwhile had taken its place. "The wing has lost another pilot," the colonel's words started. We had lost a great number of both pilots and airplanes in the A-1 operation, to be sure. The A-1 was rare enough at that point that every one lost was gone forever as there were no replacements. We were flying an endangered species. And, of course, the pilots were the same. More pilots showed up, but the ones that went down seldom came back. Now we were talking

167

after the fact, the usual case, not before when it was essential. It was a little like crashing first and getting flying lessons later. "A young lieutenant named Herrick went in up north."

To him it was a young lieutenant, to me it was Jim, a buddy, a living, breathing entity with feelings and thoughts. An individual person. He had just been relegated to a teaching aid on the blackboard. The colonel drew a large letter *M* on the board which he said was representative of a valley with mountains on each side. Then, chalk in hand, he said, "Now, if you're down here"—and he put a dot at the bottom of the valley—"you can't climb out this way." He drew a line into the side of the mountain. "You can't because you'd hit the mountain," he said, turning to us as if it were a revelation. It was embarrassing. "You've got to go up until you have enough altitude to clear the tops. Use the old rule—a thousand feet higher than the terrain."

Most of us were totally unfamiliar with that postulate, and Ron turned to me and said, "The *old* rule?" "Yeah," I said, "those *old* boys always knew that *old* rule. Now you do too." It was too bad that Jim hadn't been one of the old boys, although I'm certain he could have made a coherent statement about not flying into mountains. The colonel was once again going through the motions of what he thought it took to be a commander. Chalk in hand, obtuse words streaming from his mouth, the colonel was again making a fool of himself. There was no such old rule, and we all knew better then to fly into a mountain. The man had a few more words. "Everyone should know these things, and here's a letter which has just come out from *my* commander on the subject." He held it up and read. "'Pilots will not fly down through holes in overcasts over mountains.'" With that terribly inspiring message, the meeting ended. We all stood and the procession commenced. Jim had been dismissed, and the remnants of the episode were strewn across a mountain in northern Laos and represented in white chalk on a green blackboard. It was over for the leadership who could get a fast answer, cover their fannies, and move on to more important things. The real reasons, the basic laws, the discussions that had to take place never did. The fact that Jim had gone down to get a truck, that he had spotted the enemy and was attacking, that Jim had been fighting in the war, was never mentioned. We were sick at how his bravery was treated, even though he shouldn't have broken formation to attack. That was what needed to be discussed. And, of course, one other item escaped everyone. Jim thought the war was for real.

As we walked down the hall, there was another loud statement that had been forgotten in the formal meeting. It was about those haircuts again. "Why do I always have to go into this subject again and again?" the voice said. I stayed well behind the crowd so I wouldn't have to look. "See my hair? *This* is a military haircut." For the majority of us it was impossible to see any hair at all, and that was the point.

We walked into the evening air and solemnly went back to the hooch. There wasn't a lot said because we were sad at what had just happened. We were living in a situation so incongruous that it was difficult to keep one's sense of perspective. It was as if a very few sane men were being controlled by the vast insane majority.

It was near this time that I finally came to see

169

that I had no reason to stay in the Air Force, that I could no longer put up with the ways of the organization. There were great moments in the airplane, times when we were out there slugging it out with the enemy, days of immense fulfillment in flying the last of the great prop airplanes and sharing it with some fine buddies. But those were few and far between, and even those times were being taken away. I went to personnel and filled out the forms for my resignation as an officer in the Air Force. I wasn't alone. Many of the younger pilots and officers, even some who had been in the Air Force a very short time, were doing the same thing. Even Academy graduates were disillusioned and considering resigning. The "new" Air Force had required all their people to be "educated," have degrees, be the "cream of the crop." In acquiring such people, it neglected to treat them accordingly. It questioned why it was losing so many good people, yet wouldn't seriously try to cure the cause. The system really wanted only those who went along with the program without question. It didn't really want fresh thought from the intellectuals and capable men it recruited with its new image concept. It didn't want people who loved to fly, even though the recruiting posters still showed the airplanes and the fighters turning amongst the stars. It also didn't appear to care all that much about those who wanted to fight a war and win, or at least it did everything to discourage such thinking. Every day the system's operatives told us that flying wasn't important, that doing a lot of empty work was, and offered themselves as examples of what the Air Force wanted. It was thus easy to see that it wanted people who would agree to embellish a few things here and there and who would put up with the piddling tasks assigned to fill time and paper. Those at the top, those hidden men of greatness, were not using their heads. How can someone ask a man to put his life on the line for a purpose that can no longer be explained, to fight for a charade, to go into battle while the "leaders" march about trying to collect their medals and a combat tour? Many of us realized that we were there now by choice, because we wanted to fly that airplane and fight the war, and it had relatively little to do with the Air Force anymore. The organization just happened to own the equipment we needed. Respect is a valuable thing, but there were few people we could find worthy of that sentiment. I felt as though I were fighting not only the enemy but the Air Force and U.S. government as well.

Sitting in the pilot's lounge a few nights later, I saw one of the FACs come in drenched, his poncho dripping rain on the floor. He took a paper cup and started to get some coffee, but the container was empty. He threw the cup and tossed his poncho on the floor as he poured himself into a chair. "You going out?" he asked me.

I looked up from my paperback. "Yeah, supposed to. Another fifteen minutes or so."

"There's nothing there," he said. "The weather's so bad I never saw any ground at all. Flew around for three hours in the storms for nothing. There's no reason to go out there now. It's rained so much that the Trail is closed anyway, no trucks, nothing. I'm sure you'll be canceled. Just taking off and landing is bad enough." He closed his eyes and sank into a sleep full of fatigue.

I looked at my watch. The time was near for getting the survival vest and helmet and moving out to the aircraft. I put the paperback into my leg pocket

171

and zipped the pocket closed, grabbed my poncho, and walked past the hulk of a man strewn out across two chairs.

A voice called after me, that of a lieutenant colonel from the command post. I thought he was going to say that we were canceled, but he didn't. "Thought I'd just let you know that you're still going, in case you thought otherwise," he said.

Most of us had our opinions about the command post personnel. The general consensus was that they were not really involved in combat and just getting a good report for having served in such a "vital" position. I don't recall ever having taken one of them very seriously about anything.

"You know, sir," I said, "it's really silly to go out there. There's a FAC right there in the other room who just came in who says it's lousy, no targets, no holes to work through, nothing. Just lots of bad weather. And we both know that even the enemy doesn't do anything when the weather's this bad. I spent last night out there in a storm. And for what? If there were a good, meaningful target, then it would be different. I'm ready to go in that case. But this is plain stupidity, sir."

He folded his arms across his chest, which was apparently his way of assuming the superior attitude and position. "Obviously you don't understand the big picture, Captain," he said. The use of rank in the conversation told me I wasn't going to get anywhere. "If you knew what was really going on, you'd see why you're going out there."

I leaned against the wall, really looking forward to what was coming. "Explain it to me."

"It's simply a matter of dropping ordnance an

172

flying sorties," he said. "The more we drop the better we do, and also the Defense Department looks at what we used during this time period and projects our future finances and allotments on that figure. If we cancel flights, then we drop less ordnance, use less fuel and oil, and get less next time. But if we keep the figures high, then we get the money and supplies again next time. And, of course, the more we drop the more damage we do to the enemy. Think of their morale knowing you're up there, even in the storm."

I looked at the man through a grinning face. "The enemy is most likely laughing at us," I said. "And as to that other stuff, I would have been embarrassed to have said it. You don't really believe that's our real mission, do you? I mean, that's all rather a dumb reason to risk lives and these airplanes."

"Like I said, Captain, the 'big picture,' that's what you need to see."

I shook my head. "Sir," I said, "that just doesn't make any sense. If we drop tons of bombs on nothing, then we get absolutely nothing in terms of the war. It already looks like the moon out there from the holes we've put in the ground. And if we can't drop because of the weather, like tonight, then we've wasted lots of gas and oil and risked lives for nothing. It's bad enough when there really is a good target and the weather's clear. And I'll bet you'll get what you need in fuel, oil, and bombs when the time comes. What good is it to waste what we have?"

Then he made a great show-biz statement. "Well, that's war."

In a storm of my own, I went out into the rain and wind. Jim Bender, my wingman, said something about what an interesting takeoff it was going to be, and I agreed, still shaking my head.

"You wouldn't believe the reason why we're going out tonight," I said as the van rumbled across the metal ramp towards the aircraft. "We're going to perpetrate fraud on the Defense Department. That is, according to the colonel in there, and we're going to win the war by dropping bombs through the weather on random pieces of ground."

Jim always took things in stride with a calm, mature attitude. I had started calling him Uncle Ben on account of it, finally shortened to Ben.

"Sounds about right," he said. "Maybe we can enjoy the flying somehow and make up for it. Think of the experience you're getting in flying in thunderstorms."

I looked up through the rain which came through the open door of the van. "Yeah, that's the sort of experience I can do without. See you on 55.55 FM." That was our personal FM radio frequency. I trudged out and under the wing of a black-bellied A-1 which was shedding water like an unconventional shower mechanism. The wind was whipping the rain through the cockpit, so I closed the canopy and jumped down under the wing. The crew chief came up and huddled beside me, his hands in his pockets, water dripping from his nose and ears. He wasn't wearing a shirt because even in the rain it was still very warm. "You actually going to go, sir?" he asked, still looking forward into the rainy night.

"Yeah, sure am. Want to go along?"

He turned with a smile. "Nope. You go right ahead. I'll just stand here and watch."

"Thanks," I said.

The sound of wind and rain gave way to the belch and roar of the Wright Whirlwind, and the storm was visual and tactile from then on. Sound was engine sound and radio sound. "You up, Ben?" I asked on 55.55.

"Hi there, Rick-O. Ready here." He sounded rather jolly for such a venture.

Inching the throttle forward, I moved from the parking spot and started a crawl to the arming area. Once in a while a gust would move the aircraft on the metal ramp which was covered with grease and oil, and I would be just a passenger for a distance of a few feet. "Easy taxiing, Ben," I called. "A bit slippery on the ramp."

"Yeah, I know," he answered. "I'm kinda sideways right now. Be right with you."

The runway stretched out ahead for a short distance, then disappeared into the heavy rain. Someday I'm going to remember what this looked like and felt like, I thought. And I'm going to wonder how I ever did it. That is, if I get back and have a future to think in.

Tailwheel locked, I put the power in and started the ordeal down the runway. I left the landing lights on so I could see well enough to keep a fair semblance of a straight line. Around a hundred and ten knots I got off and was immediately lost in a dark and violent rain. It was solid instruments from the ground up. I relaxed after I had a thousand feet of altitude, started the turn out of traffic, and hoped Ben was doing OK. I never saw him. But for two hours we drove through the night. The airborne controller was amused that we were up there. "Moonbeam," I said, "you wouldn't happen to have any targets for us, would you?"

175

"You're kidding," he replied. "There aren't even any FACs up here now. Everyone's gone home. Weather's lousy. We were wondering why you even came out."

"You wouldn't believe it," I said.

"Probably not, but you might as well go home. I don't suppose you want to dump that stuff through the clouds. Thanks, anyway."

A strange and stupid game, I thought. I could go back and say, "I told you so," except that they didn't care. It wasn't worth it. "Ben, I don't want to appear silly or anything," I said, "but the weather's really bad and we aren't going to drop, so we'll be going home now. You heard the man."

"I knew that before we took off," he said, "like you did. But the takeoff was worth it. Pretty exciting, huh?" Ben had a way of making things easier to take.

"Glad you enjoyed it, old buddy," I said. "Hope the landing excites you as much."

With the great weight of the full ordnance load and the drag it caused, I kept final approach speed up and touched down on the main gear with the tail high, around one hundred and ten knots. I had my hands full; it took complete displacement of the controls to maintain direction, the wind gusting violently and the runway slick. "Practicing a pilot's art at its best," I said over the radio. Ben's landing lights emerged from the wet night sky and settled to the concrete. There was a slight swerve which ended abruptly as he caught it with the rudder.

"Not a fit night for man or . . ." he said, trailing the sentence off in jest.

Back in the lounge I got a cup of coffee from the fresh gallon that someone had just made. There was

176

a puddle of water where the FAC had fallen asleep in the chairs before we had gone out. I had taken his place, wet and fatigued. Ben came up and put his arm around my shoulders.

"Well, I have nothing to say," he remarked.

"Let's go home, then," I said.

We turned and walked back out into the rain.


We were soon treated to an official briefing on the war, and as I listened to the man from Saigon, the puzzle palace of the Southwest Asian war, I was aware that people not directly involved in the prosecution of that war were totally ignorant of the facts. In many cases they had apparently invented fictions that pleased them and their superiors who required positive fictions, not negative reality.

The man said, "There are three methods which have ensured our success in this conflict. These are tonnage, sorties, and the body count." I mulled that over and arrived at my same conclusions. The kingdom of the Saigon general and the Washington elite was still surrounded by fragile, opaque glass. It was a one-way view at best. In a magnificent "tour de farce," the higher echelons had deluded themselves. If one dared to question the regime, then exile to SAC bombers or the like might be anticipated.

Unfortunately for the generals and those with charts and graphs, none of the "scoring" methods applied reflected an accurate picture of the real war. Tonnage dropped on nothing gained precisely nothing. It did cost lots of money, though. So empty plots of jungle were redefined as "hidden storage areas," and "suspected truck parks." A great deal of tonnage was dropped on such targets. Sorties flown were meaningless, due to weather, no targets, emergencies, or the other infinite number of things adding up to an unproductive flight that netted nothing. But there were impressive charts that pointed out the terrific number of combat sorties and hours flown over enemy territory. Body count was worthless in a war where the opposition cared nothing about bodies and even said they could well afford to lose people because there were too many anyway. And when the body count was repeated, multiplied, and guessed at, when the ground FAGs consistently called in their "you kill one hundred bad guy," we ended up with worthless data. But it did fill up the papers and was impressive when documented with flawless charts and graphs which allowed the chart maker a good combat tour effectiveness report.

What it meant to the people participating in the charade was that if there were fifty airplanes sitting on the ramp, then fifty airplanes had to fly since we would be winning the war if we flew all we could and dropped all the bombs we had. It could be defined as "one hundred percent utilization" and "maximum effort." But someone in that big school for leaders forgot to mention that a well-placed strike on a true target might be worth fifty worthless ones. We were not hurting for true targets. The supplies were there, the harbor at Haiphong was full of ships off-loading to the enemy, the airfields were there, the lines of communication were there, but we were relegated to "suspected truck parks" and "probable storage areas" for the most part. There was no way the war could be won against an enemy we refused to fight except on its own terms, whom we helped supply, whom we appeased with our lack of drive and determination.

That night I flew another mission to Barrel Roll. The weather covered the ground and we flew over solid overcast. The only terrain visible was the tip of a mountain which came to about ten thousand feet. The controller said, "I have a target for you. I'm going to give you a radial and distance from the TACAN. Just fly out there and drop your stuff." The TACAN was essentially a radio transmitter and we would just fly inbound or outbound on one of the radials. I couldn't believe it. We weren't B-52s which radar-bombed through the weather, nor were we cavorting about for hours just to dump through the overcast. I said that rather than dump we'd just take the ordnance back home, which we did.

Sitting at the debriefing desk, I grabbed the form and started with the "remarks" section. I wrote: "If it were known what is going on out there, you wouldn't have to fight the NVA or the VC. You'd be fighting the irate taxpayers, the citizens of the United States who are financing this stupidity." Then I signed my name and left.

Very early the next morning I got a phone call. It was stated that the debriefing form was for official statements only relating to the mission flown and was not to include personal opinion about the war. Unfortunately for some, the trend caught on, and several lieutenants were caught making personal statements and were assigned menial jobs in the briefing room and command post. We tried to laugh it off, most of us finally aware that the war was no war at all in the overall scheme of things. It was serious to those of us who were being shot at and killed, to those of us who truly believed that the Communist and totalitarian threat was a real danger, but it was no more than a political

179

stageshow to everyone else. What should have been a worthy and noble cause was now a shoddy racket benefiting the corrupt and bankrupting our country. And the worst, everyone knew it. While the pilots could see the war, saw the enemy's progress, watched as we tied ourselves to a no-win policy, felt real guns firing and hitting, no one else cared to hear about it. While the "leaders" made song about our feats of valor, the enemy advanced, infiltrated, marked time, moved again. There could be no doubt about the outcome of such a travesty.

A brighter light than we had seen before arrived in the way of a change of command. There was nothing regal in the ceremony. One day we would simply have a new squadron commander; that in itself was cause for rejoicing without pomp and circumstance. But for a few minutes I still had to listen to the antics of the departing creature. For an egomaniac whose eye found few people worth regarding, he managed to devote lots of time to me. I had a statement thrown at me which was perhaps the highlight of my day, or even many days. The colonel had sauntered through the squadron looking for and finding those who had violated his haircut and sideburns precepts. "Drury," he said, as if I didn't know I had become the subject again, "I thought you would know by now how I feel about haircuts." I said nothing. "As far as I'm concerned," he went on, "a person's intelligence is directly proportional to the length of his hair." I looked up, wondering if he was talking in jest or if he really didn't know what he had said. He surely meant "inversely" proportional. No, after another brief tirade, I saw that the man didn't actually know what he was saying.

Orders arrived and the time came. Our commander was leaving. Things were suddenly wonderful around the squadron. For the colonel, problems disappeared. Living was simplified with a new rank and a new place to go. One of his final gestures in the squadron was to remark that one shouldn't hedge on reports, that awards and decorations were serious business not to be toyed with or exaggerated. In grave terms he talked as though he could clear the air by admonishing others and gain the favor of the celestial powers. In my mind, he needed help, but the system would only sustain him, as it had already made him a full colonel with a chest full of medals. Then he left, and a great relief came over us.

Our new commander was Lt. Col. "Lucky" Lowman, a silver-haired fighter pilot who could fly with the best of us and do it night, day, and on almost any schedule. We called him the Silver Fox. He did what every commander secretly wishes he could do. Lucky got respect because he was a pilot's pilot, a man's man, and people did for him because they wanted to. If anyone sluffed off, the feeling was that he had let the "old man" down. Nothing really had to be said. We talked with him about P-51 Mustangs and listened to stories reminiscent of our dreams. He was a man whom we could arm-wrestle on the bar, yet simultaneously respect as the commander. His flavor came to the fore one·evening after we had raided the multiengine establishment across the street. The multiengine pilot has traditionally been rather subdued and not inclined towards the ragged edge flying of fighter operations. So we occasionally went across to their hooch and showed them what spirit and camaraderie were all about. It was peculiar. Those of us who went out into

181

true combat where the shooting was were a really happy lot, given to song and good cheer. The transport pilot was quiet and not disposed to much in the way of laughter and joviality. One would think it might be the other way around. When we finally came back to our hooch, Lucky shook his head and smiled. "You guys are really going to get me in trouble tomorrow at the briefing. That many-motor commander is going to chew my fanny again." We cheered him for his bravery and hoisted him to our shoulders. He raised his glass and offered a little philosophy, after which we knew we had a good man. "Well, if I didn't have to look out for you guys once in a while and run a little interference, I wouldn't have a squadron of fighter pilots." He enjoyed the free ride around the hooch and all the drinks Pete could make. We finally had a commander we could talk with, but true to the system, Lucky eventually got passed over for promotion. He was just too nice a guy. And besides, he loved flying.

# NINE

HAND LAVENDER came into the squadron building, checked the future flying schedule, and sat down beside me. "Looks like you start the Sandy program with me next week," he said. It was the voice of a flight leader who once again had to contend with a novice. It was another apprenticeship since every facet of combat flying is a new art and requires a starting place. In between night operations and day strikes, as the rainy season was nearing its end, I was a wingman again, learning the rudiments of search and rescue.

John Flinn had explained the rescue role to me long ago and had cherished it as *the* mission. While Hank was talking I reminisced about that night when John sat next to me explaining what it was all about. Considering the things that had gone on with our leaders and the nature of the strikes we had, rescue sounded like the last noble role we had. John would have been happy to know that I was becoming a Sandy.

Hank explained the system in pilot terms; that is, what it would mean if we had a rescue and what we would do in each position. "As you know, there are six of us on alert. Numbers One, Three, and Five are the flight leads, and Two, Four, and Six are the wingmen. If there's a call on the first day, we'll be alerted to go as Sandy Five and Six. Sandy One and Two will have gone out already, and Three and Four will be escorting the helicopters. We will then be ready to relieve Sandy One if the event takes very long. It often takes many hours, and fuel and oil will be the consideration. We may well have to go out there if Number One gets low on fuel. If there is no activity before the afternoon, then we take off and fly an orbit over Steel Tiger which usually lasts about four hours. During that time if anyone goes down we become the on-scene Sandy force, and it will be our show. Otherwise we come back around sunset, and that's it for the first day.

"The second day we will be Sandy Three and Four. The same plan goes, except the orbit is flown up north in Barrel Roll and is normally longer, sometimes over five hours. During that time, the new Sandy Five and Six will be doing what we did yesterday, flying the southern area. If anything breaks while we're on the ground, then we escort the helicopters to the scene. This way we cover the entire country of Laos. Again, after the orbit if there is no activity, we come back after sunset. The orbits are really nice because you get to tour about the country and just enjoy flying the airplane for a few hours.

"The third and last day of the tour we are Sandy One and Two. We sit ground alert all day. If anything happens before the afternoon orbit flights launch, then we scramble and head directly to the place where the pilot was shot down. If not, then we're pretty much through when the orbit flights get off the ground. But I'll tell you now, when you're Number One and just sitting around, you'll be a nervous wreck. It means that no matter where the survivor goes down, even if it's right on the Trail itself and he's next to every gun

184

in town, you still go. And that means broad daylight at minimum altitude. Think about that for a while."

I did. I thought about it all the time. It meant that at certain three-day intervals during every month, I would have the dubious pleasure of potentially visiting Uncle Ho's Trail under a bright sun in an airplane which could do perhaps all of 150 knots with its full load.

John's words kept me company. "This rescue thing is the best, most rewarding operation in the entire war. It's really great to actually get someone out after he's been shot down. That's a great feeling."

I knew it would be. But for the time being, I could admit to harboring more than a trifle of concern. I kept thinking about a picture in the hooch which showed Ron Rounce's airplane after he brought it back from a rescue attempt. It looked like an open-air sculpture, one which could be aptly titled *Space*. There was more air than airplane. The metal had been ripped away like flimsy wrapping from chewing gum. The fuselage that felt like hard metal as I climbed into it was no more than butter to a well-placed round of high-caliber groundfire.

Ron explained his incident in humorous terms. "It was my first rescue, and I was pretty nervous. We were circling through the area when I took some hits, or at least I thought I had. I couldn't see close out the right side, since I was in an 'E,' so I didn't know what had actually happened. I called on the radio, but lead said to be quiet because there was a rescue in progress and not to tie up the radio. So I just flew around with the airplane full of holes, thinking it must be normal procedure. No one seemed concerned at all. The airplane didn't fly all that well, but I just kept on circling

185

after lead. Then, after it was all over, lead kept calling for me to speed up the rejoin. I had everything full up but just couldn't get the airplane going very fast. So he turned around and came back beside me, probably thinking that those new young lieutenants couldn't fly. I guess it was some sight. So I pointed the thing at the base and flew along while my lead flew alongside all the time amazed at what miracle was keeping the thing in the air. When we got back over the base, people said they could see lots of blue sky through the wings. But it kept flying and I landed OK. I had a flap completely gone, but the airplane's a good one and it brought me back. There was a huge hole in the left wing, enough for several people to stand in while we took a picture, the right flap completely gone, and a great number of holes in the fuselage. The worst part of the whole episode is that the downed pilot was dead when we got to him."

It was another apprenticeship, but certainly more dramatic and immediate than the others. And the results would be worth the trouble. ". . . to get someone out after he's been shot down. That's a great feeling."

Hank led me through my first Sandy tour, a fairly uneventful three-day session. We were all out at dawn preflighting the airplanes, each man finally checking in with Sandy One over each of three radios. The afternoon orbit flights gave the opportunity to take a junket around Laos, chase each other around cumulus, or even sit in trail formation reading a book as the hours droned on. The C-130 Airborne Command Post checked in with us infrequently while we occasionally flew alongside the Jolly Green helicopters which were also on orbit. We were aerially poised, but there was no action. Our heavily laden airplanes flew sluggishly, the immense aerodynamic drag from the pods and tanks noticeable with any tight turn as the aircraft buffeted and shook on the edge of stalling. I tried to picture what we would do if a call came in but realized that each rescue was different. Weather, terrain, antiaircraft fire, survivor's condition, even the time of day, made each rescue unique. Only three basic rules remained the same: Find the survivor, suppress the groundfire, and get the survivor out. Beyond that, each Sandy lead had to improvise as required. There was no amount of training that could pass for the real thing.

Although I wasn't on Sandy alert when the next rescue operation started, I was selected as part of the backup force. The Sandy pilots on scene would be needing close air support, so a number of us prepared for a trip to Tchepone, a very heavily defended area on the Trail in southern Laos. It was another three-thirty-in-the-morning wakeup. To motivate myself to get out of bed I told myself that a downed pilot was waiting out there for us. I hit a quick shower and made my way to the large briefing room. Once again, the hall was filled with the chatter and hopes of first flights. I looked at the last known position of the survivor on the large wall chart and knew it would be a long day. Two men had gone down, one hurt for sure.

I took off and joined up in an eight-ship formation. We had been relegated to the chore of laying a gigantic smoke screen for the rescue helicopter in the final moments of the effort. We moved behind each other in a long trail formation and finally held in a wide circle above the only hole in a massive overcast. The Sandys were below, unseen to us, but talking it up on the radios. We listened in a semidetached way, circling like buzzards but hoping for the saved life of another comrade.

An hour moved passed like a day. I kept yawning in the heat and vibration of the cockpit. It was already a hot day, so I poured cool water from my canteen over my face and opened the canopy for airflow. It was soothing. The terrain below was mountains up to some three thousand feet, and the cloud layer was covering the peak tops. So it was a busy atmosphere underneath, with so many aircraft packed into a small area. The guns were firing, and the one physically intact survivor made infrequent radio calls reporting groundfire. The other, with a broken leg and arm, only managed to say that he was in great pain and wanted to go home.

We kept circling, the chain of eight aircraft alerting from a circle to a large oval as weary pilots tried to relax and fly less exact formation. There was a change in my engine sound, the fuel pressure dropped, and a red light came on. Tired, I reached to my left and behind to turn the large fuel selector handle to the centerline fuel tank. There was a cough from the engine, then smooth running on the new tank.

Another hour passed. Slight turbulence started, and I was incarcerated in the single-place cockpit like a prisoner held in the sun and glare through hours of interrogation. I felt like falling asleep and dozed off a few seconds. I woke with a jerk which the airplane mimicked, but I saw that my airplane really hadn't moved from relative position. I decided I mustn't fall asleep. There was a hypnotic vibration through the airframe, a slight yawning in the turbulence, and it chanted to me ... sleep ... sleep ... sleep. I decided to keep my mind active somehow, looking at the clouds, rehashing old memories, anything. The clouds in the distance looked like lenticulars, and I took myself back to glider flying when I was a young boy, the swish of wind around the silent machine, the bubbling of the winds, circling in convection currents, feeling like an escape from the schoolyard prison...

"They're shooting at you, Sandy One," the voice said on the survival frequency. "The gun's at your five o'clock now!"

The milieu went on below with the excitement and tedium, havoc and slow passage of time. I stretched as best I could and moved to my side to try paralyzing my other cheek from sitting so long on the hard seat. The canteen water got warm, the oriental sun turning the ice into tepid water. I splashed it on my face, jiggled my helmet around, and opened the canopy again. Then I remembered the paperback in my leg pocket, so I took it out and closed the canopy. I thought that if I could read a few lines now and again I could stay awake better. I checked the instruments for the thousandth time, read two sentences, looked out, read, and got into a routine that lasted yet another hour.

My book was an old Nevil Shute novel about a commando operation by the British in World War II. I pictured the gunboat disguised as a fishing vessel and began to read longer and longer passages. Finally I was totally engrossed in the book. I was thinking how it must have been a truly exciting time, how the drama must have been unbearable, how the people must have known such intense living, and I wished that I could have been a part of that sort of thing. I could just about taste the salt spray and feel their boat moving through dangerous waters. My mind then wandered to the airplanes of the time, the Hurricanes and

Spitfires, and the Battle of Britain. It was all high excitement in that book.

I looked up sharply to be certain I was still in relative position and, seeing that I was, immediately started laughing. I put the book away. There I was flying at nine thousand feet in a single-engine prop fighter waiting to drop down below the clouds in a massive rescue attempt for two downed pilots. My paper story suddenly wasn't all that exciting. How much of our lives was spent in wishing and dreaming of what we thought was better or more interesting while we were actually engaged in novels of our very own? We were all leading characters, for that matter. I was tired and had lost my perspective again. The Battle of Britain was surely exciting, but some of the greatest and most dangerous and heroic flying ever done was right there in Laos in old A-1 Skyraiders.

The gauges checked, my glance into the rearview mirrors elicited a pair of reddish eyes staring back from an unshaven face. It had been too early to contemplate shaving, I had thought.

"OK, Smoke Flight, let's get it moving." The chain of Skyraiders suddenly straightened out into line and then snaked down through the hole. Dropping down to fifty feet, we spread a long smoke screen which ended just beyond the survivors. Yanking the stick hard over and pulling back, I climbed in trail with the other airplanes beside the mountains and back out the hole into clear sky and blazing sun. The helicopter ran in under cover of the smoke, grabbed the survivors, and whirled up and away. The hole closed up and the ground disappeared as we all turned back to Nakhon Phanom. We entered a downwind pattern eight across and broke off for individual landings. I thought it was possibly one of the most exciting sights I had ever seen, as if great chunks of life had gone past me greatly unnoticed until now. Not only had the survivors been rescued, but I had learned something valuable as well. It was a good day.

The Sandy tour came at regular intervals during each month, evoking mixed emotions each time. Day flights of a couple hours' duration were generally pleasant and fun to fly. The A-1s didn't venture on the Trail by day, so there wasn't the constant exposure to the big guns. The night flying was terrifying if you thought about it, since the orders were to fight on the Trail, generally. There was nothing but big guns and night dive-bombing. But rescue duty carried with it the eventuality of flying on the Trail in broad daylight at low altitudes, from fifty feet on up. Losses were very high during rescue missions. But I noticed as the tours came and went that what bothered us most, more than the groundfire perhaps, was wondering at our ability to actually make the rescue when the time came. There were so many variables, so much to consider, that I personally hoped I wouldn't be overwhelmed. A rescue in its entirety meant the planning, the organization of forces, the sweat and blood of finding the downed man, then fighting the groundfire until it was safe enough to bring in a helicopter, and then amassing the forces and making the final plunge ... thereby, hopefully, plucking the survivor from the enemy's hands. But the questions compounded. What if one of us went down during the attempt? What if the chopper went down? Bad radios, weather, and so on added to the problem. I recalled one rescue when Sandy One just called in and asked for a replacement. He said that he was unable to function any longer, that it was just

191

too much for him. I thought that to be an honest move and a sane one. But his superiors thought badly of him for doing what he did.

It was easy to understand how one could get overcome with so much going on. It took courage and honesty to do what that man did. I had to trust that when the time came I would be able to function and do the best I could.

As I flew on the wing for one of the last times, Maj. Nelson Moffatt and I flew formation on a perfect day on the northern orbit. Rather than top the mountains, we were contour flying along the valleys, skimming the ridges, traversing the roads, trails, and meandering rivers. The terrain was rugged, mountaintops reaching two miles high in places, the jungle a solid canopy of greens and browns, landing places so remote as to assure a nylon letdown by parachute if anything happened to us.

We followed the ridges until coming to Route Four, a dirt road appearing from the depths of the jungle, circumventing an eight-thousand-foot mountain area, and heading for the Plaine des Jarres. The road was silent, or at least we couldn't see any movement. Where Laotian homes once stood were charred frames. Where once rested a rice paddy or garden there was now scarred earth. Where the simple and untouched Laotian life had gone on in its same basic and simple way, slaughter had taken its place. North Vietnamese troops had made every village in the area a ghost town. While our newspapers and other media carried accounts of our aggression, we vividly watched another picture completely.

We flew to the remains of Xiang Khouang Ville.

"That must have been a beautiful place to live," I said over the radio.

"Yeah, it sure is pretty," Nelson replied.

We slipped into trail formation and dipped our wings left and right to see the dead village. The people had gone, had become refugees from the swarm of murders, and would do the same from their next shelter and the next, unless the army of men stopped marching like a tidal wave.

Route Four became a thin line dotted with bomb craters where fighter after fighter had tried to stop the trucks and tanks and troops of North Vietnam. And then we came to the Plaine itself, still glistening from rainy-season moisture. It was a haunting sight, a plateau some three thousand feet high resting between severe mountains which spiked into the cool air over a mile up. The landscape was bathed in a sort of emerald neutrality, a color never seen before or to be seen again, one constructed and painted for only that place on the covering of the earth. The Plaine was a place of a thousand faces, an ancient burial ground where earthen jars had become priceless museum pieces but too heavy to be moved, an ancient battleground where mangled and charred skeletons of trucks and airplane frames rested on ground drilled with the circularity of craters. Yet a single tree would stand nearby on the simple shore of a minute lake, a lake formed by rain in the cavity made by the detonation of a five-hundred-pound bomb. There was an absolute and undeniable beauty, a remarkable contrast to the horror man was able to perpetrate. A herd of wild horses galloped across the thick green tapestry as the sounds of our own thundering horses echoed from the hills. Following their ivory-colored leader, the herd stampeded by gutted hooches and empty trenches. There was a beauty in so-called flaws, in the "imperfect," as in a slab of marble valued for the gashes and lines inherent in its face. An old airframe stood blackly, its skeleton looking like a whale's bones in the sand. There was the hurriedly constructed runway where Laos and Meos were attempting to gather enough supplies to fight for their homes, where a handful of ill-trained troops would march off to meet their deaths, where waving arms greeted us as we flew overhead at fifty feet. Air America and Continental Air Services airplanes were ferrying supplies in and out of the various strips on the Plaine, but even so the little fortress of tents and trench lines and smiles wouldn't last long. That land had changed ownership at regular intervals so the people of the land were driven from their homes to the same schedule.

We covered the Plaine in low flight, monitoring the various radio frequencies, switching fuel tanks, and observing the fervent activity of a small force of men assembling for yet another battle. The land looked serene, but it wasn't.

When the rains came, motorized traffic slowed to a stop, and so mounting an offensive militarily was just about out of the question. The PDJ was "friendly" in the rainy season for the most part. Came the dry season, the area was a traditional battleground and "unfriendly." When I first arrived in the Laotian air war, the Plaine was full of high-caliber antiaircraft weapons and was considered a bad place to overfly. But for a brief moment in time it was ours, and Nelson and I flew over its majestic expanse. Whether it was an ancient burial ground, the large earthen jars being tombs, or not, the site was precisely what the gods must have wanted. For those who have seen the PDJ green and lush, there are few sights to compare. We flew between the buildings near Arrowhead Lake and brought the wind of our machines across the Road-runner Lake, all so named because of their shapes. These were once areas so unfriendly that their mention brought a shudder. We entertained a vicarious thrill by buzzing those places in daylight, seeing firsthand what was only on a briefing chart before.

And finally we started the turn towards home and toured yet another area of mountains and valleys, virgin land relatively untouched by foot, seen in any detail only by air. The peaks were spires sharpened through years of weather wear, solid scupltures that had far outlasted such foolishness as all the wars and hopes of domination below. It was as if when men gave up thinking, their blood was spilled at the mountain foot and the trees grew larger, the soft green of the valleys spread, and the old battlegrounds were eventually covered. It was a scene rushing past as though we were suspended over a revolving drum of landscape.

We descended across Pak Sane and turned to follow the Mekong River, down to the water along the banks. There were naked men in fishing boats, waving. Large white birds skimmed the trees which towered one hundred feet high, the water rippled behind our aircraft. The other airplane was there steady beside me. As we raced from the sunset, it was the earth that appeared to be moving past. We were still.

With the dry season, the rescues increased as the gunners apparently wiped away the grease and oil and preservatives, then swept the roads clear so that ammunition and men could traverse the network more easily. The guns were pointed skyward, and we showed up as usual. It wasn't much of a surprise when the first airplanes started dropping and the rescues went into high gear.

One morning there were the cries of a gathering rescue force and heavy footsteps banged on the wood planking outside my door. Someone else had gone down and another rescue was launched. Pilots tumbled out of bed to receive their briefings, as the lead rescue aircraft were taking off. That morning, two F-4 Phantom pilots had ejected near the Trail. There were telephones ringing all over the base as pilots and ground crewmen went about preparing aircraft and making changes in the routine. I had previously been assigned to cover some helicopters that might have to help an important ground team on an entirely different mission, so I wasn't released for the SAR. I went to the briefing room and waited anyway.

It wasn't long before the large room was full and everyone was listening to the loudspeaker which was tuned to the rescue frequency. We could hear as though the operation were taking place right in front of us, like the old motion pictures of fighters in a dogfight and everyone in the headquarters tent listening on the radio.

Pilots sat with their vests and guns and helmets, maps were spread around the room, people were sleeping, waiting. Dots marked the place as the intelligence officer pointed out the best bailout areas, probable and reported areas of groundfire, and what had happened during prior flights. A call came and two more pilots rushed out the door, a lead and wingman clanking buckles and helmets down the hall. Soon there was the sound of two more A-1s roaring east.

The radio crackled, "OK, they've got one man

in sight. The chopper's going in for a pickup now. Stand by!"

There was a heavy silence in the room. Static crackled. The same voice returned. "The chopper's taking groundfire! He's been hit! He's trying to pull out!"

We shook our heads. Another group of pilots went out trailing equipment behind and marching solemnly down the corridor. The weathermen brought in another chart with an updated view of the situation. They went through a revised briefing of the cloud cover, density altitudes, and forecasts. For helicopters, there was a critical relationship between altitude and temperatures. When the air got hotter it also got thinner, and the heavy machines couldn't get a good bite of thin air. It was possible for them to get to the pickup site and actually settle down but lack the power to get back out if the temperatures made the air less dense. Since the ground was already around one thousand feet high, the soaring temperatures could thin the air considerably. The forecasters left and we poured more coffee.

There was soon the same rasping static on the speaker. The controller's voice returned. "The Jolly is heading out. Sandy One wants more cover for him." This meant that the huge Sikorsky CH-53, camouflaged and known as the "Jolly Green," couldn't get in close enough because of groundfire. They were critical also on the amount of groundfire they could absorb. The helicopter engine and transmission system is complex, and the addition of stray bullets does nothing but cause a sudden decrease in performance.

There was a distant voice from another airborne command center. "We've got some fast-movers we can send." That meant jets as contrasted with our "slow-mover" force of A-1s.

The SAR controller replied with some in-depth knowledge. "No! No! We want accuracy here. Send more A-1s." There was a majority nod from the crowd in the room.

The day wore on slowly. Three A.M. turned to nine and eventually noon. A truck came with hot dogs and soft drinks. We sat. The helicopters were waiting to go in, and the NVA gunners knew it. Sometimes they stopped shooting and waited for the low Sandys and the Jolly Green to come in. It would appear that resistance had been stopped. But once into a hover and the Sandy force was flying low cover, it became a deadly game of survival for not only the survivors but also the rescue force itself. The gunners would open up, and everyone was at his most vulnerable point, low and slow.

Another hour went by and more strikes pounded the area. The radio blasted familiar voices through the room, many of them in high pitch. Then came another pickup attempt. "OK, they're trying it again. Will keep you advised."

It didn't work. Aircraft started dropping like lead weights, and in the span of one hour five A-1s had gone down! That was a devastating loss—five in one hour! I figured it was only a matter of minutes until I would be released from my original mission and called for the SAR.

I was tense even on the ground. Fortunately the damaged A-1s had managed to turn away from the immediate area and everyone got picked up—except one who went in with his plane.

Another pickup was organized for the downed jet

pilots and started into operation. We waited while the voices pieced the story together for us. "The helicopter's in a hover!" I caught myself holding my breath for a second. "They've got one out! They're taking groundfire, but they've got one out!"

There were cheers around the room and then silence as attention turned to the other survivor. The radio was quiet. I turned another page of the book I was reading, something about World War I SE-5As over the front lines. My coffee got cold.

The helicopter tried for the remaining survivor. The first one was heading back to base, the rescued pilot alive with scratches and cuts.

The controller's voice returned. "The Jolly is going in now. He's going down the valley behind the lead A-1. He's slowing just a few meters away from the survivor. He's almost on him!"

There were people standing like on the last play of the game. It was late afternoon. It was like the biggest game ever, and no one could leave.

"He's lowering the penetrator now." That was a heavy, streamlined device that could penetrate dense foliage to the survivor. It went down on a cable and, once within reach, the survivor could lower two or three arms and sit on them as he wrapped a strap around his back. Even if he took a hit, he wouldn't fall off the seat. The winch in the helicopter would reel the penetrator and survivor up as it turned away and climbed from the area. But it was initially a slow process requiring a steady hover, not pleasant when bullets were flying.

The picture was in our minds. There had been a time when each of us had been out there watching in similar circumstances, circling the Jolly as the attempt went into effect. The minutes passed. "Why aren't they talking?" someone asked.

Then the voice returned. "He's got him! I repeat, he's got him! They're turning back to base now!"

There was a loud roar from the pilots in the room, and we started filing out to return to the hooches. I put my book back in my leg pocket and went back to the Hobo hooch. My group was finally released from its original ground team and helicopter escort duty.

It was night. With the exception of the one of us who hadn't returned, everyone was at the bar, the cluster of waving hands describing how it was and ever-increasing excitement slowly turning the real events into near fiction. That was standard procedure. Reality on the Trail or an SAR was so far out as to be considered fiction by most people anyway.

I tried to sit back, detached, and take it all in. The roar and the cloud of smoke mingled with the airplane photos and the nostalgia of great aerial events. The thoughts of every pilot were bounced from the walls. Even though we would leave that place physically, we would never be able to leave it mentally. There was no denying the warmth and greatness involved in men who rolled out of bed to rescue another human being and fly yesterday's aircraft across a land that attempted to kill them every minute. It was an honor to be there.

It wasn't too many days later that we had perhaps the most memorable and dramatic SAR. An F-4 had gone down near the ill-famed Mu Gia Pass, an area called Ban Phan Hop. Both pilots had ejected but had come down on different sides of the river that meandered through that area. The rescue forces launched as usual and spent the day in fierce battle with the gunners and ground troops. Flaming projectiles of every caliber filled the air. Bullets flew like swarms of iron flies and the airplanes were ventilated with jagged holes. We couldn't even get close to the survivors. The machines settled back to earth, rudders shot away for the most part, punctures and immense cavities in the wings and fuselages, a wingtip gone, a shattered canopy, one 20mm gun barrel bent and twisted where a 37mm antiaircraft shell had hit it, and a loss of some A-1s altogether.

That first night the hooch was filled with smoke and serious talk. There would be no way to get a helicopter into position if things remained the same. A series of night flights by the multiengine FAC aircraft attempted to stay in radio contact and soon relayed that one man had apparently been captured and killed. The lone survivor said he heard the screaming voice of his fellow aviator across the river. We cringed, thinking how the man must be shivering with fright as the damp night settled on the jungle, the cries and screams of his friend ringing in his ears. We would go back at first light, but he probably wouldn't be there.

But he was. At dawn the sky was again filled with the sounds of every available A-1, the sounds of rockets and bombs reverberating across limestone hills already blasted by the thunder of a thousand other raids. There were heavy gun emplacements hidden in caves, bunkers full of machine guns, and troops roaming the area trying to get our lone survivor. The survival frequency was at once filled with his frantic voice. He had indeed made it through the night. Strikes went on throughout the day, weary pilots dripping in

201

sweat changing from one weary airplane to another, .38-caliber pistols swung from our hips, grease pencils marked the spot, gun enplacements were drawn to accuracy with red threat circles, and pilots sprawled on chairs in semisleep waiting for another turn. And still it went on and on. Finally, tactics changed, another rescue attempt was made. The A-1s blasted the area and brought in a helicopter. It looked good. The giant CH-53 stayed low and the A-1s led it around the hills, kept it hidden for the most part, then rounded the final corner and made for the survivor. It looked better and better. The survivor ran out and leaped for the hanging cable, but it was just beyond reach. Then the ground-fire started up again, worse than before, the helicopter pilot yelled, then turned his machine around and left. The survivor ran back to cover. It was like a last grasp from a plunge down a mountain and finding that the grip went into soft sand that gave way. We could imagine his tears, his pounding heart.

More strikes went in, the day wore on, more airplanes were treated to crushing antiaircraft fire and returned to sit on the hot ramp, hot oil dripping circles around fuel tanks, waiting for yet another flight. The rest of the war had almost ended for a few days so that we might get one man back, that he would live a free man, not die running from a merciless mob. The sun moved down into the horizon. The bullets kept spraying the air and the survivor kept calling for help. But it was soon night again.

The hooch filled with smoke and the subdued sounds of spent pilots. "If he's still there in the morning it will be a major miracle," someone said.

One of the helicopter pilots turned to me and said, "I sometimes wonder why we do all this. We've lost a lot of airplanes and people. And it's all for just one guy. It doesn't seem right. Why in the hell do we do it?" He learned forward and put his head on his arms.

It was a valid question, one difficult to answer when the aircraft was whistling air through holes, when the helicopter was sitting in the middle of a cross fire, when people were falling from the sky in burning chunks of aircraft. But it was something that we would do again and again, for reasons developed long before the event actually took place, because our philosophy was one of value for people, diametrically opposed to the thoughts of those we were fighting. It was a tribute to intrinsic value that we went to rescue one man. It wasn't that we had lost five airplanes in the attempt but rather that we went and tried. In doing so, each individual man became what he was inside, what he could be, like a hero blossoming from what had only been flesh and bone.

A figure sits in his chair, a lump on a cushion. He avoids discomfort, abstains from maintaining any convictions requiring action, sits limp. What is that figure? A man? Living is nothing if one doesn't acknowledge one's dormant power. Another man walks from a placid room, from the comfort and warmth of a bed, and attaches his body to lifeless metal. He takes off into a storm or night or rescue and in so doing becomes Man. That is why men go, that is why they must.

Morning found the first flight looking resolved to finish the job. Standing in the briefing room draped with their gear, they gave the impression of solid rock, firm against a gale. They folded their maps and sorted them into thin black cases, tossed their empty paper coffee cups into a trash can, and disappeared through the door, clanking once more the sounds of buckles and helmets down the hall. The booming, rolling sounds of starting A-1s filled still darkness, and the flight took to the air just as a trace of sun cut across the sky. We readied our things and sat idle, listening to the crackle of static on the room speaker, wondering what would happen on the third day.

The survivor was still there, racing on foot to keep one hiding place ahead of troops intent on his destruction. It had been a wretched night, one in which he told the world to go away and let him die, to forget it because it was going to be over shortly anyway. We didn't pay any attention. And when the morning's light came across his burned and smudged face, the sounds of A-1s came with it. But something strange happened. The groundfire was less intense, the strikes cut into the resistance like a solid steel knife slicing through paper, and towards the end of the day, a voice with the sparkle of glory came over the radio, singing into our ears with joy "We've got the survivor on board. Now let's get the hell out of here!" And we wheeled a huge formation of aircraft and helicopters from Ban Phan Hop and headed on home. A *three-day* rescue was over!

It wasn't long before we started receiving newspaper clippings praising the rescue and reporting its intensity. But they either asked the question of where it had all taken place, or said it was in Vietnam or Southeast Asia. Factually, Woody Bergeron, Jr., ran for three days and two nights in Laos, evading NVA and Pathet Lao troops at his heels. The horror of it all, the fatigue and sorrow mixed with the elation of his rebirth, was to be seen in Woody's eyes when he emerged from the rescue helicopter back at Nakhoc

Phanom. I looked into his eyes, and what I saw penetrated me to the marrow.

Before the party started the hooch became a haven for exhausted airmen. Pilots who had flown through three days of solid fighting in one of the worst areas of the war sat like weary soldiers of fortune, cold beer in one hand, the other hanging aside and covered with the oil and dirt of fervent cockpits. One of the helicopter pilots stood at the card table wrapping a package with Christmas paper. We hadn't thought much about it, but it was December. He finished with the brown covering and the address and string. He turned to leave. There was a huge oval of white salt around the back of his flight suit from hours in the Jolly Green, where his perspirtion drenched his clothes and smeared the controls. "I'm going to mail this," he said. "I want my daughter to get it in time for Christmas." Then he opened the door and left.

Within a few minutes he came back, package still in hand. We looked at him as he sat down with the thud of tired body meeting wooden chair. His eyes were wet, the package sat on the table. "I couldn't mail it," he said. "They were closed because this is Sunday and the sign said it isn't a working day."

There was a quiet interval after that three-day event, a welcome span of minor battles and some quick and successful rescues. On the second day of a Sandy tour, Jim Bender and I flew like tourists around the northern mountains, visiting places we had never seen before. Laos haunted us with its landscape no matter how many times we had flown across its mountains and plains. "Not much longer today, Ben," I said on the radio. We didn't even know what day it was, not that it mattered. We worked every single day and really didn't consider it as work, per se. Flying airplanes to those who love it is beyond work.

Jim was weaving back and forth under my airplane, enjoying the flight. "Yep, what do you figure, another half hour or so?"

I glanced at my watch. The sun was sinking into the haze and the sky was turning bright orange again. "Yeah, that's about it. We can start heading south now." I had become a Sandy lead and was enjoying the sense of accomplishment and solid feeling of leading a flight.

Then we got a call. "Sandy, there's a Raven FAC going down. He's east of your position, over Route Four, heading for the Xieng Khoang Ville area." The Raven was one of us, an Air Force pilot flying as an FAC in Laos, nothing really strange to us but a super secret otherwise. The Ravens lived in Vientiane and dressed and acted as though they were civilians. They generally flew either the single-engine Cessna O-1 or a T-28. It was the living and operating in Laos that made it all so secret.

I immediately turned and pushed up the power. "Push it up, Ben," I called. "Let's get over there."

Xieng Khoang Ville was on the southern outskirts of the Plaine des Jarres, a questionable area in terms of enemy troops, Laotian forces withdrawing rapidly and the NVA and Pathet Lao rushing forward, swarming over the terrain almost at will. The changing of the guard was at hand as the dry season was in effect. We dodged around and between hunks of cumulus clouds until the little dirt strip at Xieng Khoang Ville was in sight. The O-1 descended in a wide circle, planning for a touchdown on the landing strip if possible. I switched radio frequencies and was soon in touch with the FAC.

"I took some hits in the engine and the oil pressure's now reading zero. I sure do appreciate the cover, you guys."

I flew past him and scanned the ground below around the runway. There wasn't anything moving, but that didn't mean much. There wasn't any way of knowing if troops were there or not. That situation fluctuated so much we just couldn't be certain. If there, they would most likely wait for the helicopter, then open fire. I called for a helicopter, and Air America responded. This was generally the case. The Air Force helicopters often took a great deal of time to get to an area since there were so few of them and those were so widely scattered. Air America was flying a great number of aircraft throughout Laos and usually had someone close at hand. As one arm of the CIA's organization, they were darting from the area dropping rice, ferrying the Meo troops, and hauling supplies to and from the various sites. Their flight experience was such that the pilots were first-rate and could be depended on to know their way around and help when needed. While the military hampered itself with its policies of requests and subsequent waiting for replies, Air America could simply move in and make a pickup in minutes. It could often take an hour or so for the military to determine the need and make the decision. That process could prove fatal.

The silver helicopter with the Air America lettering on its sides circled down through the hole in the clouds and settled near the end of the runway. Jim and I flew down the strip, giving cover as the Raven raced for the helicopter. There was no groundfire. In a swirl of dust, the machine lurched into the air and turned away to Long Cheng, the large CIA-operated base in northern Laos.

"Thanks, you guys," the voice said. "Appreciate the help, and see you again sometime."

Jim joined on my wingtip and we climbed together through the sunset-tinted clouds. There was cooler and calmer air above. I turned on the navigation lights and watched the sun dip into a gray line of haze, then disappear. I looked over to Jim, who was sitting there off the wing, solid, stable, only his propeller hinting at our motion. "I'm sure glad that we've had our rescue for this tour," I said. "Now we can look forward to a quiet day tomorrow."

"You never know," he said in return.

Yeah, you're so right, I thought to myself. Over here, anything can happen.

Some fifteen minutes out from the base, I gave the command post a call. Their job was to keep track of the missions, where the airplanes were, maintenance status, and so forth. They got my attention with, "Roger the aircraft status and get right in here after landing. We have to talk with you."

"Wonder what that's about," I mused to Jim on the radio, looking over to him.

"Dunno," came the reply.

The night air was smooth, and we descended in formation like floating on water with an incredible lack of effort. I heard the brief wail of a survival beeper, but assumed it was one of those which went off for a few seconds in the personal equipment shop when someone checked his radio momentarily. "Say, you don't suppose there's a rescue on, do you?" I asked Jim.

208

"I kinda hope not," he said. "You'd think we would have heard about it if there was."

My thoughts rushed out like glue through a punctured tube of model-airplane cement. We might not have heard if someone had gone down in the southern section of Laos. It was night, so the Sandy force wouldn't be going out until dawn. (That was because the helicopters had some difficulty keeping orientation at night in a hover.) So we probably wouldn't be involved until the next day. If that were the situation, then I would be Sandy One on my first such rescue in that position, and it would be a full, exciting, and dangerous day. I rather hoped I had just used the wrong color ink on some form or angered someone in power, or some such thing. Then again, the feeling gnawed at me that I'd like to get out there and effect the rescue if there was one. I called the command post back for more information, but they wouldn't say anything on the radio to give me a clue.

I walked into the building and confronted a barrage of people and conversation. It was close to eight P.M. There was obviously a rescue attempt scheduled. There was a huge map on a board with the survivors' positions noted and the marked threat circles from neighboring guns throughout the area.

"Well, Rick," Col. George Miller said, "so you finally get yours." He put his hand on my shoulder and led me to a cup of coffee. "The situation is this: A Navy A-6 from the U.S.S. *Ranger* went down this evening on the Trail. The call sign is Milestone 516. Both survivors are alive and up on their radios. They're down right on the road and it's not a pleasant situation, as you know. You'll be Sandy One, so get your briefing together after you study the situation and be ready to brief the rescue force at 0330." I was flooded with information and immersed in my first SAR as Sandy One.

In the command post, George lit his pipe, going back to work amid telephones ringing and pads of paper with all the data displayed. I sat down and looked at the map. It was obvious that gun enplacements were covering the area and that it would be a long day with lots of shooting and lots of sweat. A phone call came in with the news that one of the survivors had a broken arm and probably a broken back, and some leg problem as well. That meant that someone might have to be lowered from the helicopter with the penetrator to assist the injured man in getting up and aboard, a very important consideration in terms of time in the battle zone.

Lt. Col. Al Martin was acting as the SAR coordinator and came to ask what I would need. He would then get on the phone and call the various bases and units, telling them what aircraft and ordnance I would be wanting for the rescue operation. I thought back to previous rescue attempts and remembered what things had gone wrong. The problem was often not enough firepower, particularly in the high-threat areas. The enemy had to be worn down quickly. The use of napalm often ended a lot of the shooting, the savage heat and burning compound well disliked by anyone who had been around it. Its roar and fire had ended resistance many times. "Let's have napalm stacked to heaven," I said, "just in case. And I want A-1s in the main, as many as we can generate. Also, let's have an FAC go out with us at first light so he can help put in some extra fighter strikes on surrounding guns while we work mainly with the survivors and the helicopters.

210

I'd also like the fast-movers to work well outside the survivors so we don't bomb them in the meantime." I was recalling a recent incident in which an F-4 had killed our own man by mistake. The minimum safe distance for a five-hundred pound bomb for an unprotected man was about seven hundred meters, and two or three times that distance would be just fine for jet flights. The jet squadrons used the excuse that their people had come from all commands, transport and bomber outfits, and that they just weren't the fighter-pilot types. The Air Force really didn't understand or care about the psychology of the fighter pilot, so it was indeed sending everyone around for a tour in fighters and combat. The results were obvious. But that didn't help our rescues. I wanted the accuracy of A-1s, which came in low and slow enough to keep everything in sight and hit with great precision, not a Phantom at a few hundred knots, nearly out of fuel since they burned it so quickly, flying at an altitude well above the service ceiling of an A-1.

Colonel Martin turned back to his desk and picked up the phone. I went back to the chart and my pad of notes. Jim Bender kept saying that we ought to have something to eat and go to bed. The furthest thing from my thoughts was going to bed. "I'll stick with the coffee and my notes, Ben. You can go on and I'll see you at the briefing, or in the shower about three in the morning."

He laughed and shook his head. "There isn't all that much you can do now. You'd be better off with a good night's sleep."

I motioned him away and went for another cup of coffee. Someone said, "Say, you're too short for this sort of thing, aren't you?"

I nodded. "Yes, less than ninety days to go," I agreed. When you said someone was "short," it meant he had a short time left to go before going back to the States. I secretly hoped that night wouldn't be my last night, and that I would, in fact, finish my ninety days alive.

The FAC came in and we chatted about what we would do, how I wanted the rescue to go, and what the basic plan was. He would use his call sign of "Nail," which we all knew as common to Nakhon Phanom FACs. There were two areas of high ground over which I would have the helicopters hold and move across to keep them protected. The actual crossing of the Trail network would be at a point of minimum threat, and I would plan on laying a smoke screen for the pickup. That was the general picture. It also assumed that the survivors were at the point plotted on the map. Anything else would mean a change of plans after arriving on the scene. That was not the preferred method, but then a rescue was not always a by-the-book operation. Every one was different.

My imagination wandered. I felt as if the entire world were waiting, looking, going to judge, and that two lives were at stake as well as a multitude of others who would place themselves inside my plan and live or die there. It was an awesome responsibility, and I was quite aware of what the others before me had gone through when faced with a rescue from the Sandy One position. I checked my notes until they were memorized.

Eating wasn't very interesting; I left the plate and walked off. Back in the room, I plopped on the bunk, took out the pad of notes, and started in again. It was nearly midnight. There was still the question of how the various radio frequencies would be used, how the strikes would go in, how I would work with the survivors, how I would bring the helicopter in, what I would I do if the plan didn't work, and a few thoughts about what I would do if I went down myself. It was twelve-thirty in the new morning, three hours before the briefing time, four hours before I would start the takeoff roll, about four hours and thirty minutes before I would start talking with the survivors and trying to locate them.

Out of respect for the antiaircraft gunners in broad daylight, I started packing my important belongings. I put valuables into envelopes and boxes and noted on the front, "If R. S. Drury killed or missing in action, please mail this envelope to the following address." Then I put them in my locker side by side. It was a strange sensation, as though I were attending my own funeral rites. Everything had a fresh significance, the breathing of my roommate then asleep, the white glow from the table lamp, the smooth pages of my books, the tinkle of the bamboo curtain we had erected in the room, the little pile of letters from the States, the model airplanes I had built, and the photographs which were on the wall. I perused the last letter from a friend and sat in a pensive atmosphere for half an hour. Then I slipped into the cot at one A.M. and turned out the light.

At one-thirty I snapped the light back on and picked up my copious notes which were beside the pillow. I rearranged them into a neater form and looked them over for the hundredth time. I was possessed of so many thoughts that I couldn't read the papers with any clarity. I fell asleep.

\* \* \*

The alarm blasted staccato notes into the warm and dark room. It was two-forty-five, and it felt like it. It felt as if I hadn't slept at all, which was also about right. I trundled out the door into the black morning. There was a white light outside the door, which was swarming with flying creatures and crawling spiders. Jim was walking down the wooden planking, rubbing his eyes. "Mornin', Rick-O," he said. I waved and walked into the latrine behind him. There was plenty of hot water for a change, because no one had been using it yet. It was usually gone by nine or ten in the morning. We took showers and shaved in silence. Jim showed me the new shaving mechanism he had received. It was an electrical device for serving hot lather. It seemed a strange delight considering the morning's situation.

As I arrived at the briefing building, a jeep pulled up beside me. It was the chaplain. His jeep was all regulation blue with white nameplates and the like. He jumped out and walked beside me through the gate.

"Going out to the rescue?" he asked.

"Sure am. I'm leading the affair."

As the sentry inspected our identification, I looked out to the chaplain's jeep. The white lettering said GOD SQUAD. I looked back at the chaplain, who was apparently enjoying being part of the excitement.

"Well, give 'em hell," he said.

I walked into the large briefing room at three-twenty. The room was filled with pilots and briefers and weathermen. Officialdom sat in the front row, and the wall-size map was rolled out across the stage. My very own little episode-to-be was traced in red and black on the green-hued chart. There was a silence at three-thirty and the briefing started. In a matter of

214

seconds Lieutenant Colonel Martin introduced me, Sandy One, and I went to the podium, turned, and faced the audience. I was nervous, not a cinema hero, tired, not the vision of a bright young fighter pilot, and not particularly erudite. The notes which had accompanied me to bed were creased and rumpled. I set them before me and started to talk.

I told the helicopter crews what the plan was and where they would be holding. They made notes and circled the high terrain on their personal charts. There was never a more nervous group than the chopper bunch. Even though they had the best holding areas, the most cover, and never really went in until the rescue force of fighters had pounded the area for hours in many cases, they were still jittery. But consider: While we in the A-1s were slow, the helicopter had to come to a stop and wait for the survivor to ride the penetrator. They seemed pleased with my selection of high ground and smiled when I mentioned my plan of copious quantities of napalm. It made their job much easier if enemy forces were consumed with their own problems rather than shooting at helicopters. I gave everyone a separate radio frequency and traced the route across the map. Then we named the survivors "Alfa" and "Bravo," A for the pilot, and B for his radar operator. There wasn't much else left to do. There were no questions, and Jim and I left after the briefing. I felt relieved just exiting the building.

"I think I'd rather take off and fight the guns than stand there and talk in front of those guys," I said.

Jim laughed.

I then made a stop at the latrine and had a quick case of the dry heaves. The mounting tension was nearly unbearable.

We sat at the end of the runway while the arming crew connected the wires and checked the ordnance. Both machines were fully loaded, and an additional fuel tank was mounted on the right stub. We would take off at near maximum gross weight and arrive in the battle area still heavy. That meant lots of aerodynamic drag and reduced maneuverability. It also meant increased loiter time with the added fuel, and more firepower with the big load. We had decided in favor of the time and power rather than turning and climb capacity. The airplane weighed about twenty-five thousand pounds.

There wasn't even a hint of dawn yet, and the effect was that we were commencing another night flight. The takeoff was long, and I struggled from the ground after rolling about four thousand feet, then stayed low trying to gain climb speed, which was slow in coming. The machine was my own, #257, patched from a previous SAR, the cowl painted in bright gold, proclaiming MIDNIGHT COWBOY, with my name below the port canopy rail in Old English lettering. I had given 257 that name because I had made so many near-midnight takeoffs. I also liked the music from that motion picture.

The exhaust flames licked the pitch-colored metal inches away from me, and Jim pulled alongside shortly, his instrument lights a dim red through his canopy. I could barely see his dark helmet behind the panel, the airplane a black shape a few feet away. Then he moved out and blended in with the dark, and I was alone again. My radio navigation system went out, so I told Jim and took up a heading and noted the time. I wasn't about to abort the mission for the loss of navigation equipment. "Keep me posted on our distance out," I

216

said. "Sure will. Showing twenty miles out now," Jim said.

A lighter shade of black let the sun through into the new day, it soon looking as if someone had left a door slightly ajar and the light was coming through the crack. "About fifty miles now," came Jim's voice again.

I glanced down at my notes which I had attached to my knee clipboard. I felt I had lived with them for a lifetime. I had also cut a small portion of a map of the area and inserted my own information as to ground-fire, gun locations, and the like. It looked as though anything could be expected, from handguns and ZPU through 23mm and 37mm.

A hazy dawn was evident. Jim called out another mileage figure, and shortly we were in the general area. I switched to the survival frequency, which the survivors would have on their tiny emergency radios, and attempted contact. There was no response. The sky was brighter, and I turned the instrument lighting down. The ground was beginning to emerge from the night as a few chunks of higher ground loomed from a murky deep.

Jim's aircraft took shape as a fleeting image through the haze, and the terrain became raw earth through my already tired eyes. I descended until the ground was fairly clear and started a radio search, hoping to ADF on the transmissions from the two survivors. During a turn I noticed that my gyrocompass had jammed and the dial was failing to move. I was forced to use the magnetic compass with all its limitations and inadequacies. "Milestone 516 Alfa, this is Sandy One. Good morning. Are you awake yet?" I thought some humor would be acceptable under the circumstances. I might put the guys at ease somewhat, since a night in enemy territory produced such tension and fear.

"Hey, Sandy, this is 516 Bravo! Good morning! Sure glad to hear from you." The voice was scratchy on the radio but understandable. As he kept talking I worked the radio and managed to finally home in on his signal. "My arm is pretty bad and my back feels like it's broken," he said. "But I'm ready to get outa here any time."

His voice was that of a man who had spent a lonely and painful night on enemy ground. He was scared, and rightfully so. As I got closer I began to hear the other survivor, faintly at first, then with increasing volume.

"Sandy One, this is Milestone 516 Alfa, this is 516 Alfa!"

I twisted the volume knob to the maximum and called him. "Roger, roger, this is Sandy One. I can hear you loud and clear."

The ADF needle hardly wavered from the first position I had picked up from the other transmissions, indicating that both men were fairly close together. I descended lower until low altitude and the new bright sun combined to allow clear vision. The winding section of the Ho Chi Minh Trail was a foreboding sight complete with varied-sized craters and barren ground. The road segments crossed at a large X where several clumps of trees remained in skeleton form against the incessant bombings, the miserable weather, and the bleaching of the sun.

The pilot, 516 Alfa, gave away his flying background as I flew over him. "Sandy One, you don't

218

know how damned good it is to hear a Spad! You're beautiful!"

I wasn't aware that he had over a thousand hours in the Skyraider himself. The A-1 was known as the Spad to the Navy, and it sounded good to hear this name.

There was close resemblance between my map section and the ground, with roads in proper position as indicated by the cartographer and the contours drawn to precision. The survivors would be near the road crossing, most likely in the trees.

I orbited the area but gave it a wide berth so as to not pinpoint the survivors for the enemy, in case he was trying to locate them as well. "Is there any evidence of hostile activity in the area?" I asked.

"Nothing at present," was the answer. "Last night I did hear something that sounded like distant voices, but nothing actually close."

Turning back towards the area, I pointed the nose of the airplane at the road intersection and said, "What I want you to do is tell me when I fly directly over you. I'll keep going, but just tell me when I'm directly overhead." If I turned or dipped my wing for a period of time, I would also be telling any ground troops where the man was. We had to use the radios to locate the survivors and determine the overall situation, as well as to execute the myriad details of the pickup finale. Radio communication was a necessary evil, but we were careful not to pinpoint exact position since we assumed the NVA and Pathet Lao had VHF radios at the very least. We also changed frequencies and used UHF and FM radios in conjunction with our VHF. Unfortunately, survival radios were generally preset to one standard emergency frequency.

"You bet I will, Spad," he said.

I dropped down to a hundred feet and roared over the trees and roads. "Now, Spad! Now! Now! Now!" His voice continued and he would have been located on a line a mile long if I hadn't looked down at the first "now" signal. I dipped the wing slightly and got a mental picture of the area, then continued ahead and finally turned away. I called the other survivor and located him in the same manner. There wasn't a shot fired. There wasn't a hint of activity, and there was a peculiar aura to the situation. I didn't want it to be a trap, so we flew throughout the area trolling, trying to elicit some sort of response. There was absolutely none.

The airborne controller called to give me the personal authenticator information pertinent to our survivors. Every combat pilot had some personal information on file in case he went down. Of course, only the right person would be able to give the correct answers. It wouldn't be the enemy luring us into a pickup slaughter. One of my questions related to a pet dog apparently owned by the pilot. I gave it a try. "Say, 516 Alfa, what's the name of that dog you have back home?" The wrong survivor heard me. His response led me to believe that the situation was real and typically American. "Look, Sandy One, I don't have a dog, but if you think I should I'll get one right away. But I'd sure like to get the hell outa here right now. Damn it! Get me the hell outa here!"

I turned back over the road. "OK, Alfa and Bravo, I want you to get your flares ready for use, but do not ignite them until I tell you. Do you understand?" I wanted the devices ready for the pickup to give the helicopter a precise target as well as some kind of wind information.

"Understand, Spad, we'll be ready."

Then the pilot, 516 Alfa, made a statement which held a premonition of things to come. "Last night I came across some electrical cables. They led to a little radar van. It's quite a ways over to the west of me. You might be interested in that."

I was! Everyone was. Radar-controlled guns were beginning to appear more frequently in Laos and were deadly. If a pilot didn't see the muzzle flash and tracers from the onset, he would in all probability be hit. Radar meant accuracy. The van was obviously a matter of great concern. I recalled the words of motivated pilots who wanted to hit the supplies as they came from the Russians in Hanoi, at the Haiphong docks. We couldn't do that, for some political reason. And now we were faced with the sophisticated equipment in Laos.

The pilot spoke up again as I flew across the trees. "Spad, are you sure you have my position?"

"Yes," I said, "I've got your location."

"I'm out in the open now!" he yelled. "You ought to be able to see me!" he screamed into the little radio. "I'm waving an orange flag. You're over me now! Can you see me, Spad?"

He was in the open, really open ground, out of his cover, waving a bright orange piece of cloth in an increasing frenzy. He was so excited and anxious to be rescued that he had given up his cover to be certain we knew where he was. "Get back in the trees!" I yelled. "Get back under your cover."

The waving figure stopped waving and darted back into the foliage. I hoped that he hadn't given himself away, although I could well understand his

221

exuberance. I was also thinking about his flying companion with the broken arm and the painful back and leg. Then there was that radar van, or what he had described as such.

Jim Bender called from a position further west. "Hey, I've got the van in sight." It was time to break the lunar silence.

"OK, Jim, go ahead and put some ordnance in, and I'll be behind you." Before I could get there he called again, his voice high-pitched and faint. "I took a hit! There's a big gun over here. I'm turning back west. I think I can make it home!"

His voice faded away as the aircraft began the trek homeward, pieces of aircraft metal beginning to fall off and drop away, hydraulic fluid spewing into the air, a huge hole punctuating his starboard wing. From then on he was known as "Jink" Bender. He would always remember to jink hard and often in enemy territory from then on.

I called the airborne controller and got a wingman to escort Jim back to base and requested a wingman for myself. It was suddenly quite lonely out there, hostile too, for small puffs of gray began to dot the air, framing the *Midnight Cowboy* with pieces of exploding metal. So it happens now, I thought. Other guns opened up and the air was filled with tracers and bursting 37mm shells. Both survivors confirmed with audio what I was seeing visually. "Hey, Spad, they're really shooting at you! I can hear them all around!"

"Yeah, I know. Stay down and we'll put in some strikes as soon as possible." I twisted the machine as hard as I could, feeling the burble of a stall as I reached three Gs in turns. All that ordnance made things a bit sticky, hanging there in the wind. My low altitude didn't help, and the brilliance of daylight didn't offer any assistance in concealment. It wasn't a great place to be flying. I called the FAC and we located several gun emplacements, me getting them to fire as I flew overhead, him spotting them as I did so. The planes I had requested the night before were coming in on schedule, diving from the heavens and pounding the earth with all manner of ordnance, napalm splashing and burning black, five-hundred-pound bombs sending dirt blasting into the air, machine-gun fire rippling the calm like pneumatic hammers. And then the groundfire stopped.

"Say, Sandy One, it looks quiet," the FAC said.

It had stopped too abruptly for me. It had all the flavor of an ambush. "OK, I'll drive back over the area and see what happens. Keep your eyes open." I turned back and called the survivors again. "516 Alfa, this is Sandy One. I'm going to fly over you again. Let me know if you hear any shooting and from what direction it's coming. Understand?"

"Yes, sir, Spad," he said, still watching as his old Navy mount flew around the area. "I'll let you know."

I pushed up the power and plowed back into the heated air. Trolling for groundfire was necessary but risky. I got about half a mile from the survivors when the guns opened up once more. The machine bounced in the turbulence and the gray puffs of explosions started trailing the airplane again, the gunners not leading me quite enough.

"There's something big to the west of me!" Alfa yelled. "It sounds like a thirty-seven-millimeter or fifty-seven millimeter size to me."

The FAC reported that he could see it, and I jinked away hoping to avoid holes in the airplane and holes

223

in me. I caught myself holding my head down and morbidly snickered at the act. A 37mm didn't care about a lowered head. It tore the metal quite easily. I might have avoided small-arms hits, though. I meandered to the higher ground while another bunch of strike aircraft pounded the guns. My new wingman arrived, and I quickly briefed him on the situation, pointed out the location of the survivors, and went over what I wanted done in the near future. I watched the smoke and dust drift in the wind, observing what the smoke would be doing when I went to put down the smoke screen.

"It looks reasonably quiet again," the Nail called, so I pulled a few strands of courage together and set out once again to see if I could draw groundfire from the area. There was very little, and Alfa reported what he thought was a light machine gun firing at me. I sprayed some rockets in the general direction and called the Nail. "Put in another strike flight on that area and I'll prepare the choppers and smoke flights."

"Roger that, Sandy," he said, turning his twin engine OV-10 away to put in a smoke rocket for the next group of fighters.

Then I called my new wingman. "Sandy Two, I want you to get the first two helicopters over here to the high ground; get the lead smoke here also." I then called the survivors, who reported things fairly quiet and added that they were more than ready to get out.

The Smoke Flight leader checked into the area, and I had him fly to my position. "Here's what I want you to do," I radioed. I had him follow me around the general area so he would know the terrain and see the situation firsthand. "When I tell you, I want your flight to come in trail down a line to the east of the survivors.

Lay a line of smoke right...down...here," I said, dipping a wing, pointing to the region I wanted covered.

"OK, got you," he said. He climbed away and went back to brief his flight. Then I chatted with the lead helicopter pilot. "I'm going to put down a large Willie Pete marker for you which will be your initial run-in point," I explained. "That's where you'll start. I'll cover you all the way in and give directions all during the run. You'll be in heavy smoke, but I'll be able to see you from above. Stay low and follow my instructions exactly. Any questions?"

The Jolly Green pilot was a familiar voice. It was Maj. Ed Robbins, who lived in the adjoining building near our hooch. He was a competent veteran. "No questions, Sandy. We're ready."

I glanced down and saw my carburetor air temperature gauge indicating full hot. Just what I need, I thought, something else going wrong. Hoping it was only a gauge failure, since nothing else indicated any problems, I elected to continue. It was no time to be leaving on account of the peculiarities of a gauge. The time was at hand for the first pickup attempt, and I wasn't going to miss it, having organized and run it so far. I was going for broke.

The FAC terminated the strikes, and I had him draw a line down the side of the survivors' area with his remaining smoke rockets. Then I called the Smoke Flight leader. "Smokes, this is Sandy One. There's a line of Willie Pete rockets where I want you to lay the smoke screen. Do you have it in sight?"

There was a pause. Then: "Got it, Sandy One."

I looked around and took a deep breath. The time had come. It was immediate, exciting; my stomach

225

climbed to my throat, my heart pounded, sweat ran down the rivulets of my face, the oxygen mask chafed against my cheeks and under my chin. "Let's go, Smokes!" I yelled.

"Smoke's in," was the call.

From above me I watched a steady stream of A-1s diving in trail formation. I nodded in excitement. It was a great sight, knowing the pilots, watching the plan unfold, hearing the voices on the radio.

"Let's move it around, Smokes, the area's a hot one," the leader called. Smoke started erupting from the canisters and a line was formed precisely on the mark. "Lead's off, breaking west." The call was followed by the others. "Dump your empty canisters, Smokes, move it around, let's go."

The thread of aircraft weaved away jinking and climbed out leaving a perfect white smoke screen. The wind caught the billowing line and started it across the survivors. I called the helicopter. "Move to the initial point, Jolly Green." He raced to the IP, which was the white phosphorous bomb I had just dropped. "OK, Jolly, we're on our way." I charged out in front and had him follow me. "Fly low and on the eastern edge of the smoke screen, Jolly."

"Roger, roger," came Ed Robbins's voice.

The smoke was drifting exactly over the area. Visibility into the hiding places was obliterated by dense white man-made clouds. It looked good that far. "You're coming to a small road up ahead," I said. "Do you have it in sight, Jolly?"

"Got it," he said.

"OK, I want you to make a left turn and follow it into the smoke. Do you understand?" He did. The helicopter came to the road, executed a sharp turn, and plunged into the smoke. I called the supporting A-1s. "Form a circle around us, guys. Lay down some ordnance and give us lots of cover." A huge daisy chain started, and I put my attention back to the helicopter and the survivors. I can see from above," I said. "Come left about ten degrees, Jolly. You've got about two-hundred meters to go now." It was like controlling a model by remote control. The chopper turned, slowed, and moved as directed. The wreck of the A-6 sat ahead and was an easy mark for the helicopter to navigate over. Then there was the parachute of Alfa which stretched and pointed in a line to where he was hiding. He had hit the ground and started running immediately. The parachute looked like a big arrow pointing to him, or at least the direction he had initially run.

Then I called the first survivor. "Milestone Alfa, this is Sandy One. I want you to pop your smoke flare now!"

"Great! Great! Popping it now!" was the response.

Dark red-orange smoke started ascending through the white smoke. "OK, Jolly, there's his smoke directly ahead of you. Go to it!" The helicopter slowed and finally came to a halt. There was a huge and empty silence. The A-1s were still circling above, strafing and putting rockets into the surrounding terrain and old gun positions. Smoke drifted across the scene, the red smoke faded away, and there was still silence. Then came a happy and fervent voice. "We've got one survivor on board! Guide me to the other one!"

"OK, Jolly, turn ninety degrees right and proceed about a hundred and fifty meters," I instructed. The huge machine turned and churned through the smoke.

"Milestone 516 Bravo, this is Sandy One again. Pop your smoke now!" Another cloud of red smoke climbed and mingled with the white. "About twenty degrees to your right now, Jolly!" I yelled.

The helicopter descended and was swallowed by the smoke screen again. I twisted over the area, breathing hard, looking for a trace of any groundfire, my guns charged, switches again ready, rockets poised. There was another macabre silence during which there wasn't a single voice on the radio. Then Ed Robbins called me, and it was the voice of joy. "Sandy One, we've got both survivors on board. Get us the hell out of here!"

"Make a ninety to your left, Jolly, head for the smoke at the IP. We'll all be covering you."

"Roger, roger," he said again.

"Cover his exit," I yelled to the rest of the A-1s. There was a mass of CBU, rockets, and machine-gun fire as everyone pounded the exit route. The helicopter reached the IP and started a climb over the high ground. I sat back, not really relaxed, just infinitely fatigued. "Jolly, this is Sandy One. Let's go home."

"You bet, Sandy. Thanks. Great job!"

We all joined and set out to the west, leaving a miasmic cloud over the location of our five-hour scene. It hung there, and I kept looking at it as we climbed away. Such a small point in time, such a tiny plot of land, all over, everything said and done. Our exodus home was marked with radio chatter, and I rolled over the helicopter and did a split-S to the ground. It was a very satisfying feeling.

I sat in the de-arming area and watched the helicopter settle to the ground and the pilot wave. I waved through the propwash of my own airplane and taxied back to the parking spot. Jim Bender met me with a jeep. He shook my hand and held up a jagged hunk of torn metal. "This came from my wing. Quite a souvenir, don't you think?"

"Yeah, Jim. Keep it on your mantel in remembrance. Glad you made it home," I said sincerely.

"Good to see you, too," he said with his big smile.

We jerked to a start across the metal ramp, the tires making a metallic rattle as we headed for the helicopter, passing the ambulance which was heading posthaste for the hospital with the injured survivor. There was a large crowd, a normal thing after a successful rescue attempt. It was always good to see one of us plucked from the enemy and standing there sipping champagne after a heroic fight. I walked through the crowd and someone said, "There's Sandy One."

I took off a glove and my hand was grasped by a lieutenant commander with a huge mustache. "Sir, thanks for my life. I mean, really thanks!"

Although he outranked me, I ignored the "sir" and only commented in jest about his nonregulation mustache. Then we all laughed and the inevitable bottle of champagne appeared, the cork flying into the pattern overhead, the liquid splashing down dry throats. Returning A-1s roared overhead, their vibration shaking us. God, it was good!

"Name's Pee Wee Reese," the man said. "Milestone 516 Alfa to you." He was short, perhaps five six, and the mustache consumed most of his face except for the huge smile underneath. He limped a little, and his flight suit was covered with dirt. He talked like a man just rescued from the very hand of death, and he never stopped talking and laughing. He was alive and he sincerely liked it.

229

I languished in the combination of hot sun, bubbling champagne, and a mellow feeling tempered by five hours of emotionally and physically hard work. The crew chief came up with my helmet and said he had found a few small bullet holes in my aircraft. Jim and I then drove off to the maintenance debriefing, where I gulped two cans of beer, and then to intelligence debriefing, where we had to re-create the episode and construct the milieu on paper. Lieutenant Commander Reese was working out the details of his ordeal on tape next to us. He was still high in spirits. We later discovered that his survival water flask had been filled with whiskey and that his night had been a fairly comfortable one.

On arriving back at the hooch, I found it most pleasant to discover that such things such as flowers and fresh breezes still existed. My room, a citadel from outside travails, took on a new meaning. There in the gray metal locker were the envelopes, sealed, the words about my death or missing status printed on the outside. That small chamber had never looked so pleasant. I sank into a chair and watched the model airplanes turn on the end of long thread as the air conditioner spun them back and forth. Everything was incredibly nice. I had a strong feeling of what Pee Wee Reese was suddenly knowing. Being alive and *knowing* it was precious.

There was the usual party. Pee Wee was still in his soiled flight suit, still limping, still drinking. We borrowed a six-pack of beer and a jeep, then headed for the hospital to see his radar operator, who had perhaps even more awareness of life than we. He was sitting back in bed, his bandages covered in blood, his arm bandaged, several cuts and bruises evident, and

230

there was a sharp suggestion of pain across his face. Still he smiled and shook my hand firmly. We plied him with beer and his pain diminished, or at least the tension seemed to come from the face. The doctor finally had us leave, so I shook his hand again and watched him lie back. Even with such pain he had climbed on the penetrator hanging from the helicopter and had effected rescue alone. It must have been another story for him. He missed the champagne on the ramp and the party. But it looked as if he was primarily delighted to be back from the morass of terror he had known during the long night and morning. We squealed away in the jeep under some extraordinarily bright stars. We all noticed them.

Lieutenant Commander Reese went back to his ship a couple of days later. It was a great memory for me, but one evening we got a surprise. A plane had flown in with two packages from the U.S.S. *Ranger,* one for Jim and one for me. I opened the brown wrapping paper, and there was a flight suit like the one he had worn, his squadron emblem on it, and the blue T-shirt he was wearing during the rescue. Across the front was printed *New Jersey Recreation.* It had been some joke since that morning. Without knowing it, I had worn my T-shirt which said *Coors: Breakfast of Champions.* There was a small photograph attached to the flight suit. It was a picture of two A-6s in formation over the *Ranger.* On the back was Pee Wee's writing. Although I eventually received the Silver Star for the rescue, my most valuable memento of the event was that bit of writing on the picture. It said, "Thanks for bringing me back to the land of the living. Thanks for my life. Lt. Commander Evan P. Reese." There was a reflective silence during which I thanked him in absentia and understood more about the common bond among those who fly and those who put their lives on the line for each other. Another day later his commander flew in from the ship to meet those who had taken part in the rescue. Just before he left he took out a small button and gave it to me. "This is for you," he said. "Sandy One is certainly the man to get it." He pinned it to my shirt. In red lettering on a white background were the words *I'm Fearless*. He also laughed and said, "By the way, that orange flag he was waving at you—that nut stole it. Those were the curtains in my room!"

My name was on the schedule for another night mission, Nelson Moffatt was sitting on the steps reading a letter from home, Jim Bender was playing Ping-Pong, and two A-1s took off, their position lights turning east under a bright gunner's moon.

# TEN

THE SUN BURNED INTO ME for a while, then some clouds passed by and dropped a mist so soft as to be likened to snowflakes. Then it was steaming hot again. I sat on the grass with my notebook, selfishly hiding the results of a minor clandestine operation, a small tin of Vienna sausage and a microbial bottle of mustard. It was a rare pleasure. To complement my banquet there was the haunting refrain from José Feliciano's "Rain" from the hooch speaker. I made several notes in my book, then luxuriated in my small feast.

I was spending a few relaxing hours in the sun, pondering some of the latest news from around the world. In particular, I was taken aback by one clipping that had been sent to me. It stated that we, the fighter pilots of the Southeast Asian war, were a bloodthirsty lot strafing orphanages for pleasure, bombing villages for lack of any better target to kill, and gunning down animals for sport. This would have been typical and amusing from the Communist countries, but it was disheartening as it came from home. In yet another clipping, an American actress, of all things, was standing by a North Vietnamese antiaircraft gun emplacement, smiling, looking skyward as if to anticipate firing at one of us.

I looked to the walkway where the day fliers were

returning in the afternoon, tossing their hats in their rooms, heading off for the hooch and the refrigerator of cold beer. None of them appeared to represent hometown newspaper villains. As a matter of fact, they were a surprisingly gentle and fascinating collection of men. None of us had done any of the things said about us, and as for shooting animals, there were times when heavily laden water buffalo, ammunition and military supplies strapped to their bellies, were targeted the same way as a military vehicle would be. And they were precisely that. But such characteristics of the enemy were disregarded by our Western culture. Killing animals was repulsive to those back home, and we couldn't convince the television audience otherwise. They were not in Southeast Asia except vicariously through the news media which selected what they would show. Since the media needed flavor, excitement, and action to keep ratings and jobs, they showed just that. The enemy was careful to conceal its actions. It showed only little old ladies sipping tea, inquiring why the mighty U.S.A. would bomb them. The propaganda schemes were old hat to us, but if one hadn't seen them for himself, things always sounded way out of proportion and certainly at odds with a traditional American upbringing. Our enemy always played on those emotions, confident that our heartstrings would betray us rather than straight analysis cutting through their chaff. They laughed that we would expend so much to rescue a man, just a simple man. They laughed that we would set rules for ourselves and allow so much freedom to the enemy. They laughed as selected U.S. representatives went into Hanoi and broadcast what amounted to enemy propaganda to au-

234

diences in the United States. They laughed as those people gained respect and listenership back home.

Joe Leonhardt walked past, made a glib comment about the working class, and returned a few minutes later to join me in the sun. Joe always smiled. Even when things went wrong, he just laughed. In that respect I thought he was a very smart guy. Things never bothered him. There was a tattoo on one arm, and I asked him about it. He said that he had been in the Merchant Marine. "Yeah, I sailed the Caribbean mostly," he said. "It was really a good life. I used to chip some paint, paint, chip more paint, and paint some more. There was lots of sun, and there was the ocean. It was good. And I was always surprised. You'd think only us idiots would do that sort of thing. But I found teachers, writers, lots of people like myself who just wanted to get away and think and read, and mull things over. It was pretty interesting."

I asked him how he ever got to be a pilot and end up in the war with an old prop fighter.

"Well, I was driving a truck for a while. Then a buddy said that we ought to join the Air Force and be pilots. So we did. It was kind of a spur-of-the-moment thing. After a while, I saw the A-1. And with that airplane I thought there would be emphasis on the individual, not computers and transistorized technology. It was like working on the ships; I could still feel accomplishment in what I was doing with my hands and my mind—my life. It was an airplane, the last of the sort I suppose, where a pilot still had to face a forced landing once in a while, and smell the oil and gas. When you get to flying most of the jet stuff there's only stop, go, and eject. That really isn't what flying is to me. So I figure I just got on the last of the real

235

stuff. It's going away, but at least I did it while it lasted."

He sat back and absorbed a little sun, perhaps with the same feeling as he had known on a freighter from a time past. Then I asked him what he was going to do after it was all over.

"Think I'll open up a liquor store. How about 'Joe's Liquor'?"

He laughed, and I didn't know if he was serious or not. Then I figured that a man who had sailed in the Merchant Marine, driven trucks, and piloted prop fighters in combat was most likely serious. It also might explain why he always laughed.

Nelson Moffatt drifted by, looking as if an army of men had marched over him. After flying test flights from sunrise to late afternoon, he wasn't inclined to flaunt any bright spirit. He moved slow and easy, carrying his inevitable letter from home. I imagined that his wife did nothing but write letters, apparently long ones. He sat beside Joe and me, and Pete brought out a couple beers for us. Nelson started reading, and I made a few notes in my book. Nelson was another surprising personality, the squadron, I reflected, being full of surprising people. He even had a couple thousand hours in crop dusters. Nelson had spent his military life flying fighters, and fly well he did. I secretly considered him the consummate pilot. He was a quiet sort under most circumstances but became sharply articulate when anything false was spoken about flying. He just liked being an excellent pilot and didn't feel the need of reward other than the freedom to fly. I had witnessed him explode from silence with a one-hundred-dollar bill when his aerial prowess was challenged. He would win any bet. Because he was good and just wanted to fly, he saw his future military career as a static affair. Nelson didn't care one iota for the supercilious and would be inclined to say so. Accordingly, he was popular with his peers and less so with the management. One got the impression that he didn't really care.

Randy Bertrand came up like a steam engine, two hundred and twenty-five pounds that was as quick as it was solid. I had once tried grabbing him and forcing him to the floor in the hooch. It had been a night of cheer and high spirits. But as Randy stood on my chest I realized that a few drinks did not in fact make me his size. Randy had come to the A-1 from pilot training, which meant he was good enough in his class to get such an assignment. He was a fairly good-natured fellow who was genuinely sweet and likable. But after a few drinks it was most important that he be on your side. I had watched him actually lift a jukebox from the floor and throw it, followed by a pool table and its assorted components. Through some delicate questioning we discovered that Randy, or Bert as he had come to be known, was once a bouncer in a Miami nightclub. He said he didn't like facing guns but that once he got them from their owners things went just fine. He had a deep voice which bellowed from under a black mustache, and even when he talked on the radio, his voice got results. If one were possessed with the notion of going downtown or to any ominous place, Randy was a particularly good choice for company. What surprised me most was that he was a gentle man at heart who would do anything for his friends.

Ron Rounce walked to his room, then emerged a short time later in civilian clothes. He pulled up a hair, and we chatted briefly about flying. He still talked fondly about putting the dope on an old J-3 Cub. "I used to go out and fly patterns, one after the other, and make landings all day long," he reminisced. "It was really great, a yellow Cub and clean air. A guy can't ask for more than that." Ron went to the Air Force Academy but didn't shine his shoes all day, nor did he come on with garrulous military patter. He had somehow survived the system. I thought it might have to do with the fact that he still loved aviation.

Two A-1s entered the traffic pattern and roared over us, each of our heads was upturned, and not a word was spoken. I made a mental note that whenever I had been with fliers, and no matter how many hours aloft they had, they always looked at the airplanes overhead. "I just don't feel worth a darn unless I can fly," Ron said. It was a comment pertinent to us all.

There was a nice sunset, and everyone else went into the hooch. I showered and dressed and went to join them. There was a moon sitting overhead like a freshly minted quarter. I walked into the building and penetrated the bluish smoke. There were little huddles of pilots, their hands describing patterns in the air, mugs of beer sloshing about the furniture. It was a place for pilots, and most interesting, I thought, that the guys I flew with were not at all the subjects of our magazine and newspaper articles. They were quite the opposite. Ron was describing a fantastic sunset from ten thousand over the PDJ, and Loren was reading about the rigging on some ancient schooner. The intrepid night fliers finally left and the excited hooch atmosphere calmed down, until at nine P.M. there was soft, tranquil music and a few nostalgic drinkers. It was a good place. They were good people, real, alive, interesting. It was a moving experience to live among

238

them. One remembers those things. I knew I'd never be able to forget the companionship, drama, life-and-death existence we shared. I wouldn't have traded it for anything. And with these thoughts I headed for bed and a few hours' sleep before an early-morning mission.

I awoke around two in the morning. My roommate was talking in his sleep, vocalizing his dream. I surmised that he was on a particularly memorable mission. He tossed to one side. Then he started again. "Getting low. Got to pull out! Pull it out! They're shooting. Pull ... out!" He calmed, then turned to his other side, facing away from me towards the wall. His breathing was heavy. I lay back in the dark and guessed that he had pulled out. Someone once said that if you don't wake from such a dream and actually do crash, or whatever, then you die, really. I wondered.

As I closed my eyes, the door to the room opened. I kept motionless in the heavy dark. The only sounds were breathing and the eternal air conditioner that moved warm air around. Someone tripped over the little table, then finally stood by my bed. I knew where my large survival knife was, but didn't budge. Then the person sat down beside me. There was a mumbling that was incomprehensible, but I recognized Walt Davis's voice. He reached out, picked up my arm, and looked at my watch, which was glowing bright green in its strange luminescence. "Humpf," he said.

"Hey, Walt," I said, "what are you doing there?"

He stopped shuffling around. "My room," he said.

"No, it isn't," I stated. "Yours is at the other end of the building."

"It is?" he groaned.

"Yep, sure enough is," I said.

239

There was another pause. He scratched his head. "You sure?"

I didn't say any more. He got up. "Had some martinis after the mission. They were really shooting out there. My God, they were really shooting." He stumbled over the small table again, found the door, and tripped out into the hot night. I shook my head at what that place was doing to people and formed a smile without humor. Even when we were really scared, we always went. There was always the lure of the mission, the solo sortie into the battle in the night. But when you came back, it sometimes hit hard. I looked over to Joe, who had apparently completed a successful mission and was finally sleeping easy. I tried to shake the madness from my head and sleep, but there was only half an hour to go and I only sweated with my eyes closed until the alarm went off.

There wasn't even a hint of light, just a soft black velour everywhere embracing warm and humid breezes. I stood on the wooden walkway and yawned into the dark.

My movements were silent. Everyone else was asleep except the man who was going to fly with me. The other night fliers were still out, still on the Trail. I grabbed the old shaving kit, the soap, the towel, and strolled to the common latrine. A formation of moths and other creatures were convening with me under the lights. I kept yawning.

Ken Ohr dragged in with the slam of the door, not as quiet as circumstances called for. He still looked asleep as a vague "Hi" emerged from his mouth. There was the sound of water in the washbasin at three A.M. My flying partner stood almost asleep in the shower, leaning on one wall while warm water poured over him. Our combat pilot's world was a curious place, missing sleep yet being able to witness the sunrise over mountains from ten thousand feet, chasing through streaks of cloud over a dozing stretch of the Far East. There were times when we wanted to eulogize pilots everywhere, bow to the sun, drink in the warmth from two miles up, laugh, be free. But at three A.M. that was often difficult to realize. Yellow water continued to gurgle down the drain. Finally Ken turned off the shower and stood there naked, eyes closed, yawning. We didn't look much like eager fighter pilots.

The night looked quiet but it wasn't. It only appeared to be sleeping. The night was Charlie's. He moved in it with great finesse and superb agility. We tended to own parts of the daylight hours, but somehow Charlie kept the night. His trails and rivers and footpaths let him wander through the dark hours with relative ease. That was why we were there, at that hour, to help take his nights away or at least make them wildly unbearable. That was the military reason I was shaving at three in the morning.

My metal locker banged open because the door stuck, as always. I tried to be quiet, but that damned door crashed open and the little padlock tapped on the metal with a cold sound. I dressed in my flying garb, the sounds of my dog tags tinkling through the dark as I put them over my head and tucked them under my flight suit. I surveyed the room quickly before leaving. It was lifeless under the sparse light of the gray table lamp. Light out, I left.

Since aviation's infancy, authors have engaged themselves in attempting to shape emotions into literary expression, to crystallize and reveal the flier's world. All who echo the songs from Icarus to Saint-

241

Exupéry, who have seen the titan of the heavens conduct that symphony with all the variations of hue and drama, those who have and will assimilate the pageant from their airplanes amongst the clouds, all of them who have been and will be impassioned with it, a pilot can call friend. But none have put on paper what can be drunk from the cockpit.

The evanescent majesty from 10,500 feet was unrestrainably delicious to the accompaniment of my Wright R-3350 engine. Every little problem of my life, every minute and inane detail of "busywork," vanished into its true insignificance. The inner voice counseled me to apprehend true prosperity. I looked through the plexiglass canopy across the sky and saw only an infectious good. In harmony with the sky there was perspective, that something which shades our lives every second, that changes it from despair to joy. The mad artist and the frenzied conductor poured out their life's creative work with giant swaths of infinite blue-black which gradually became a blue-pink. There were no edges of separation, only a soft blend of color. Then there was a pause as the brightness increased. The artist asked, "Now?" The conductor said, "No, not quite yet." The sky was bursting with promise, glowing with pearly pink color. I opened the canopy and stuck my hand up into the wind, feeling the cool blizzard down my sleeve. Then, smiling, the conductor said, "Yes, you may do it . . . now!" And the most magnificent sun I had ever seen loomed from the depths of the artist's palette. Driven by artistic passion, the two virtuosos careened between the stars from the horizon to the zenith with their devices of joy. We applauded in our own way by smiling and waving and rolling through the display singing with the vibrating intensity of our secret existence. Ken and I, Ken with his little blue hat with *The KID* on the back. The Kid and I were out to taste the nectar of the morning.

The mountains and valleys were garnished with white fluff far below. A few of the pointed peaks impaled solitary disks of white mist, and the sight was that of snow like we had known back home. I clicked the mike button. "Don't get to see snow like this up here very often."

"Yeah," The Kid said, "it's sure nice."

It was our applause again. We were two individual pilots, in two individual airplanes, yet each seeing the morning with the unique appreciation of pilots. It was a pilot's morning once seen through the goggles of Lindbergh and Wiley Post, through the eyes of Richard Byrd and Roscoe Turner, through a million cockpit windows, and finally through The Kid and me. It is as though pilots are alive long before the rest of the world, way above in cool and quiet air, the first on hand to see what will happen in the universe, frolicking in the world available only to a very few. It was a proud legacy given to every man deserving the name of aviator.

We approached the deep valley and circled over what appeared to be a small fire. Ken called me over to the VHF frequency, and we started calling the ground FAG. Working with the FAGs was frustrating, yet often humorous. They directed strikes into areas where they *thought* ordnance would be effective, but they seldom followed up and moved on with their men to occupy a position once held by the enemy. They seldom advanced at all, usually backing up if anything. Even the Lao soldiers carried tennis shoes in their packs so they could run away faster. It was disconcerting to try and work with such people when three-quarters of them still thought the earth was flat, made up only of Laotians, the round-eyed white people from the sky birds, and invaders from North Vietnam. It was a pretty land deep in eleventh-century culture, steadily retrogressing.

And so we called the FAG again by his call sign. "Hello, Pogo, this is Hobo. How you hear?"

There was a barely audible voice. "Hello, Hobo, I have bad guy all around. You help me."

I moved into trail formation and chased Ken around the area. "OK, Pogo," Ken said, "you show us where bad guy, and we drop bomb for you." The early-morning scud was breaking up, and we could see the hills clearly. But we couldn't see Pogo. Then he called back with a suggestion.

"Hobo, this is Pogo. I shoot mortar to bad guy. Then you see where drop bomb." We tightened our circle and banked steeper to see. "OK, Pogo, go ahead." There was a second's silence, then a bright white flash came from the trees and a tracerlike trail arced across the ground and landed in dense foliage. Just after it hit there was a return flash and a trail of smoke which arced back into Pogo's position. There was silence on the radio.

"Pogo! Pogo!" Ken yelled. "You OK, Pogo?" There was no reply. There were no further smoke firings or smoke trails. Ken called me on the interplane frequency. "I sure as hell hope they didn't get Pogo." Then he went back to calling him. There was still only silence on the radio, broken by momentary static. We circled for ten minutes without Pogo's voice contact. Then came a crackling static, followed by an extremely high-pitched voice racing for words.

"Hobo! This is Pogo! Bad guy shoot at me! Bad guy shoot at me!" The voice was coming through heavy breathing as if the man had been running, which he probably had been.

"We understand, Pogo. We clear drop bombs now?" Ken asked.

"OK, Hobo, you drop bomb now, please." Ken rolled in immediately, releasing a five-hundred-pound MK-82 into the enemy mortar position.

"You drop number one bomb, Hobo. You do same, same again." Pogo thought it was a nice gesture to return the NVA warmth with a few thousand pounds of ordnance. I set my intervalometer and pressed on down into a steep dive pass, overlapping Ken's hit with my own bombs. Pogo was appreciative and sat through a twenty-minute strike in relative comfort. We finished with some strafe through the area, and Pogo called afterwards. "Hobo, this is Pogo. You drop number one bombs. Bad guy no shoot at me now. I want thank you. I see you again maybe."

Ken flew past me rocking his wings, which meant that his radio had gone out. I joined up with him and looked over to his cockpit. He held up his hand and moved it back and forth across his mouth and ears, indicating radio failure. I moved into the lead with The Kid on my wing and headed on home, the smoke from our strike drifting through the valley below. I opened my canopy and Ken did, too, and once across the river we descended into the heat below. There was a new day, life stirring in the open, the world waking up from the night. We had been there before it had started.

We walked into personal equipment, handed over our guns, and hung up our vests and helmets. It was nearing nine in the morning. "Sure hope we helped Pogo," Ken said, emptying his .38 shells into the supply bin. "Sounds like he had a long night to me."

We took the trolley back to the hooch and grabbed two beers from the refrigerator. The last I saw before going to sleep was Ken's body stretched out in the sun, a Feliciano record blaring from the hooch, and the Thais sorting out laundry in the bright morning. It was as if the war only existed for several hours a day for us. Pogo's war was a twenty-four-hour-a-day affair. The sun burned through the air like a furnace, every window crying dripping water from the humidity. The artist who had painted the morning could sleep, too, his work and ours finished for another day. I pulled back the covers and sprawled out on the simple luxury of cool sheets.

I managed a few hours' sleep before Tom stuck his head in the door. "Hey, Rick, phone call for you. Get it by the latrine." I rambled down the walk attired in a towel and shower shoes. The receiver hung at the full length of the cord and I reeled it up like an anchor.

"Drury here," I said.

"Hey, this is George. How about cocktails at six?"

I took the receiver from my ear and looked at it. Then I brought it back and said, "George, this isn't Beverly Hills. You OK?"

There was a subtle laugh. "Sure, I'm just fine. We might as well be civilized, you know. I'd like you to stop by at six, and then we can head out for dinner." I agreed and hung up. Ron came by and said, "Hi, Rick-O, we're going to have a few drinks in the hooch, then go to the Thai restaurant for dinner. Want to come along?"

I turned to go to my room. "Sorry, I've got an

appointment for dinner myself—and cocktails at six. Mustn't be late for those things, you know."

There was a trail of laughter as Ron walked on, saying, "You are kidding, aren't you?"

I waved. "Nope, not at all. It's all very high fashion over here, as you know."

He shook his head and took off for the hooch. It was a true pleasure for me to join Colonel Miller. Not only was he a good friend but he was a squadron commander at that point, heading the A-1 squadron known as the Zorros. He restored my faith that somewhere in the Air Force was a good man steadily progressing to the top. I changed my garb from chic terry-cloth towel to passable slacks and shirt, a welcome change from a flight suit stiff with sweat. The sun sloped behind the horizon and a warm and wet darkness settled on the base. Following a two-truck Army convoy trailing dust, I vaulted two ditches and walked across the dirt to George's room. Two stairs lifted me to a walkway in front of the rooms and the many doors with pilots' names on them, just about like the Hobo Hilton. George's room was near the northern end, and I knocked twice on the wood. Squadron commanders, if they deigned to live amongst their men, had a room to themselves which afforded more space than usual. The door opened and George stood there with a pitcher of martinis, a gentle smile under his mustache. "Why, Colonel Miller, how nice of you to invite me for the festivities," I said, shaking his hand.

"Why, certainly, Richard, enter and have a seat."

There was a tape recorder playing soft music and several chairs about the room. I sat and George opened his icebox, grabbing a handful of ice cubes which he placed in a plastic container. "Gin and tonic, Scotch, or would you like to try the world's greatest martini?" he asked.

"If it's the world's greatest, then I really ought to try it."

"You won't be sorry. They're very special."

He poured two and we toasted something, then sat to talk. It was a totally incongruous feeling to sip martinis in a fairly nice room after a combat flight, sitting in relative luxury a few hours after the world's best antiaircraft gunners had tried to kill us.

"Funny thing happened today," George said. "I met a guy who has flown only in Vietnam. He said that we were lucky being stationed in Thailand and not being really involved in the war. I asked him where he flew, and then I asked him about the groundfire. It was crazy hearing someone who had such limited knowledge. He said it was really terrible, that every VC had a rifle and sometimes they had fifty-caliber machine guns. Then I asked him about losses, which he said were none. I also asked him about flying on the Trail, which he admitted he hadn't done. And I really got ticked off. Imagine, someone getting medals for shooting up trenches in a jet fighter, and us out on the Trail in prop aircraft fighting thirty-seven-millimeter guns! I took over a thousand rounds last night myself. You know, there's a simple matter of probability involved. If you go out there often enough, you're going to get it. And that's not a pleasant thought."

He poured another drink. I passed my glass and said, "Perhaps someday people will recognize what went on here. Right now they are ignoring the whole thing. For that matter, I've kept newspaper clippings that deny we are here in Laos." George handed my glass across the table and leaned back in his chair, lighting his pipe. The martini seemed good. It might well have been the world's greatest, although I wouldn't know. I normally don't drink them.

"You know," he went on, "it's going to be real murder if we ever send forces into Laos without them really aware of the situation. I don't believe even some of the higher-ups in government are truly aware of the severity of the situation. It is almost as if the briefers are playing it down or ignoring it entirely. Hell, I'm not telling you anything you don't already know. The antiaircraft fire is the worst anyone's ever seen anywhere, and it's all big stuff, not just small arms and bow-and-arrow type. But we've been out there so much that we're getting rather blasé about the whole thing. I mean you go out there night after night and take thousands of rounds, dodge all that junk, and come home. You finally accept it and keep going. And you go around making as much a normal life as you can with a few peculiar hours of people trying to kill you in large doses. If some of those pure Vietnam fliers could take a few trips on the Trail or spend a few hours on a Laotian SAR, they'd probably have heart attacks. But as I said, we're getting blasé about everything. We pull out our funny money and wonder which country it came from or where we can spend it, we've been so many places. The same with the groundfire, the losses, everything. Blasé."

We raised our glasses and drained another tumbler of joy. George was mixing another batch of the world's greatest when there was a knock outside. He carried the pitcher over and opened the door. One of his squadron pilots was standing there in the dark. "Colonel

Miller, sir, I thought you might like to know what just happened."

I got up and went outside. The night was broken by a candelabrum of flares in the southern sky.

"Sir, I thought you'd like to know that Lieutenant Frisbe just bailed out. His engine came apart after takeoff and he got out. His seat system worked OK, and he's apparently in good shape. Those flares are over him now."

George took a drag on his pipe, then asked, "You sure he's OK?"

"Yeah, he's even directing the helicopter to his position for a pickup. I just thought you'd like to know."

"Sure, thanks," George said.

The pilot walked off, and I stood there looking at the flares for a moment. They hung under small white parachutes and settled slowly in the pitch black. "Almost have this pitcher ready," George said. "Where's your glass?" We closed the door and poured the gin.

I gave a quick thought to Noel Frisbe, who had gone through my A-1 class in the States, and formed an instant picture of him fighting that engine, then making the split-second decision to pull the handle and extract in the night. It could have been any of us since the engine reliability wasn't a great record one could put his trust in. It could very well have been me. It could be in the future.

"As I was saying," George went on, "we really do get downright blasé about what is happening over here."

George and I dined and chatted about what we had learned, how we had changed. For my part, I could see that I had become a more decisive person, more attuned to what was really of importance to me, and much more appreciative and understanding of life in general. The Air Force had shown itself to be far less than I had expected, and I was finally certain that I could not be a part of it much longer. I had come to realize that everything has a price, and that I was paying one for being myself, for living as I wanted, for flying a truly great airplane. My paperwork was in for the resignation of my commission as a Regular officer. I was fairly unpopular with ranking officers, none of whom I respected in the least, and it mattered not. A tremendous burden had been lifted. I had discovered a basic truth, that we grow by overcoming difficulties, by meeting challenges head on. For me, I had to fly A-1 Skyraiders in combat to realize such things. It was the hard way.

George had many of the same feelings gained from combat flying but was going on in the Air Force to big things. If we, the younger and well-educated officers, were getting out, he said, how would things be changed? Who would do it? I admitted that his feelings were valid but added that it would take longer than I cared to give it. Military discipline was important and valuable, and none of us was disputing that point. But we were disputing the need to fill time with inane jobs just to keep people busy. And we were averse to being treated like a herd of children who had to be constantly reminded about haircuts, mustaches, and that sort of thing. None of us had been lacking for spirit, motivation, and desire to fly and fly well in the combat environment. But it was as though we suddenly had a training academy at Nakhon Phanom. Where our officers and military system had to be above reproach, we had been faced with "leaders" whom no intelligent man could respect, who pulled the strings for a good report and a few medals, who were not at all averse to pretending and adding some fiction to a report here and there. And rather than see the system prosecute those men, we watched them rise in grade and stature instead. It was no wonder many of us were bitter and disillusioned. George admitted that it was tough in many cases we had seen. As it would turn out, George would become a general soon after we left the war. It was good to see someone we respected make it to the top.

It had been a warm meeting, and we departed early as George had things to study before morning. Back in the Hobo Hooch, I found that the new class of A-1 pilots had finally arrived. We thought our workload might be reduced with more people available and they had just checked in. It was reminiscent of the day I arrived, the tan uniforms, the new faces, inexperienced A-1 pilots wondering what real combat was like. We introduced ourselves and tried to make everyone feel comfortable, but I realized the same chasm that had existed the day I walked in new. Now, almost a year later, I was one of the "old heads," watching those new pilots the same way I was eyed at first. If you looked carefully, you could tell which of the new pilots would make it and which would not, or so word had it. I didn't want to make such judgments and went about shaking hands and answering questions but wondering who looked at me when I arrived and what those life-and-death judgments were then. I just hoped the new bunch loved to fly and that the A-1 and their combat tours would be as profitable for them as it had been for me. So we talked combat mainly, explaining that the basics still held true: Come in out of the sun if possible, don't go in the same way every time, keep eyes and head moving, slip and skid to confuse the gunners, and know the airplane as well as possible. The more a pilot understood his machine, the better he could use it.

Their other questions, when they asked any, still trying to act evenly and knowledgeable, centered on the usual things: being afraid, how about the killing, the losses? Those things each man faced differently, but there were common grounds. We were all afraid, one would be nuts to think otherwise. But a certain event took place once we put the chute on, strapped in, and hit the starter. The machine, the sounds, sensations, the sky, all combined to somehow make the fear subside. I had begun to like the feeling early in my combat career. Sometimes, when the groundfire was particularly heavy, one could get pretty nervous, and I related the story about a rescue when Bob Pohl followed me down onto a gun emplacement. There was so much cross fire that Bob couldn't believe I had made it through. But I had been so uptight that I had set the armament panel incorrectly and, trying to fire rockets, had dropped the entire pod off the wing as I had the selector in "bomb" function. I had nearly cried. They all laughed as though this was, after all, a human situation and feelings were allowed. About the losses— when my roommate went down I had sat alone and cried. But a year later it was more analytical, more questioning of the mistake or circumstances, a more calloused shrug. After all, nearly fifty airplanes had gone down during my tour and a lot of friends with them. I mentioned that we often drank a toast to those who had departed, our glasses held high, and it was not really sad, but an honor. They saw that we couldn't answer their questions precisely, as they were not answered for me that first day. Certainly it was a language and knowledge learned by doing rather than by listening. We could discuss the mechanics of a mission, the nuts and bolts of an A-1, but the rest, the substance of what was really going on, was something they would pick up on their own. It just wasn't possible to explain.

While the raw, fresh pilots conversed about combat aviation, hoping to assimilate everything known to civilized man through osmosis in a few hours, four of us made our way to bed, a first-light briefing at hand.

We sat alert all day. A special ground team had been inserted behind enemy lines, and our mission was to escort helicopters in for a pickup if the ground team got in trouble. Such missions were interesting and exciting. The teams were often dressed in North Vietnamese or Pathet Lao uniforms so that they could blend in with the enemy, probe for the direction of their movement, their plans, and then disappear from their ranks to a designated pickup point where we waited. The helicopter pilots said it was often very exciting when a team of soldiers dressed like North Vietnamese came charging from the jungle towards the sitting helicopter. They had to hope they were the "good guys." If not, it was all over. I was glad to see that at least we were doing something effective in combat and applauded such team infiltration techniques. Of course, the enemy was most likely doing the same thing with better results.

Nothing happened. There were no calls, only waiting while everyone else flew. Then, in late afternoon, word came down that we were released, the team was going to spend the night, and we were free to fly a strike mission. Randy Bertrand was lead of his flight, and I was leading Dale Townsend. Bert came over and in a low voice mentioned that we might join up and fly a four-ship once away from the field. There was a brief discussion as to where we would meet. There were those disposed to incite riot when someone deviated from the norm, which happened to be a standard two-ship formation unless otherwise officially specified. We thought such a rule was most likely made by more administrative incompetents who thought a formation was simply two airplanes going the same direction. After deciding on the small points we took the blue van and got our gear. We took off in the manner of a two-ship, plenty of spacing and all that, but were already grinning in anticipation of a meeting point a few miles ahead.

"OK, Bert," I said on the FM radio, "we're coming up on your right." His wingsman slid over to the other side and we moved neatly into position, Dale hanging in smartly to my right.

"Hi, old buddy." Bert's voice was deep on the radio. "Nice day, huh?" Whatever the day was didn't really matter. We were talking about the nice day flying airplanes.

"Yes, I say quite nice, old chap," I said in my best British accent.

"Yes, I say, merry old England looks different these days, don't you think," Bert chanted in an English accent. "Say, I suggest we make it in time for tea. What do you think, mate?" he asked. The game was fun, fun because we were deep in Spitfire country, turning on to real flying, playing the elusive parts of our lives once a dream, now lodged in reality. Al-

255

though we weren't there physically for the Battle of Britain with Hurricanes and Spitfires over the English green, we were in similar machines slicing through the air over Laos, in our own special war, feeling the same sorts of things, though, as any pilot would who has flown a recip type fighter aircraft.

"Certainly, old man, lead on," I said. I could sense the smiles behind the oxygen masks. And that was what it was all about, doing something we believed in, doing it perfectly, not worrying about the paper rules or tin medals, and reaping the personal rewards of our convictions.

There was a call from the airborne controller after we all checked in. "Hobos, get on down south of Saravane. We've got some friendlies being attacked, and they can use air support." Starting a turn back south, Bert said, "Roger, we're on our way." Continuing in a wide sweeping arc, our four machines moved as one unit, side by side, steady as if welded together by some invisible construction.

A few miles ahead there was a massive layer of clouds, stratus, white and polished by the afternoon sun. I'm sure we all thought the same thing, but it was up to lead to make the decision to descend and fly in the tops. He did. "Say, let's move it down a little to the tops of that stuff." Still as one entity, the formation settled into the top sea waves of foaming whiteness. It was an ocean of chalky foam, the wind churning tall wisps of spray. Immersing ourselves in the moisture, we had entered a new world. We could sense speed as the stratus clouds raced by, sometimes a wisp covering us for a second.

A gigantic hole drifted precisely over the ground team's location, making the hills easy to see. In trail, we circled our prey and got instructions from the team leader. Then Bert peeled off and started on down. "Lead's in," he called. Contrails streamed from his wingtips as he started the climb in the humid air. "I'm off, turning north," he said. His Mark-82, a five-hundred-pounder, went directly into the designated area. His wingman called in and we followed each other in a constantly diving and climbing daisy chain. It was a contest to see who could be the most accurate. It was easily a draw. The ground team was happy; we had bought them another night of life. We joined overhead and took out to the northwest. How distant that jungle looked, a place where safety was a mound of dirt and help was a flight of A-1s and voices on a radio. And how strange that some of those down there wouldn't fly in combat for anything. They had said to us that it was too dangerous, that they would rather be on the ground.

The trip home was over familiar terrain, and the ADF needle confirmed our direction. That lavish sheet of cloud still covered the horizon, so there was no further climbing. We simply leveled on the tops and went home. But the ocean was gone. To us, a limitless expanse of sand had taken its place, pure and reaching as far as our eyes could see. Each grain sparkled starlight until the satin became a world of visual fantasy which held us captive. In the clouds were four travelers exploring the dunes of time, the sands lying open to our probing, extending through every age, yielding the secrets of man's learning. We saw the monuments of struggle and conquest, the tombs of kings, the pyramids tall and pointed, the statues crumbling in the dust, winding rivers of antiseptic blue, the wind chipping away at once-sought material things.

257

We were no longer going anywhere but traversing our minds. I could visualize airplanes in the distance, and we soon came to a camp of Spitfires, MK Vc versions from number 601 Squadron, Merlin 46 engines bared to every tempest of the desert, four-bladed propellers solid silver in the sun, elliptical wings, the respondent monuments of aerial sculpture now hidden in a desert bivouac.

Miles further we dipped our wings to a group of Messerschmitts from JG.27, Daimler-Benz engines the color of dark gunmetal, mechanics probing inside like surgeons, the aircraft in their mottled camouflage of the African theater, sitting like model memorials. The camp was lit with small fires, and the pilots waved as we thundered overhead. Our shadows followed, chasing us across the desert, racing along the riverbeds of history. The pink settled on the undulating hills, the color borrowed from the last glimmer of sun. We turned further west until the sands receded completely and we leaped off the cliff edge and were transported back to northern Thailand.

"OK, let's close it up," Bert said. I hadn't realized that Dale had broken off and was turning back and forth over the clouds, and that I was on his tail. We formed as a four-ship once again and descended towards the lights of Nakhon Phanom. At perfectly timed intervals we broke off and landed, not really caring any longer if someone saw us wingtip to wingtip as a flight of four. There was a thumbs-up signal from each of us in the de-arming area and a formation taxi back.

"Hey, I saw you guys. What's the idea of the four-ship?" I didn't even look to see who made the inquiry. Loren was still working on his huge A-1 model as we walked by his room, and the Beethoven piano music was creeping out from the old door. Nelson was on the concrete steps like clockwork, reading his letter from home. A flight of two A-1s passed overhead, the returning Sandy orbit flight, and the four of us stopped to watch it go by, the position lights blinking, exhaust flame proud in the night wind. I could have saluted, cheered, perhaps cried. There were but two more flights left to me in the Skyraider. In short time I would pack up, and the world of intensity in a combat cockpit would be gone forever. It was difficult to accept. How could those people in those circumstances ever be replaced? How would I ever adapt to being back home? And, of course, the hard part was knowing that aside from memories, our mental retreats, and maybe a buddy who would stop by from time to time, it would be over forever.

With that final flight to go, I was enjoying the precious minutes of the next to the last. It was a routine strike followed by some in-trail aerobatics. And coming home I wanted to be alone for a while. It was near sunset, and the calm pervaded even the cockpit. I took the aircraft off by myself, the other A-1 going on to make a practice instrument approach. My machine knew what I felt, or so I thought. It responded to loops and rolls like a true lady, responsive, and I delicately touched the worn knobs and levers and caressed the canopy rail, the old dials and gauges. I had often wondered why people got so much pleasure out of a lock of hair, an autograph, touching some renowned person. In a way it made sense. By feeling those things I was hoping they would linger, that I could somehow take those feelings home. I was in love with an airplane

259

and what it had taught me. I wasn't ashamed of it or embarrassed.

As I looked beyond my camouflaged wingtip, the sun turned to crimson and the zenith changed to pink, like clear rosé wine through crystal. The clouds changed from frosted white to pearl, and the wind through the cockpit changed to velvet around my neck. The mountain loomed like charcoal drawings sketched above the gray haze of burning rice fields, and euphoria came through the cockpit and into me like water into a sponge.

Thoughts of things past and present drifted around like poetry, of leaves floating on a pool, picking out special clouds, reading. There was immense happiness warming the cockpit, partly in seeing romance in what most people took for granted, partly in having a childlike rapport with the universe. I wished I could bottle the essence of it all and send it to those who couldn't see yet. It was something worth all the effort, all the desire, whatever prices had been paid. There was eternity for those who understood what those moments concealed; wild, overwhelming experiences, oceanic floods of truth through the sun, the sky, tree, rock, heat, sound, the total greatness of any microsecond, united and understood. It was what the false premise of drugs and pills and mainliner philosophy hoped for and promised but never delivered. Those things couldn't help because they buried the essence even further. This was being "on" because of being alive and knowing what it meant. It came in realizing individual worth, seeing that the most valuable piece of existence wasn't diamonds or money but Mind.

I rolled the aircraft on its back and plunged two miles down through color-splashed sky, swimming in the roar of sound at fifty feet above the ground, grabbing the wind, hungry for more.

The machine raced above the trees, the gear doors opened, the struts lowered, and the tires brushed concrete with a purr as we landed. The sun winked, then disappeared. I walked off across the ramp, supremely happy.

# ELEVEN

**M**Y LAST FLIGHT I viewed with sad elation, if there be such an emotion. It would be a big letdown never to climb into the cockpit of a roaring radial-engined fighter, canopy back, the wind spilling through like an ocean. But then, it would be ever so nice not to get shot at day after day, night after night. The odds were bad if one elected to stay on. Many pilots began to believe they were invulnerable. After a year that was survived fairly well, they began to get bolder and bolder, often taking wild and dangerous chances well beyond what was necessary. Several volunteered for another tour and went back into battle armed with thoughts of their invincibility. Many of them never returned. One could hope to fly through thousands of rounds of groundfire for only so long. They would eventually catch up. The decision to pack up and go home was the wisest decision but bittersweet as well.

Last flights for fighter pilots have traditionally been a time for great rejoicing, of a last pass down the runway with a smart pull-up into the pattern. After landing, there was the waiting fire truck and a heavy hosing down. As the pilot stepped from his cockpit, the water was turned on and the hot and happy pilot was liberally doused. Then the bottles of champagne. Everyone always turned out from the squadron; it was a preview for those left to go, those hoping they would also make it through the tour and have a farewell. For me it marked the end after two hundred and twenty combat missions in the A-1, a few over Vietnam, the rest in Laos. I began to plan that last pass when a deplorable yet understandable thing happened. The wing commander made another set of rules. And since he wasn't a fighter pilot, he wasn't particularly interested in the reaction. Only the operational pilots were interested.

The new rules came down on regulation paper in a regulation form. Summarized, they simply said that there would be no more low passes on last flights, nothing out of the ordinary, not even a hint that it was a last flight in tribute to a full combat tour. The rules further stipulated that should anyone desire to do something a little extra on the last mission it would have to be presented to the commander for approval. Of course, everything we submitted was quickly disapproved. There were four of us ending our tours on the same day, but all four-ship formations were outlawed. That was ridiculous since one of the basic fighter formations was the four-ship and it was even the sole method of A-1 combat training we had used. So we were officially divided into two-ship flights, scheduled at different times, and told to do nothing out of the ordinary.

Our morale hit a small low once again. It was not only my last flight affected, but last flights of many to come. The old fighter pilot business was slowly being drained of substance. I asked why the former commanders had flown low passes and the like but was put off by excuses of their experience which was further defined in terms of hours flown. The entire trend of thought was rooted in the concept that except for the privileged few, one pilot was essentially the same as the next, or as bad as the next. Of course, the hours method of computation doesn't signify much of anything unless time is spent in small or single-engine or fighter-type aircraft because hours there mean lots of landings and hand flying and quick thinking. In a transport, for example, hours mean autopilot, coffee drinking, maybe a snooze, and perhaps one landing in five or six hours. The commander had no concern with our motivation, no thoughts on aptitude, no consideration that among the four of us were nearly one thousand combat missions in the A-1, nearly three thousand hours in the airplane, certainly evidence of adequate ability to make a flyby and land thereafter.

There were two easily visible options. The first was to ignore the stupidity of the decree and fly the last flight in the traditional way. The second was to come back and land as specified. We talked it over and decided that since we were scheduled at different times we all might not meet up anyway. We also knew that rules in the military are not to be violated at will. It is clearly a dictatorial environment, and the punishments are severe and swift. But I found myself in the dilemma of generally being regulated by those who had lost all of my respect and by a system gone to hell. So there were no real plans. We'd do what had to be done when the time came.

The aircraft sat blistering in the hot sun, so hot that my hand was burned in the scorching handhold as I climbed onto the wing. I stood there for a while, looking across the expanse of the field. A delicious scent came windward from the other machines. It was the aroma of oil smoke and fuel. I wouldn't be breathing that alluring fragrance much longer. Of course, it would end one day soon for everyone, and then we would be talking about how it used to be. It would be like the old men who told me about the delights of a Jenny in a grass field when they were young. It had been good to capture some of that flavor. At least I would have a scrapbook of good times in good airplanes from the last of a good era.

Dick Nordhaus and I flew together for the last time on May 6, 1970. That in itself was a singular experience. As he flew alongside, I mused on an incident that took place years before. I was finishing pilot training and was scheduled for my final formation checkride back in August of 1966, at Williams Air Force Base in Arizona. I marched myself solemnly into the check section office and was faced with a young lieutenant who would be giving me the check. It was Dick Nordhaus. And we were somewhere around thirty thousand feet over Arizona chasing another jet through the clouds. Dick grading my flying. That had been a long time ago. As we flew together four years later, I thought about saying something to him like "Hey, close it up. Think you're a fighter pilot?" But I didn't say anything because he was perfect out there, his canopy back for the last time. It was strange how we had met again. Fellow pilots always have a way of showing up in time. It is a very special world.

We worked our way through some gigantic cumulus and flew through some clean rain as we neared the Plaine des Jarres. Then we turned east and made contact with an FAC. He was keeping an eye on some Laotian troops who were battling it out with the NVA again. We rolled in under the clouds and through the rain, doing the best we could with such natural obstacles. It wasn't spectacular, and we finished the strike within twenty minutes. But we didn't make a direct line for the base. We both felt much the same, that we didn't want it to end quite yet.

Dick headed across the expanse of the PDJ, and I followed close in trail. We were taking a look at everything for the last time, putting our thoughts together, trying to form some acceptable conclusion.

There were the familiar landmarks: Arrowhead Lake, Roadrunner Lake, the "Chinese Cultural Center" in the southeast PDJ composed of several white buildings with reddish roofs. It was often a haven for NVA gunners who knew we wouldn't fire back into the "historical landmark." To the northwest was Muong Soui, and thoughts of our friends there resting eternally in their aircraft came to mind. It had been a long year.

We crossed the high mountains and I skimmed the top of the tallest peak, rolling over on a wingtip to watch the trees flash by. Then we started a long descent aimed at the Mekong River. I looked through the cockpit at my attire, gloved hand on the stick, face in the mirror, the other airplane flying near me, sun and sky, the clouds and the infinite sky which we played in like children at a park. By what incessant instinct did pilots brave the storms, the night, the wind and rain, the tribulations of old and worn cockpits? I thought it must be much the same as those who knew the sea and ships, twisting roads, or mountains, yet it would always be just a little better to fly. Once fully experienced it wouldn't be necessary to describe. It had to do with being alive, with not accepting the man-made limitations of distance and space and time. It was performed because of the need to discover the world, ourselves, reality. This feeling was nothing new;

it had been acted on as long as there were wars and airplanes. There was once the lure of the Lafayette Escadrille with multiwinged fighters and the smell of hot oil, helmet and goggles. And the same man said, "Mum, I've got to fly a Spitfire," and so went off to the skies over England. And there were the shark's teeth on P-40's in China, the Flying Tigers. There were the grand names of great machines, Thunderbolts, Lightnings, Mustangs, Bearcats, and, to us, Skyraiders. We, being the same man, had to fly them. And putting his life on the line for his vision, this man has always seen everything else as paltry tasks. He flings himself into battle, into a night sky full of blistering ammunition crisscrossing and enveloping his airplane, jinking and reeling about the sky behind lashing exhaust flame, where the moon lights the land in silver, in a conflict when said and done, may well mean very little in itself. The life gained and known to the fullest is the treasure known to few. Even those departed, gone down in their cramped cockpits, trailing smoke and flame, went as they wanted, did it the way they hoped, went out with something men seldom know called glory and fulfillment and peace. The man who lays his life on the line finds life. He has found death not real. The curtain has been lifted. He has been set free.

Those with this affliction would do the same thing again and again, anywhere, just to be there. We would have yet another chance to be free and fight for it, to know heroism, comradeship, drama, the smell of cordite and the sound of engines. And we would still believe in those vanishing thoughts about freedom. We would still fight slavery, suppression, the philosophy we call communism. These are not men gone mad or cold-blooded killers. Deep inside, each knows that without true freedom he would die a death inside. He has seen men hunched over desks or chasing nothing, finding nothing, chained to self-imposed limitations. We elect to slip those bonds and be free to control our destinies. Summarized, there were no regrets. It was worth it!

Warmth filled my body as Dick and I knocked about the sky, stunting around the cliffs and bluffs of clouds, negotiating right-angle turns down cumulus corridors, rolling upside down and falling through the tears of angels, tumbling from the clouds. I pulled up the sleeves of my flight suit and bared my arms to the elbows. With the canopy back I took off my helmet and let the Wright engine combine with the hurricane wind, feeling as if the substance of the universe were flowing through my fingers and arms and head. The moment was complete, one in which all the things of value, all the ideals and desires of my life, were as they ought to be. It was a sky I just needed to experience. It was a singular moment of satisfaction in chiseling dreams into solid gold. A pilot couldn't come away from that cockpit without acquiring wisdom. If he just looked it was there. Through the machine, we acquired a perception founded in the roasting heat of the days, the muddy nights, storms, winds—holding destinies in our grasp.

We crossed the Mekong and raced along it, being charitable to fishermen in sampans and flocks of large birds. Through a small aperture in the clouds a shaft of light beamed down, settling on a small village nestled in the corner of a deep valley. It was a finger of gold pointing to an enchanted city hidden from the agony of war. While I knew there wouldn't be any more solo cavorting at midnight under Arcturus and the Pleiades hunting the elusive jungle soldier, I also knew that every village would be abandoned or overrun in time. We would leave and they would all change. During a quiet and concealed slaughter, the world would call it peace.

Then we climbed to near ten thousand feet and prepared for the last landing. I closed in on Dick, and we decided on a simple pass down the runway with a pull-up into downwind. It wasn't such a great tribute to our year, but it was the most we figured we would be allowed. Our pass commenced from altitude, a dive which leveled over the end of the runway with a roar and the sound of cyclone winds. Dick pulled up, and I followed a few seconds later. Reaching downwind altitude, I opened the canopy and set about lowering the gear and flaps. As Dick neared the end of the runway I started my descending turn to final approach. It was only a light wind that swept through my cockpit carrying the fleeting images of a way of life on a humid wind. The ghosts waved farewell, and I brushed the concrete as gently as I could. The plot to steal my life had been foiled, but the life given by a great airplane was gone as well.

Nelson and Stan were waiting for us in the de-arming area. They had landed just a few minutes before us. They had, we later learned, been more daring on their last pass. They had turned opposite directions from their initial pass, fanning out in a large climbing Y-shaped pattern.

The arming crew jumped onto my wing to remove some rounds from the breaches of the wing guns. While they were working, the four of us chatted over our interplane frequency. It was the general opinion that since we hadn't been allowed to make our last flights together in the more dramatic fashion, there was really no reason why we shouldn't fold our wings symbolically and taxi back in formation. After all, the Navy had been folding those wings on carriers for twenty years. So we did. It was a beautiful sight, four aircraft in close taxi formation with the wings folded. We turned onto the ramp, and I donned my leather helmet and goggles and threw my white scarf over the side. We turned into our parking places and lowered our wings together. It was tearfully gripping. There was no other way to describe it. Then the big props stopped turning, clouds of oil smoke blowing away in the late afternoon. There was the familiar metallic crackling sound of the cooling engine and the whir of gyros still turning. The fire truck pulled up and the squadron pilots were there, the guys smiling and taking pictures. We all got the shower of cold water from the fire hose, followed by bottles of champagne. Lucky shook my hand, but there was a general air of discontent.

The wing commander had driven out to see how his empire was performing under his reign. He witnessed four pilots who apparently didn't care much for his book of rules. To put it politely, refuse rolls downhill in the system, and rather than say anything to us, the commander had started in on Lucky, who was naturally torn between the thrill of watching A-1s race down the runway and arc upwards into the traffic pattern and the knowledge that he would also catch hell for not better controlling his men, or whatever the military would call it. I was only saddened because Lucky was affected. Other than that, none of us cared at all. The champagne was good in the sun and didn't take long to make its presence known internally. Someone mentioned that we were to report immediately to the wing commander's office, but after the champagne and sun and heated tempers it was decided to make it the next day. That was a wise decision. We would have said what everyone wanted to say but kept inside. The gist of the situation was that we had not only flown a low pass down the runway but also had done something that, in the commander's words, "had never been done before"; we had folded our wings. And quite often, in the new military, if something hasn't been done before, doing it is complete sacrilege.

I turned to Nelson, who was covered in champagne, laughing his biggest laugh. "Great way to run a war," I said.

He just kept laughing. Then he said, "Buddy, I'm going home to my wife and family. And right now I don't give a damn what anybody thinks. Man, we're through—it's over!"

There was only the order to report to the wing commander for some sort of disciplinary action, then the going-away party.

We showed up at the commander's office at the scheduled time, but the man had decided not to be there. Instead, he had appointed his deputy to say what had to be said. And that was good. The deputy commander had been a longtime A-1 pilot who greeted us with a smile, the sort that said we had been caught with our hands in the cookie jar. He said that, as we knew, such things as willfully disobeying orders could lead to bad records and so forth. We nodded. Then he said, "Well, I didn't get a chance to see it. How'd it look?" And we told him.

A going-away party at the hooch was a cheerfully

disconsolate affair, a mixture of gay expressions and nostalgic reflections. While we were laughing at our exploits we were also recalling that we wouldn't be flying there anymore. The round engines and fourteen-foot propellers belonged to the other pilots from then on, ours only in memory. There was the feeling that we were past history and time was going on regardless, like the senior class graduating and the juniors saying that it was good, that it was time for a new group of old-timers.

The last party was normally attended by the wing staff as a matter of formality, except in our case. Since we had violated the sacred writings, those people conspicuously stayed away as a reminder that outlaws weren't to be honored with the royal presence. It really meant that we could have a decent party without further political deceptions and could say what had to be said.

There was a cookout followed by drinks and the words of our squadron commander. Lucky Lowman called us in front of the group one at a time, saying a few words pertinent to the individual infamous deeds we had performed during our tours. As I stood by Lucky there was a moment of real sadness for me. It was something I didn't want to end. It was an instant in which I felt the love I had for the man, the place, and the camaraderie. It was a split second in which I absorbed the model airplanes hanging from the ceiling, the pictures on the walls, the fervor that had been lived in that place. Lucky hadn't anything to say in regard to my additional duty accomplishment or devotion to political ascension. He mentioned the only things that were of any importance to me: my disdain for the man-made book of rules and limitations, and my passion for flying which had been evident in the air. He said,

"Rick doesn't care one damn for the book of rules. He flies because he loves it, and one would be hard pressed to tie a tin can to his fanny in the air. He just loves to fly." As far as I was concerned, that would have been a fine epitaph. Lucky wiped a tear from his eye and his speech broke. He set his glass down and turned to face me. Then we suddenly found ourselves clenched in a bear hug which was the most honest expression I could imagine.

I couldn't find much to say. Lucky handed me the usual plaque which was the large brass number one symbol of the First Special Operations Squadron. The inscription said, *In appreciation of a fine Hobo*. We also received a scroll and lapel pin which signified that we were members of the vanishing breed of aviators who hadn't even really approached the speed of sound. It was known as the "Mach Nix Club."

There was nothing left to say, words being ineffective at that point. The greatest statements were made with glances and smiles, handshakes and arm-around-the-shoulder embracing. Then, because it was late and the new "old-timers" had to fly, the party dwindled in attendance. The four of us sat like strangers in another place and time. The morning missions and the airplanes didn't belong to us anymore. It was time to leave.

I went back to my room, the wooden, boxlike contrivance, just one of a series of similar rooms, always damp, far too small. I had thought of it as a confining prison on first inspection, standing there beside my B-4 bag, perspiring under the sun of a new world. But the room became a haven instead. Returning from a steel-filled sky, through the heat and dirt, I arrived to that wooden box as if it were my palace.

It became that. For into it I had stuffed remnants of my existence, pasted pictures on the walls, nailed boards into bookcases, and had gained solitude when I needed it. It was a veritable museum of books, airplane models, piles of magazines, various pipes and tobaccos, boots and shoes, and a drab minimum of military furniture. My treasures were my books and papers, which littered every available space. I had bought and read books in the same manner as one eats popcorn. In ten months I had read over one hundred books and innumerable magazines. The enemy had given me something not intended, a certain appreciative way of life. A book might have remained just a book, a picture just a picture, a glass of wine simply something to drink. But things changed as I changed. A book became a delicious blend of thoughts and places, and the delicate printed page was a luxury. My glass of wine was priceless nectar, friendship with my aerial comrades seldom known elsewhere. In that little stuffy room I gained more and more of my sight. The cubicle became a cathedral.

Row after row was the same. Room after room was filled with the ultimate substance of living. Everything was there—life and death, joy and pain, laughter and tears. In one, a pilot readied for a sortie while his comrade slept from a recent mission. In another, a pilot who was just missed by a hundred bullets drank Scotch and read a letter from home. All the pathos, the drama, the meanings of lives was contained there.

My room was, after all, a cathedral to life. When my wooden name tag was removed from the door and a new one tacked to its place, the same evolution would take place. Someone else's books would line the crude shelves. Another temple would have been erected.

Alone in my room, I had a sensation much like coming to the last pages in an absorbing novel. The last flight was over, the farewell party had passed, and the handshakes were memories now. I sat uneasily that last night, my thoughts going back to the day I had first walked in. What changes, what insights, what learning had come about there. I wrote for a while in my ledger, trying to capture those lingering images. I reflected across my life in the air, to the first solo when I was fourteen, to soaring in Belgium a few years later; looping biplanes into the sun, watching the aurora over Canada from thirty-seven thousand feet, to all the unique raptures experienced from a cockpit. Then I thought about people I knew who had lived much the same, barnstorming a biplane through the Midwest, sailing alone around the world, writing books. I saw them all as vividly as if they were there with me. Perhaps they were. Then I read for a while, realizing that it would be the last time I would have that pleasure in that room.

When I was through and set down the books, I noticed a folded page which I had inserted among the last pages of my journal. I opened it and the familiar lines greeted me like old friends. Type from my borrowed and humble typewriter offered two quotations, the first by Plutarch. Two lines said:

> The measure of a man's life is the well
> spending of it, and not the length.

Those lines were followed by the pleasing words of Mr. W. Beran Wolfe. They summarized everything

I had been thinking, and they were all that had to be felt on that last night before leaving, a time when I knew that I wouldn't trade any of my tour for anything, that I would do it again tomorrow, next week, next year—problems, contradictions, flimsy policies included. The words were simple:

> If you observe a really happy man you will find him building a boat, writing a symphony, educating his son, growing double dahlias in his garden, or looking for dinosaur eggs in the Gobi desert. He will not be searching for happiness as if it were a collar button that has rolled under the radiator. He will not be striving for it as a goal in itself. He will have become aware that he is happy in the course of living life twenty-four crowded hours of the day.

I put the papers away, then stepped outside into the hot night air. There was a most brilliant gunner's moon, cold, piercing, a stark symbol of our nights in combat. It had become something rather special to me, a universal eye from an unemotional, uninvolved cosmos, a spotlight illuminating our stage, probing, looking at us, the eye we could never escape and which made me feel that I must inspect and make sense of things. The one lustrous eye examined me, and I was forced to examine myself, forced to dig into the hidden recesses of my mind. That eye I would never forget, that moon would forever capture me in an exclusive spell.

Back inside my room, I packed and then took a

276

last nocturnal glance around. I wondered who would put his name on the door next, spend a little of his earthly existence there. I also wondered if he would live or die with his airplane. Those would be things I would never know. I turned out the gray table lamp for the last time.

# GLOSSARY

*Abort:* To cancel or stop a flight, mission, or takeoff.

*ADF:* Automatic direction finder; a receiver which detects signal strength and provides bearings to low- and medium-frequency transmitters. The A-1 had ADF capability to receive bearings to an ultrahigh-frequency (UHF) transmitter.

*Attitude:* The position of the aircraft as determined by the relationship of its axes and a reference such as the horizon, or an instrument presenting an artificial horizon.

*Barrel Roll:* An aerobatic maneuver in which the nose of the aircraft performs a 360-degree turn around a point on the horizon.

*BDA:* Bomb-damage assessment, which is essentially the "results" of an air strike. The appraisal is generally given in terms of troops killed, buildings destroyed, trucks destroyed, or other such effects.

*BOQ:* Bachelor officers' quarters, where single officers live on a military base.

*CBU:* Cluster-bomb units. This is a special-type ordnance, mainly antipersonnel in nature.

*Charlie:* One of the slang terms which refer to an oriental enemy.

*Close Air Support:* Air attacks against hostile troops which are flown to support friendly ground forces. These attacks are usually in close proximity to the ground personnel and require extreme accuracy.

*DCO:* Deputy commander for operations.

*DME:* Distance-measuring equipment. This instrumentation provides the pilot with accurate distance measurements from a ground station. The information is presented in a digital readout, in units of miles.

*Drag:* The force that resists forward movement of an airplane through the air. Whatever interferes with the streamline flow of air around the aircraft constitutes a form of drag, blunt surfaces causing higher drag then streamline ones.

*Ejection:* An escape system which shoots a pilot from his aircraft.

*Extraction:* An aircraft escape system in which a pilot is pulled from his aircraft by a rocket device (as contrasted with an ejection). The extraction system was used in the A-1 aircraft.

*FAC:* Forward air controller. Essentially a spotter role, in which a pilot locates a target and directs air strikes against it.

*FAG:* Forward air guide; generally an indigenous soldier who directs air strikes from the ground.

*FM:* Frequency modulation. A radio which operates in a specific band which is relatively free of static.

*Formation:* A method of flying a number of aircraft together with each airplane in a designated position with respect to the others. *Trail* refers to a one-behind-the-other position as in a line; *wing* position meaning a side-by-side position. The number of aircraft involved determines the designation of the formation, such as two-ship, etc.

*G:* The acceleration produced by gravity. In a four-G pull-up, for example, a body weighs four times its normal weight, a 170-pound pilot weighing 680 pounds.

*GCA:* Ground-controlled approach. This is a radar landing system operated from the ground. The ground controller talks the pilot to a landing while the pilot flies on instruments and follows the instructions.

*Groundfire:* Antiaircraft artillery used to shoot at striking aircraft. Various-sized weapons were used in Southeast Asia, pilots over Laos normally encountering 23mm, 37mm, and 57mm. The shells are usually fired with tracers and explode either on impact with the airplane or upon reaching a certain altitude. The pilot sees a black puff during the day and a bright flash at night. Also known as *flak*.

*Ground Pounder:* Essentially one who does not fly and holds a desk job. (Also known as paper pusher, pencil pusher, and strap hanger.)

*Guard Frequency:* A specified radio frequency pilots use in emergency conditions.

*Gyro:* A mechanical device which uses the angular momentum of a spinning rotor to sense angular motion of its base about one or two axes at right angles to the spin axis.

*Hooch:* Term applied to dwellings in Southeast Asia,

and also applied to certain wooden buildings on military bases in the area.

*Intervalometer:* A cockpit device for selecting which piece of ordnance is to be used and at what rate (interval) it will be fired or dropped.

*Jam:* An attempt to render radio or radar ineffective by countertransmission or other means.

*Jink:* Maneuvering the aircraft sharply and continuously so as to become a more difficult target for gunners to hit.

*Jolly (Green):* Name applied to the large USAF rescue helicopters.

*LF:* Low frequency; signals which can be received on the ground or at low altitudes. It is the type of frequency used by most commercial radio stations.

*Loop:* An aerobatic maneuver which is simply a vertical circle accomplished by climbing to the top of the circle where the airplane is upside down, followed by a dive back to the starting point.

*Mach:* (After Ernst Mach, Austrian scientist): A number expressing the ratio of the speed of a body in some medium to the speed of sound in that medium. A Mach number less than one is *subsonic* and greater than one is *supersonic*.

*Mag; Magneto:* An electrical generator which supplies current and voltage for the ignition systems of reciprocating engines.

*M.A.P.:* Manifold pressure. The pressure within the intake manifold. The manifold pressure gauge tells the pilot the exact pressure in the manifold and enables him to determine the amount of power his engine is developing. The pressure is measured in inches of mercury in barometer increments, such as a reading of thirty inches of manifold pressure.

*MEO:* One of the Laotian tribes. The Meos came from China somewhere between the sixteenth and nineteenth centuries. They live in the higher mountains of northern Laos and are predominantly animists. They have a strong sense of family and home ties and made the best fighters in the clandestine war. Their leader was General Vang Pao. The majority of Meo men have been killed in the Laotian war.

*Meter:* A basic metric unit of length, approximately equal to 39.37 inches.

*MIG:* A Russian fighter aircraft of which different models were flown in North Vietnam, presumably by North Vietnamese pilots.

*MIL:* A unit of angular measurement equal to approximately the angle subtended by one yard at one thousand yards range.

*Mixture:* The fuel and air combination which enters the cylinders of a reciprocating engine for combustion. *Rich* denotes more fuel than air, while *lean* refers to allowing more air into the mixture. The pilot can control this mixture by use of a cockpit control.

*Napalm:* A jellied gasoline mixture used in incendiary bombs. (Also referred to as *nape.*)

*NVA:* North Vietnamese Army.

*NVR:* No visual results. A term used in expressing BDA.

*Ordnance:* Aircraft guns, ammunition, bombs, rockets, and other explosives carried and delivered by aircraft.

*Pather Lao:* Communist Lao rebel troops advised, supplied, and often led by the Communist Vietnamese. The organization of this force opened the door for the North Vietnamese Communist forces to invade Laos as well as enter Cambodia for a similar purpose with Communist Khmer rebels.

*Pattern:* The path an airplane flies in preparation for landing. The aircraft lands into the wind when possible, so a normal rectangular pattern may be flown, which consists of a downwind leg parallel to the runway, a base leg ninety degrees to the runway, and a final approach during which the aircraft is aimed down the runway in a descent. An *overhead* pattern is a circular pattern in which the aircraft flies over the runway, then starts a descending turn which ends at the runway. This is the quickest, shortest way to land and generally used by fighter aircraft.

*PDJ:* Plaine des Jarres. A plateau in northern Laos about three thousand feet high, so named for the large, man-sized burial jars found in the area.

*Pipper:* A dot in the gunsight that is placed on a target where ordnance is to be delivered, as with the sights on a gun.

*POW:* Prisoner of war.

*Primer:* A pump used to spray fuel into the intake

ports of the cylinders. When the engine is turned over, the fuel is drawn into the cylinders and provides a rich mixture for starting.

*PSP:* Pierced steel planking; metal planks which are linked together in constructing runways and ramps in remote areas.

*Radial:* A configuration of reciprocating engine in which cylinders extend radially from the crankshaft like the spokes of a wheel.

*Ramp:* The prepared area around the airport where airplanes are parked. Also known as *apron*.

*RNO:* Results not observed; identical to NVR.

*RPM:* Revolutions per minute; the speed at which the engine is turning, measured by a tachometer on the instrument panel.

*SAC:* Strategic Air Command, an Air Force command which operates bomber aircraft and intercontinental missiles.

*SAR:* Search and rescue.

*Short:* Term applied to those who have only a short time left in the war zone before they return home.

*Small Arms:* Weaponry of less caliber than the large antiaircraft guns, usually considered handguns and rifles.

*Sortie:* One operational flight by an aircraft or formation.

*Split-S:* An aerobatic maneuver performed by making a half-roll followed by an inverted half-loop. The result is a great loss of altitude and a reversal in the direction of flight. The maneuver generally describes the lower half of the letter S.

*Stall:* A condition which results from a radical disturbance of the smooth airflow across the wings. The airflow separates from the wing, at which point the wing can no longer generate sufficient lift to support the airplane. The term *stall* does not refer to the engine as it might in an automobile.

*Strafe:* The act of firing machine guns or cannons on ground targets by low-flying aircraft.

*Stub:* The largest of the wing pylons where ordnance is attached to the aircraft.

*Tacan:* Tactical air navigation. An air navigation system developed by the military which provides directional information to a station and distance-measuring information (DME) as well.

*Taildragger (Also TAILWHEEL):* An aircraft with a landing-gear configuration in which two main wheels are located in front of the center of gravity (balance point) of the airplane and a single wheel is placed at the tail. With the majority of weight aft of the main gear, the aircraft tends to follow sideways movement unless the actions of the pilot with the controls resist such movement. Once the aircraft moves beyond the control capacity of the aircraft, the resulting veering movement is known as a ground loop. Tricycle landing gear, in contrast, is inherently stable and eliminates the veering tendency and subsequently requires less action on the part of the pilot.

*Torque:* A turning or twisting force, as in an engine

shaft. Torque is a measure of engine power and is presented to the pilot by a torquemeter which is calibrated in pounds.

*Tracer:* A bullet which contains a chemical composition which marks the path of ammunition with a trail of fire.

*Transponder:* An electric device which transmits a selected electrical code when triggered by an interrogating signal from the ground. (Also known as *IFF*.)

*Trim:* A process of keeping an aircraft in balance without the continual application of pressure on the controls. Usually accomplished by movement of small tabs on flight-control surfaces.

*VC:* Viet Cong.

*VHF:* Very high frequency; a radio band beginning just after the commercial FM frequencies.

*Willie Pete:* A nickname for white-phosphorous rockets or bombs. The billowing, white smoke is readily visible so is often used to mark targets.

*Time and Distance:* A method of navigation whereby the pilot holds a particular heading for a precomputed time. Knowing the distance to destination and the speed of the aircraft, the pilot simply flies the time necessary to travel the distance.

*Winchester:* Term used to denote that the aircraft is out of ordnance.

*ZPU:* A relatively small-caliber antiaircraft gun effective at low altitudes due to its rapid-fire capability.

# GREAT BATTLES OF HISTORY
## from St. Martin's Press

OPERATION TORCH
The Allied Gamble to Invade North Africa
by William B. Breuer
_____ 90125-9 $3.95 U.S.    _____ 90126-7 $4.95 Can.

STORMING HITLER'S RHINE
The Allied Assault: February–March 1945
by William B. Breuer
_____ 90335-9 $4.95 U.S.    _____ 90336-7 $5.95 Can.

THE LAST BATTLE STATION
The Saga of the *U.S.S. Houston*
by Duane Shultz
_____ 90222-0 $4.95 U.S.    _____ 90223-9 $6.25 Can.

DELIVERANCE AT LOS BAÑOS
by Anthony Arthur
_____ 90346-4 $3.95 U.S.    _____ 90347-2 $4.95 Can.

THE LAST ENEMY
by Richard Hillary
_____ 90215-8 $3.95 U.S.

Publishers Book and Audio Mailing Service
P.O. Box 120159, Staten Island, NY 10312-0004

Please send me the book(s) I have checked above. I am enclosing
$ _____ (please add $1.25 for the first book, and $.25 for each
additional book to cover postage and handling. Send check or
money order only—no CODs.)

Name _____

Address _____

City _____ State/Zip _____

Please allow six weeks for delivery. Prices subject to change
without notice.

GB 1/89

# MEN AT WAR
## The battles. The blood.
## The way it was.

KNIGHTS OF THE BLACK CROSS
Hitler's Panzerwaffe and its leaders
by Bryan Perrett
_____ 91130-0  $4.50 U.S.

SHINANO!
The Sinking of Japan's Secret Supership
by Capt. Joseph F. Enright, USN, with James W. Ryan
_____ 90967-5  $3.95 U.S.      _____ 90968-3  $4.95 Can.

KOMMANDO
German Special Forces of World War II
by James Lucas
_____ 90497-5  $4.95 U.S.

BUSHMASTERS
America's Jungle Warriors of World War II
by Anthony Arthur
_____ 91358-3  $4.95 U.S.      _____ 91359-1  $5.95 Can.

FORTRESS WITHOUT A ROOF
The Allied Bombing of The Third Reich
by Wilber H. Morrison
_____ 90179-8  $4.95 U.S.      _____ 90180-1  $5.95 Can.